ADVANCE PRAISE

MW01193370

Washington State has a long history of teaching outdoor environmental education with various facilities providing for teacher and student instruction. *Teaching in the Rain* is a singular summary of North Cascades Institute, one of Washington State's most unique, successful, and sustained programs. John Miles has written an important and intriguing history of how the Institute was created and has been sustained for over 35 years. This important book is an essential guide to what it takes to direct education meaningfully in this age of environmental stress and to marshal the common ground of community to develop skills and shape attitudes necessary to address the environmental challenges we all face.

—*Tony Angell,*
Artist/Educator, Seattle, WA

Like an expert guide on a nature walk, John C. Miles knows the details, and he knows how to weave them into a story. Filled with behind-the-scenes insights, *Teaching in the Rain* is an irreplaceable history of an iconic Northwest institution.

—*Thor Hanson,*
author of **Hurricane Lizards and Plastic Squid**

John Muir said "the mountains are calling and I must go." Over the last 35 years, more than 150,000 young people have answered that calling and gone to the mountains, hosted by NCI, and were forever transformed into the stewards that this planet so sorely needs. John Miles' lessons on the origins of North Cascades Institute include vision, passion, persistence, luck, leadership, and partnerships that aligned to create one of the best environmental education organizations in America.

—*Jonathan Jarvis,*
Chief of Resources, North Cascades National Park 1985-1991,
NPS Director 2009-2017

Teaching in the Rain tells a most unlikely story, one that is far from over but has a happy outcome just the same. John Miles, as the genius loci of the North Cascades and the Institute that took their name, is the perfect person to tell it. In prose both elegant and engaging, sleek yet omitting nothing important, he takes his lucky readers through the life so far of a most wonderful flowering, from outset through evolution to its present place as an essential Northwest institution. If every eco-region had something like North Cascades Institute, and someone like John to tell us all about it, we might actually scrape through our ecological crisis in good shape. As it is, this book gives me hope.

—*Robert Michael Pyle,*
author of The Butterflies of Cascadia, Wintergreen,
and The Thunder Tree

In recounting the first 35 years of North Cascades Institute, John Miles shows how the tenacity and visions of a few can reveal the wonders and intricacies of nature to young and old. *Teaching In The Rain, The Story Of North Cascades Institute* serves as a deftly crafted instruction manual for how the National Park Service and its allies can strengthen the human connection with the natural world.

—*Kurt Repanshek,*
Founder and Editor-in-Chief, National Parks Traveler

TEACHING
in the
RAIN

THE STORY OF NORTH CASCADES INSTITUTE

Dr. MD: Thanks for your work in our field.
John Miles

JOHN C. MILES

SKETCHES BY SUSAN MORGAN

CHUCKANUT
EDITIONS

Bellingham, WA

CHUCKANUT
EDITIONS

Teaching in the Rain: The Story of North Cascades Institute

ISBN: 978-0999-5278-25 (paperback)
ISBN: 978-0999-5278-32 (eBook)
Library of Congress Control Number: 2022917727

First paperback edition June 2023

Edited by Samantha Chapman
Layout by Book House
Cover photo by Patty Direnzo, North Cascades Institute

Printed in the USA by Village Books

Village Books
ATTN: Chuckanut Editions
1200 11th Street
Bellingham, WA 98226

To request permissions, contact the publisher at publishing@villagebooks.com

www.villagebooks.com/village-books-chuckanut-editions

*To all, past and present, who have made
North Cascades Institute a success.*

CONTENTS

Introduction vii

Chapter I: Beginnings 1

Chapter II: Sowing Seeds. 11

Chapter III: A Growing Mission .29

Chapter IV: An Unexpected Opportunity: Creation of the
North Cascades Environmental Learning Center . . .39

Chapter V: The Beat Goes On 53

Chapter VI: Into the New Millennium. 71

Chapter VII: A Facility Changes Nearly Everything. 89

Chapter VIII: The Youth Movement 103

Chapter IX: Community and Other School Programs. 129

Chapter X: Adult Education 143

Chapter XI: How the Business Has Succeeded 159

Chapter XII: North Cascades Institute at 35:
Opportunities and Challenges 185

Chapter XIII: Facing the Future 203

Author's Note 211

Acknowledgments. 213

Notes 215

Index 219

INTRODUCTION

MORE THAN A HALF-CENTURY HAS PASSED since I learned there was a field called outdoor education. During my K-12 schooling experience in New Hampshire I never enjoyed a single school-sponsored field trip to study the natural world, but I did so on my own, inspired by reading and by various mentors including my parents. I learned to read with the children's nature writings of Thornton W. Burgess, an early 20th-century writer whose very anthropomorphic descriptions of New England wildlife captured my imagination. They were first read to me, then I began reading them myself. Early fascination with the outdoors and nature literally helped me learn to read. Even though I didn't, even as a young child, expect to encounter an English-speaking Grandfather Frog on a lily pad in top hat and tails and sporting a cane, those books told me where to look for him and the other animals in Burgess' stories. And look for them I did, wandering the wilds of New Hampshire alone and with my brother, exploring woodlands, swamps, brooks, and even the local river at a time when children could explore more freely than most do today. I enjoyed a wonderful "outdoor education."

After a solid liberal education in college, I found myself in graduate school at the University of Oregon, pursuing a doctorate in archaeology. However, I became disillusioned with the prospect of a life in that field. The work on site was marvelous, but in the lab not so much, so I began searching for my life's purpose in other directions. I had loved the summer I spent as a counselor at a YMCA camp in New Hampshire and was continuing my love affair with the outdoors in Oregon, exploring that amazing place in climbing boots, skis, canoes, and kayaks. I wondered if I might pursue a passion for the outdoors and nature study in my career when I discovered that the University of Oregon offered degrees in Recreation and Park Management, and even encouraged a degree emphasis in Outdoor Education. My career aspirations made a sharp turn.

Ironically, when I came to a course in outdoor education in pursuit of an advanced degree in that program, I found it was taught almost entirely indoors. This, I thought, was oxymoronic—sitting in a classroom talking about the theory and method of teaching in and about the outdoors, when Eugene, Oregon was surrounded by a great outdoors and many children itching to get out into it with someone who knew some of the wonders of that world. I resolved that when I finished my training, I would be certain to teach outdoor education in the outdoors as much as possible. I soon landed at Western Washington University in Bellingham, Washington in an even more powerful outdoor learning environment, with the Salish Sea and San Juan Islands to the west and the North Cascades Mountains to the east. Even more remarkable and fortuitous, the university was launching a new college focused on environmental studies, and I was hired to direct a project with a local school district to develop "environmental education." Broader than outdoor education and spawned by a growing ecological understanding of the natural world and humanity's place in it, environmental education was to become a part of the curriculum of this new college, and I was charged with leading its development. Here was my chance to teach in and for the environment, which included the outdoors.

The aspiration to teach outside the classroom was more challenging than I had initially thought, but my good fortune continued. I found that a core principle adopted by Huxley College of Environmental Studies was *experiential learning*, which could and should complement classroom work. The college embraced a problem-oriented curriculum and encouraged faculty to venture out into the community—and defined "community" broadly to include the ecological community as well as the human community. My colleagues and I were able to incorporate a significant measure of experiential outdoor learning into our programs. Environmental education students worked with school children in the field, developing and implementing curricula and critiquing the outcomes of their work.

My career at Huxley College began in 1970 on the bottom rung of the academic ladder. By 1985 I had become acting dean of the college, and one day in 1986 my assistant informed me I had a phone call from the superintendent of North Cascades National Park. By this time I had come to know and love the North Cascades and was pleased to hear from this leader of the Park Service, which had become the manager of a good portion of the range with the creation of the park in 1968. The caller was John Reynolds, recently appointed superintendent of NOCA (North Cascades National Park Complex). John asked if I might, as an environmental educator and dean of the local environmental studies college, be interested in joining him and a few others in launching a non-profit loosely affiliated with the relatively new national park and dedicated to teaching about the North Cascades region. The meeting would be convened to form a board and launch what would be called the North Cascades Institute. I enthusiastically accepted the invitation. At that meeting I became the first chair of the Institute Board and met Saul Weisberg and Tom Fleischner, founders of the Institute.

Thus began a new a very rewarding phase of my professional career in which I was able to observe and participate in the growth of an organization that delivered on the promises of outdoor and environmental education. I enjoyed a three-decade participant-observer experience with the Institute that deepened and broadened my understanding of this field of education, revealing potential that I had barely perceived in the beginning of my journey as an educator. My Institute experience was one of my greatest learning opportunities and certainly added to what I could bring to the students I worked with at Western. The story of the first 35 years of the North Cascades Institute must not be allowed to pass undocumented for several reasons. It is an inspiring example of how dedication to a dream and hard work, along with the collaborative talents of many people and a measure of luck, can lead to outcomes far beyond expectations at the beginning of such a journey. It is a story of collaboration and partnerships between unlikely people, especially public/private partnerships, that enhance the good works of the partners beyond what they could do alone. It is also a story that will continue to unfold, the first stages of Institute history inspiring the next generation of outdoor and environmental educators in the North Cascades region and beyond.

I hope you enjoy reading *Teaching in the Rain* as much as I did telling this compelling story, and that it inspires continuing efforts to educate about the environment so that those who come to know and love it will be motivated to care and ensure a flourishing future for this marvelous part of the Earth.

I've said to many people and I think it's absolutely true that there is no institute whose quality is any better—there might be some that are equal, but there is none that has so successfully put together such a wide array of programming.

John Reynolds, former NPS Deputy Director and
Former Superintendent, North Cascades National Park

1 | BEGINNINGS

NORTH CASCADES INSTITUTE CAME TO BE because the right people were in the right place at the right time with a good idea, deep commitment to that idea, and determination to see it become reality. Saul Weisberg, Tom Fleischner, Ed Grumbine, Jeff Hardesty, and Tim Jordan thought the time was right to create a "field school" in the North Cascades. Their knowledge of this place was growing as they traveled and studied it as field biologists, outdoor educators, mountaineers, and park rangers. As their delight in discoveries and adventures grew, the idea of sharing this special place with others captured their imagination and offered an outlet for their youthful idealism. All were conservationists and educators, and they thought they might advance the conservation of this special mountain region through field-based learning.

The North Cascades was their inspiration. A wild, gloriously scenic concentration of mountains, glaciers, deep forested valleys, and falling waters, a large part of the range had been included in North Cascades National Park in 1968. Other protected areas in the range had become parts of the National Wilderness Preservation System as the Pasayten Wilderness, Glacier Peak Wilderness, and Alpine Lakes Wilderness. Only two highways crossed the range while its southern boundary was marked by a busy interstate highway. The group thought this place, literally the back yard of a rapidly growing urban region in the Puget Sound Basin, should be better known by those who could barely see it on their eastern horizon. They believed that caring for a place required knowing it, and that pursuing opportunities to help residents get to know it would help to conserve and protect it.

While parts of the region were park and wilderness and thus protected to some degree, conservation was still needed. When the group bandied about the idea of an environmental field school in the early 1980s, Ronald Reagan was President of the United States and his administration was avowedly anti-conservation. Most of the North Cascades was federal public land under the management of the National Park Service and the Forest Service. Timber harvesting was rising to an all-time high in the national forests. James Watt was Secretary of the Interior and no one was sure what might befall the National Park Service and the exceptional landscapes in its care, like the North Cascades. Conservationists who had achieved so much in the region by protecting portions as national parks and wilderness could not rest on their laurels.

THE RIGHT TIME

THE 1970S HAD SEEN THE EMERGENCE of "environmental education" and renewed interest in "outdoor education," an approach to teaching about the natural world that had been popular on and off since the late 19th century. Environmental education embraced much of what outdoor education had been teaching but broadened it to include an ecological emphasis and emergent issues like pollution, population growth, and loss of biological diversity. Outdoor education had long embraced experiential methods of teaching and learning, moving outside the classroom to experience the environment and to learn as much as possible there about subjects ranging from reading to math. Environmental education was doing the same but broadening the content to include, in the words of one historian of the period, working toward protecting the beauty, health, and permanence of nature in the 20th century.[1] The field school envisioned by the Institute group would use the outdoor classroom to teach about the North Cascades environment, employing experiential methods to contribute to conservation.

The idea of field schools associated with federal land management agencies was also growing as these five guys thought about creating one in the North Cascades. In 1966, a seventh-grade science teacher in Jackson, Wyoming named Ted Major began taking his students into the field. With Grand Teton National Park in the neighborhood, he looked to the National Park Service for help establishing a year-round school. In 1973, the Grand Teton Environmental Education Center was born; this later grew into the Teton Science Schools. In California, the Yosemite Institute appeared in 1971 with the strong support of the National Park Service, and in the east the environmental education center which was to become Great Smoky Mountains Institute at Tremont was built in Great Smoky Mountains National Park. The friends asked themselves, why not do something like this in the North Cascades, where an ecosystem approach would involve not only the National Park Service but also the U.S. Forest Service? The latter agency had some educational programs, even though education was not as central to its mission as it was to the Park Service's. These agencies were embracing environmental education, the Park Service partnering with Major and other educators like him to expand their programs.

The early 1980s was clearly the right time and the North Cascades the right place for a group of environmentally literate outdoorsmen, highly motivated conservationists, and educators to visualize a field-based program focused on a landscape they knew and loved. Public land politics, educational theory and practice, and an opportunity to try something new in education converged to encourage the initiative that was to become the North Cascades Institute. It would be different than the other field schools, reflecting the geography of the place and the ideas and talents of its leaders.

THE RIGHT PLACE

A BIT OF GEOGRAPHICAL AND HISTORICAL BACKGROUND will help us understand how and why the North Cascades Institute emerged as it did in

1986. First, the geography. The North Cascades Mountains are unique in the lower forty-eight United States. Geologically they are a compact range with very steep topography. When huge tectonic plates collide with each other, a crumpled landscape results, and that is just what we have in the North Cascades. A jumble of peaks rise five to nine thousand feet above sea level, with two volcanoes pushing well beyond ten thousand feet. Positioned as they are just inland from the Pacific Ocean, the mountains are inundated with precipitation which drapes them with glaciers and snowfields. Trees thrive in the moist, moderate climate of the lower elevations, creating one of the world's greatest temperate rain forests. Rivers drain these forests, flowing west into Puget Sound and the Salish Sea and east into the Columbia River. Natural communities are rich and diverse. Storm clouds off the North Pacific are thrust up and drop their loads on the west side of the range. Douglas fir, western hemlock, and western red cedar dominate the forest, with silver fir, mountain hemlock, and subalpine fir rimming the steep, forested slopes. On the drier eastern side of the range, lodgepole and ponderosa pine join Douglas fir with whitebark pine, Englemann spruce, and subalpine larch on the higher slopes and ridges, all of it rich habitat for plant and animal life.

As the group knew, this environment was rich with opportunities for exploration and discovery. Initially they conceived Institute programs focused primarily on natural history—flora and fauna, rocks and rivers, meadows and glaciers, and ecological communities and processes. The North Cascades country held many wonders to be discovered and shared. Much lowland forest had been logged, but thanks to the herculean efforts of conservationists like those of the North Cascades Conservation Council (Pat Goldsworthy, Polly Dyer, Phil and Laura Zalesky, Harvey Manning, and many others), some of this forest landscape had been preserved. Included in the North Cascades National Park Complex were its two National Recreation Areas, Ross Lake and Lake Chelan, and the U.S. Forest Service managed Glacier Peak and Pasayten Wilderness. Conservationists knew what had been protected and what remained unprotected, but many residents of the Puget Sound lowlands and across the Pacific Northwest had yet to learn.

Lowland forests of the west side of the North Cascades proved a bonanza for the timber industry in the 20th century, "green gold" as some called it. The Institute could lead exploration of the stands of Douglas fir, western hemlock, and western red cedar that survived the logger's saw and achieved immense size in the moist and moderate climate. Gazing up in awe at trees towering hundreds of feet above them, Institute students could learn what constituted an ancient forest in its prime at 350 to 750 years old, and the importance of its structural and biological diversity. They might learn, as distinguished University of Washington botany professor Art Kruckeberg (one of the Institute's early instructors) wrote, "The old-growth forest eloquently dramatizes the ecological adage: 'Everything is connected to everything else.' The trees, the subordinate plant life of the understory, the animals, and all the rest of the seen and unseen organisms of the forest ecosystem, create a grand symbiosis—a self-perpetuating, mutually advantageous system of life."[2]

Photo by Nick Mikula, Courtesy of NCI

A grand view looking south from the Sourdough Mountain trail to Diablo Lake and peaks beyond.

People in Institute courses could travel trails in the National Park and in the Mount Baker-Snoqualmie, Okanogan, and Wenatchee National Forests. They could drive over passes on the few roads, especially the North Cascades Highway, through lowland forests to other natural communities as they changed with decreasing precipitation from west and east of the Cascade Divide. On the west side, hikers could climb through a climax of western hemlock and western red cedar, through mixed forest, and ultimately to alpine tundra above timberline. To the east, the climb might go through lodgepole and ponderosa pine, also topping out on some of the higher ridges and peaks above timberline. Hikers could encounter the differing effects of elevation, precipitation, topography, and aspect, and see flora and fauna, especially wildflowers during the summer months in sub-alpine meadows. Visitors could observe "snowbank communities" as plants matured at different rates with snowmelt occurring at different places and speeds. The opportunities for natural history exploration and discovery in these mountains were endless, but guides to such wonders were few.

The North Cascades contain most of the glaciers in the lower 48 states. Some of them, like the Coleman Glacier on the west side of Mount Baker and the Easton Glacier on its south side, can be reached by relatively short hikes. The "Railroad Grade," a lateral moraine of the Easton Glacier, is the perfect place to observe and explain the dynamics of glaciers, how they are created and sustained, how they advance and retreat, and how glaciers to-day are mostly retreating and why. The scenery on the Railroad Grade on a clear or mostly clear day—and there are many in summer—is monumental, the white dome of Mount Baker looming above, with unsurpassed views south across the Cascades and west to the Salish Sea. People could hike up there on their own, and were doing so, but with an instructor like National Park Service geologist Jon Riedel to explain what they were seeing, they were likely to understand much more about this amazing landscape.

A field school like that imagined by Saul, Tom, and the others could offer visitors to places like the Railroad Grade a richer experience than if they simply ventured up there on their own. Biologists, ecologists, and geologists might entice people to such places who would not go there otherwise for one reason or another. Experienced outdoor leaders like the Institute founders, along with experts like Kruckeberg, Riedel, and others, could ensure safe, rich outings and an understanding of the natural history of the mountains.

NATURE AND CULTURE

THE NORTH CASCADES ARE NOT ONLY a natural landscape. The forests, wildlife, geology, and other elements of place generated by nature are overlain with culture. They have a prehistory and a history; a time before anyone recorded events on the landscape in oral or written forms, and a time when they did. Humans have lived in and around the North Cascades "since time immemorial," according to Indigenous People, or for at least 9,500 years according to the archaeological record.

Initially the founders thought to focus their field school primarily on natural history. They were, after all, naturalists and biologists. However, they could not overlook the fact that all the lines on the land—counties, cities, the National Park, and national forests—were products of relatively recent cultural changes. They also understood that all dimensions of this unique place, its history and natural history, art, and literature, should be grist for their educational mill.

The founders were not only educators but also conservationists, and their overriding goal was to promote conservation through field-based educational experiences. "Conservation" has several versions, one of which involves wise use of natural resources like trees and water to avoid waste and depletion. Another emphasizes preservation, as of the beauty and wildness of a place like the North Cascades. This landscape had been divided up, lines drawn on it for parks and forests, by the politics of conservation. In prehistory, there were divisions among tribes—the Lummi, Nooksack, Sto'lo, Upper Skagit, Swinomish, Sauk-Suiattle, and Nlaka'pamux Nation— but the lines drawn by Indigenous People did not reflect different values of the land as those of white settlers did. Indigenous Peoples thought of the North Cascades as home. Settlers of European ancestry pushed onto the land these Indigenous Peoples had lived on for millennia and claimed title, often taking their land outright and denying them their cultural autonomy. When the American government drew lines upon the land for conservation or development, freedoms the Indigenous People and even the new settlers had taken for granted were often reduced or eliminated. The Indigenous history of the land in this mountainous place, the founders soon realized, was as ripe for discovery and exploration by the field school as its natural history.

The aesthetics of the North Cascades are exceptional. The steep, soaring peaks draped in snow and clouds are often mysterious, playing with the viewer; a ridge appears here, a summit there. Turn a corner on a trail or road or even a bend on the Skagit River, and Mount Baker appears, looming unexpectedly high above. On stormy days, the wind-driven clouds seem to be dragging on the firs as if the trees are drinking from them, streaming off them like flags. In fact that is exactly what they are doing, the trees milking some of the moisture out of the clouds and fog. The mountains sometimes seem enormous, so unlike the landscapes of daily experience that they elicit awe, even fear. Eighteenth and nineteenth century writers like John Muir often referred to the emotion evoked by their experience of mountains as the sublime—an emotional response involving awe, wonder, excitement, fear, and transport to a higher plain of appreciation. Scenery that draws such a response is as much a natural resource as timber or water and would become a rich vein to be mined by the Institute.

The founders thought of the project they would build as primarily a natural history field school but quickly came to appreciate that the beauty of the North Cascades could be explored even as the wonders of natural history were revealed. Their conception of the "natural resources" of this mountain expanded, and aesthetics became as central to the educational program as natural history. Writers, painters, and photographers would join ecologists, geologists, and other natural scientists, as well as historians and archaeologists, to explore the wonders and mysteries of this place with clients young and old.

All of this was intended to inform and inspire, but also to expose people to a special place in hopes that they would come to love it enough to actively care for it. The status of lands as National Forests and Parks provided some measure of protection to values of scenery, wildlife, and ecological integrity—the parks certainly more than the forests. But as iconic conservationist David Brower often said, the work of conservation is never done. "Victories" in conservation battles like that resulting in North Cascades National Park are temporary unless those who care for the beauty of an old growth forest, the protection of an intact ecological community, and the silence of a wild place are informed about what is at stake and remain vigilant in protecting it.

Threats to a place like the North Cascades involve big, complex issues and ideas. Education is most often focused on young people, and this was true of Forest Service and National Park Service educational programs at this time, but there was a great need for adult outdoor environmental education as well. Adults, after all, were making the decisions (and voting) about whether and how the place should be exploited. Even government agency educational programs aimed at young people were limited. The primary missions of agencies like the Park Service and Forest Service were not education but management. Agency approaches to protection of the land relied principally on regulation. A private partner like an Institute dedicated to the mission of conservation through education could add to and expand what the agencies were able to do.

The programming of the Institute might begin with adults, but the need to educate young people was also urgent. Most of the education of young people was formal and consigned to classrooms. Robert Michael Pyle, a most literate ecologist, was writing at this time of "the extinction of experience," a process in which people, especially children, do not experience rich and varied environments and are ignorant of the world's diversity. This can contribute, in his words, to "disaffection, alienation, and apathy." The concept of "environmental generational amnesia" had not yet been described, but thoughtful naturalists like the founders sensed that if one never experiences a diverse natural environment, they will never know what they have missed. These and other ideas about the importance of the experience of nature for people of all ages, but especially for the young, were part of the need for a field school perceived by Saul and the other members of what they initially called the Shuksan Institute.

Many people dream of launching an enterprise based on their youthful idealism, but few actually do it. North Cascades Institute came to be because a group of young men let their imaginations run in directions inspired by their love of nature, of the outdoors, of field biology, and of public lands like national parks and forests. They were ambitious and confident that the world needed what they had to offer and that they could provide it. They had no idea what they might be in for, but they were not afraid of the unknown. They hoped that perhaps they would be able to nurture their passions for outdoor adventure and natural history and make a living doing it. As it turned out, the time was right to pursue this dream of a field-oriented educational program in the North Cascades. The story we tell here explains how this proved to be so.

Thanks and love to Jeff and Tom and Ed and Tim—without you fellows I'd be just another bum on the dole.

Saul Weisberg to fellow members of The Shuksan Institute, 1984

II | SOWING SEEDS

Four guys gathered one summer for a couple days and nights on the Lightning Creek Float, a floating base camp on Ross Lake complete with a cabin. This was used by the National Park Service as it patrolled the Ross Lake National Recreation Area, part of the North Cascades National Park Complex. The four were Saul Weisberg, Tom Fleischner, Tim Jordan, and Jeff Hardesty; the year was 1982. All were working seasonally for the National Park Service in the North Cascades National Park Complex. Jordan was the ranger at Lightning Creek, Saul was a climbing ranger, Tom an interpretive naturalist, and Jeff a backcountry ranger. They came together that summer afternoon to kick around their idea for a field school focused on the North Cascades. Ed Grumbine, the fifth member of the group, was away working in a field school in California but would join them later for similar meetings.

As they kicked back and quaffed a few beers and some sake, gazing across the tranquil lake, they could hardly contain their enthusiasm for their ideas and the friendships forged over the years. All of them loved the landscape in which they worked. All had experience teaching outdoors. All were naturalists concerned about the conservation of places like the North Cascades and cared for nature and the environment in general. Saul, Tom, Ed, and Tim all had a connection with Antioch College in Yellow Springs, Ohio. Saul and Ed were graduates; Tom and Tim had transferred from Antioch to The Evergreen State College in Washington. Both Antioch and Evergreen were considered radical institutions of higher learning at the time, indicating perhaps that all four had in their makeup a willingness to take risks and stretch beyond the norms of conventional education.

One feature of an Antioch education was that it required students to work on jobs related to their academic interest, and this took Saul west. He worked in the Field Museum in Chicago, as a sheepherder for the Southern Ute Tribe in the Southwest, surveying birds in Sequoia National Forest, and on a salmon troller off the Washington coast. During his college years he went to climb in the Tetons, Olympics, and Canadian Rockies. After graduation he packed up and headed to join his friends Tom and Tim, then at Evergreen. Jeff was also a student at Evergreen and Olympia, Washington became base camp for all of them.

Photo by Bob Mierendorf

The five who conceived the idea for a field school in the North Cascades, reunited in 1997. From left to right: Tom Fleischner, Ed Grumbine, Jeff Hardesty, Saul Weisberg, Tim Jordan.

These five shared a love of the outdoors and outdoor adventure, but another shared experience was teaching outdoors. Tom and Tim had worked at outdoor schools in New England and had found working with young people in that setting very rewarding. Jeff had instructed at the National Outdoor Leadership School, and Ed became an instructor and then director of the Sierra Institute, an extended education field program affiliated with UC Santa Cruz. Saul taught natural history and climbing at the Foresta Institute in Nevada for a season, but at this stage thought of himself as a field biologist rather than a field instructor.

In 1980 Tim moved to Seattle to teach at Antioch University, Ed to California to work for the Sierra Institute, and Jeff to Wyoming to become program director of the Teton Science School. They remained in touch, and after Saul landed a summer job in North Cascades National Park in 1979, he urged the others to join him. All but Ed became seasonal park rangers, working in the park during the summer of 1981. During the off season Saul and Tom earned Master of Science Degrees in Biology at Western Washington University, Tim worked as a psychologist in Seattle, Ed ran the Sierra Institute, and Jeff continued to work at Teton Science School. They remained inspired by the idea of a field school in the North Cascades, and this brought them together on the Lightning Creek Float in 1982 and on several other occasions.

At this point, Jeff and Ed had some experience running programs. They all recognized that they knew very little about what creating an organization might involve but, dreamers that they were, they were not deterred. Their goals were to teach natural history in the field and to do it together. While they were tied to the Pacific Northwest, not necessarily the North Cascades, they knew this place and were excited at the prospect of spending even more time there. After exploring their ideas at Lightning Creek, they met off and on over the next three years, exploring what it would take to start an institute, envisioning programs, and trying to figure out how they could all make a living, even a modest one, teaching at the Institute forming in their minds. In the fall of 1984 they met regularly, gathering in November at the Teton Science School (which was closed for the winter) to develop their ideas further. Saul had met with Keith Miller, Superintendent of North Cascades National Park, to float their idea and Miller had rejected it outright. Tom and Saul had taught a field course for the Sierra Institute in Olympic National Park in the fall of 1983 and approached the chief of interpretation there with their idea for a field school. He was enthusiastically in favor of it. Perhaps in view of these contrasting receptions, they thought they should focus on the well established Olympic National Park rather than the still young North Cascades National Park Complex.

At the Teton rendezvous Tom, Saul, Jeff, and Ed fleshed out their ideas, compiled lists of possible programs and course topics, discussed budgets, and got down to some nitty-gritty. Their goal remained for all of them to teach outdoors in the field, hopefully with each other, but doubts about the viability of their dream crept in. Could a program support all of them? Probably not. Coming from his experience with the Sierra Institute, Ed was convinced that field programs in the North Cascades would not work because, in his words, "You can't teach in the rain." Discouraged, all returned to their winter jobs and the prospect of an institute in the North Cascades, which they were still calling Shuksan Institute, seemed to dim.

They had been working on their dream for four years. Their vision was that they would operate the Shuksan Institute as a "collective" and would form the Board as well as staff the programs. They knew of a few models like this across the country and had been told they would need a board to satisfy the Internal Revenue Service and raise money. They envisioned an organization with as little bureaucracy as possible, where they could spend the majority of their time in the field. At this point the focus was on teaching college students and adults, especially teachers who would get credit for their participation. They approached several institutions of higher education in hope of affiliating with them in some way so credit could be offered but found no takers. Tom and Saul did much of the work fleshing out the plans for the Shuksan Institute, while the others were occupied with full-time jobs. The biggest challenge was to find a way to begin, particularly to raise funds to cover initial expenses and very modest compensation for the work.

THE NORTH CASCADES INSTITUTE IS LAUNCHED

SAUL RETURNED TO HIS CLIMBING RANGER JOB in the summer of 1984. His boss was Wilderness District Ranger Bill Lester. Saul shared the idea of a field institute with Lester, finding him very interested and supportive. The summer of 1984 also saw a change of leadership at the Park when

John Reynolds became the new superintendent. A young, ambitious, rising leader of the National Park Service, John had been encouraged by his new boss, Regional Director Jim Tobin, to take North Cascades National Park Complex in some new directions. In October, very new to the job, John was scheduled to take a helicopter flight out of the Marblemount Wilderness Office where Saul was working as lead wilderness technician to wrap up the season. Before leaving, John introduced himself and Saul mentioned his idea for a field institute, unaware that John had Tobin's instructions and was familiar with the field institute idea that was already being implemented in several National Park Service areas. John flew off and the idea percolated for months.

As Superintendent Reynolds settled in, he held regular management team meetings with his assistant superintendent, the division chiefs in Sedro-Woolley, his administrative assistant, and two district rangers, one of whom was Elaine Hounsell of the Skagit District. At one of the meetings the team discussed the idea John brought up that there should be an education nonprofit associated with the Park. He suggested the idea in a generic way, not remembering his brief interaction with Saul the previous fall. As was her regular practice, Hounsell reported on the meeting to her district staff, one whom was Bill Lester, who quickly contacted John to explain that Tom and Saul had written up just such a proposal for North Cascades which had been rejected by the previous superintendent. Bill suggested that he, Tom, and Saul meet with the superintendent to explain the idea. John agreed and they met in October 1985. Tom and Saul described their proposed field institute in detail and John, seeing a new direction in which the Park could go, asked what it would take to bring their idea to fruition.

This meeting proved to be the breakthrough that resulted in the establishment of the North Cascades Institute. What they needed was support from the Park Service and some resources with which to begin work. Bill suggested that he could keep Tom and Saul on as backcountry rangers during the off season to work on getting the program ready for the summer of 1986. John approved the minimal funding needed and let them use NPS office space in Sedro-Woolley headquarters. This space included any empty desk in park headquarters that might be open on a given day, complete with a phone and an IBM Selectric typewriter. With files in a plastic file box, thus began the Institute's brief "traveling office" period. Tom and Saul, as co-directors of the Institute, began conceiving classes, recruiting instructors, typing up a catalogue, recruiting a founding board, and applying to the IRS for non-profit 501(c)3 status.

At this point in its early history the core idea for the Institute changed slightly but significantly. The year was 1986 and Ronald Reagan had been president for six years. His was a decidedly anti-conservation administration. As a consequence, conservation activism was growing in the political arena, and it occurred to Tom and Saul that no one seemed to be thinking of education as a form of such activism. Support for environmental education was increasing and had an activist ring to it, and not only might the Institute increase people's awareness of, knowledge about, and care for the natural world, but perhaps Institute programs could address some conservation issues through educating rather than politicking. The Institute would not advocate politically, but it could help people understand what they could do about challenges facing the environment. John also suggested the Institute consider focusing on the entire North Cascades ecosystem, which it eventually did, and this also considerably expanded the scope of its programming. In these ways the Institute's ambitions grew significantly.

North Cascades Institute received IRS nonprofit status in February of 1986 and programs were launched in the summer of that year. During the previous fall and winter, while moving from desk to desk at park headquarters in Sedro Woolley, Saul and Tom contacted naturalists in the region and invited them to be Institute instructors. Everyone they asked enthusiastically embraced the opportunity to teach in the mountains, and the catalog they distributed offered 23 field courses taught by highly qualified experts, primarily two or three days long. They asked the Seattle Mountaineers, Audubon chapters, and local outdoor photographer Lee Mann if they would share their mailing lists to help get the word out to their members, and they were happy to do so. A catalog introducing the Institute and the first menu of field seminars was mailed to over 5,000 people in the region. Saul and Tom waited anxiously to see if anyone would respond and admit to being surprised when registrations started coming in. When the first check arrived for a field seminar, according to Saul, they realized that they needed to open a bank account.

A founding Board of Directors had been established as a prerequisite to applying for 501(c)3 status as a nonprofit corporation. John and his assistant Margie Allen were initial Board members along with Tom and Saul. John soon invited Sylvia Thorpe, a Bellingham psychologist interested in writing a history of the village of Stehekin in the Lake Chelan National Recreation Area, to be a Board member and she accepted. He also invited John Miles, Dean of Huxley College of Environmental Studies at nearby Western Washington University, and he accepted and became Board chair. This small group assisted the co-directors in drafting the application to the IRS, and by February the IRS had responded with amazing celerity. All the pieces were in place to begin realizing the dream of the Shuksan Institute, though by this time the group was down to two. Tim, Jeff, and Ed, having continued with their day jobs, were now scattered in Seattle, Florida, and California. They remained close friends and supporters. The Institute's name was changed, and Saul and Tom became co-founders of the North Cascades Institute.

THE NATIONAL PARK SERVICE EMBRACES THE INSTITUTE

The key to realizing the dream was the support of Lester and Reynolds which, in the North Cascades microcosm, translated to the support of the National Park Service. Park Service culture had generally been inwardly focused, believing that agency professionals knew best what a park, its resources, and its visitors needed. They were the experts whether involved in resource management, visitor services, or education in the parks. The exception to this over the decades has been concessions and cooperating associations, when the NPS contracted out services such as lodging, food service, and sales of books, maps, souvenirs, and other products within the parks. Nearly from its inception the agency recognized a place in national park management for private enterprise but took upon itself the task of educating its visitors.

Thoughtful leaders recognized the need and opportunity for education in the parks early in national park history. Legislation creating the first national park at Yellowstone in 1872 stated that it "should be dedicated and set apart as a public park or pleasuring-ground for the benefit and enjoyment of the people." Establishing the National Park Service in 1916, Congress stipulated that the purpose of national parks "is to conserve the scenery and the natural and historic objects and the wild life therein and to provide for the enjoyment of same in such manner and by such means as will leave them unimpaired for the enjoyment of future generations."[3]

Nothing was said explicitly about the educational values of national parks, but early in the 20th century many park advocates argued that "enjoyment" should not be the only value of park visits. Parks like Yellowstone, while they had remarkable scenery to be enjoyed, also contained mysteries like geysers and grizzly bears after all. The more people knew and understood about things like natural history in Yellowstone and archaeology in Mesa Verde National Park, the deeper and more rewarding their visits would be. Founding Park Service Director Stephen Mather stated in 1916, "One of the chief functions of the national parks and monuments is to serve educational purposes."[4] Secretary of the Interior Franklin Lane wrote that same year, "It is the destiny of the national parks, if wisely controlled, to become the public laboratories of nature study for the Nation."[5] An educational approach called "interpretation" was born to serve these purposes.

Courtesy of John Reynolds

John Reynolds, as the new superintendent of North Cascades National Park Complex in 1985, supported the idea of a field institute in the park and made possible the emergence of the North Cascades Institute.

A park interpreter attempts to explain the essences of what national park visitors experience, be they natural, historical, or archaeological. Facts are part of this, but information by itself is not enough. Interpretation should also be revelation and provocation. It must relate to the personal experience of the visitor. Ideally it leads to a feeling of connection to what is being interpreted. The Park Service has employed field interpreters since the 1920s, but their importance in agency priorities had waxed and waned often over the sixty years before John embraced the North Cascades Institute. Interpretation was suffering one of its periods of decline in the early 1980s. Commenting on a report on Interpretation he was distributing to regional directors and superintendents in 1982, Park Service Director Russ Dickenson ascribed the decline in interpretation to a growing National Park System faced with "budget cuts, position cuts, inflation, and a 'series of special emphasis programs and initiatives.'"[6] The United States was in recession and Ronald Reagan's Interior Secretary James Watt was squeezing Park Service budgets. By the time John became Superintendent of North Cascades mid-decade budgets had improved a bit, but interpretation was still not a high priority.

John Reynolds was an unusually entrepreneurial superintendent and immediately recognized the potential for the North Cascades Institute to complement and supplement the educational programs of the relatively new North Cascades National Park. Less than two decades after its establishment, it was still early in developing its interpretation and education programs. In a 2009 interview John said, "The Institute felt right to me from the very beginning as an opportunity for a really practical, altruistic approach to connecting people with the National Park and the rest of the ecosystem in which the Park operates. We were trying to create a National Park that could respond more effectively to the kinds of opportunities and problems that would manifest themselves in the future."[7] North Cascades was and is a wilderness park, and access to its glories very limited. Thus it, along with other wilderness national parks like Olympic and Sequoia-Kings Canyon, posed different challenges for connecting with visitors than more accessible parks like Yellowstone and Yosemite. John observed, "One of the things that was obvious pretty early on at North Cascades was that it didn't have a broad constituency. It was limited to a wilderness and hiking community." How might the park constituency be broadened? He thought the Institute might be key to meeting that challenge.

That first field season, the summer of 1986, the Institute offered 23 field seminars. They were listed in the catalogue and participants had to sign up in advance. If a seminar did not "make" with enough participants to pay a modest stipend to instructors by a specified date, it would be canceled.

Of the field seminars offered, all but three enrolled the minimum and they were harbingers of things to come. "Birds of the North Cascades" was offered by Bellingham's Terry Wahl, an authority on the birds of northwest Washington. Courses on "Geology of the North Cascades" and "Mountain Wildflowers" were offered by professors from Western Washington University. North Cascades National Park archaeologist Bob Mierendorf's course was "People of the Mountain World," hosted in Stehekin on the south end of the park complex. Photography and art workshops were offered, as were Family Nature Programs and "Discovery Dayhikes." While not all of these programs made this first year, they suggested future directions Institute programming would explore.

John Reynolds, Bill Lester, and the National Park Service were essential to launching the Institute, but the educational programs were not confined to the National Park complex. Saul and Tom had taken John's advice and reached beyond park boundaries with their program ideas. Three national forests surrounded the park, and across the Canadian border were British Columbia's provincial parks and recreation areas. The Institute would teach about the North Cascades ecosystem well beyond the park. John encouraged Tom and Saul to reach out and include the Forest Service in its programming. Park headquarters were in the small town of Sedro-Woolley, as was the Mount Baker Ranger District office of the Mount Baker-Snoqualmie National Forest. A cost-cutting decision had been made to have the two offices share a building. The Institute, tied to the NPS office, found itself conveniently located in close proximity to both the Park Service and Forest Service. The two agencies had very different missions, the NPS administering its lands for preservation and recreation and the Forest Service mandated to manage its lands for multiple uses. Logging in Mount Baker-Snoqualmie was at an all-time high, clearly the agency priority in the Reagan years, but Mount Baker District Ranger Larry Hudson was receptive to Institute program ideas.

At this time in national forest history political pressures were forcing increased timber cuts, but at the same time the Forest Service was facing many new challenges. Environmentalists were protesting what they saw as unsustainable timber harvesting, sometimes physically blocking timber operations. Many in the public and even in the Forest Service thought the agency was cutting too much and neglecting the other uses of national forests. Wildlife issues in particular were increasing, with the northern spotted owl the focus of concern about endangered species in the Pacific Northwest. Winds of change were blowing through Forest Service offices from Washington, D.C. to Sedro-Woolley. The Park Service and Forest Service had long been at odds nationally and in the North Cascades—the National Park had been carved out of national forests and was strongly opposed by the Forest Service—but thrown together as they were in Sedro-Woolley, they seemed to be getting along and both agencies welcomed the educational expertise of the upstart North Cascades Institute. The Forest Service badly needed some good press, and educational programs on the national forest might help.

Reynolds and his Chief of Natural Resources Jon Jarvis were looking at the North Cascades as an ecosystem, which is also how Tom and Saul were thinking of it. New ideas about managing such a place were emerging in the Park Service and even in the Forest Service, where there was growing awareness that efforts to meet high timber targets were compromising other forest values. When the Institute proposed a seminar titled "Ecosystem Management" that would describe a new approach to forest management, Mount Baker-Snoqualmie Forest Supervisor Doug McWilliams forbade it. If this term was used, the Forest Service would have nothing to do with the Institute. Yet, soon after this confrontation, the Forest Service chief adopted a new policy he called "Ecosystem Management." These were fraught times for the Forest Service, and while the Institute had a policy against advocacy about any issue, it could explore new ideas emerging in natural resource management without judging whether they should be policy or not. Education as they practiced it could be a tool to help the public understand what all the fuss was about because the struggles over species at risk, like the northern spotted owl, and issues of forest management were very much in the public eye in the Pacific Northwest. Field seminars and day hikes took participants into the Mount Baker-Snoqualmie and Okanogan National Forests with a broad focus on the nature and management of these parts of the public lands. Leaders and instructors offered introductions to natural and cultural history and reviewed issues, often in response to questions from participants. Hikes and backpacks, all of which included content about the issues of the landscapes being explored, gave the public an opportunity to see for themselves what was at stake in the management of their public lands.

INSTITUTE LEADERS EMERGE

As the Institute grew it attracted several people to the team who proved important to its success. One was Russ Dickenson, recently retired director of the National Park Service, who had served as Pacific Northwest regional director before his service in Washington, D.C. He lived near Seattle. John recruited him, and his was a voice of wisdom and experience as a Board member. He understood the politics of federal agencies and provided invaluable insights during his several years of Board service. Another recruit was Brian Scheuch, a businessman who lived in La Conner and an avid naturalist who signed up for a course Saul was teaching at Harts Pass. Brian enjoyed the field seminar and questioned Saul about the Institute. He listened, sitting in the Pass, as Saul shared his dreams. "And I let him talk a lot and I thought, this guy is never going to make it," Brian recalled. "He's going to save the world, he's noble and a fine person, but he's never going to make it and I told him that." Saul, he thought, was no businessman and didn't even think about the Institute as a business. Too bad. Much to his surprise, Saul called him two months later and, according to Brian, said, "if you think you're so damned smart maybe you'd better join us. And that was the start of our 23-year relationship."[8] For 23 years Brian served as a Board member, sharing his business acumen and offering counsel and advice in his droll and humorous way. Saul did not aspire to be a businessman in the beginning, but soon realized that Brian was right—idealism alone would not sustain an organization with the scope and ambition of North Cascades Institute.

The key to the success of the Institute from the beginning was good instruction and leadership in the field. In the first stage of the Institute's history, the programming focus was on adult field seminars. If participants signed up for a seminar, paid their fee, and did not come away feeling good about their experience, the Institute would not succeed. Building a pool of satisfied clients who would tell their friends about how much fun they had and how much they learned on a North Cascades Institute seminar was a critical early step in establishing the organization. Fortunately, Saul and Tom recruited instructors from the very beginning who delivered these qualities and outcomes. Instructors had to be masters of content, of botany, geology, ecology, history, and other subjects pertinent to the North Cascades region. They had to be comfortable in an informal field setting, able to safely conduct outdoor experiences, and willing and able to use experiential methods in their approach to their subject. Most seminar groups were diverse in their knowledge of the topics addressed, so instructors had to be able to gauge the level at which they should address their subject and adapt their approach accordingly. Not least, they had to be enthusiastic teachers, excited about what they knew and about sharing it. They had to be enjoying the subject, the place, and the interaction with people who came out to learn and have a good time. This was a large order, but Saul and Tom proved excellent recruiters of the types of instructors who would launch the program.

In their recruiting of some instructors, they tapped people who had been their teachers. In their studies of biology at Western Washington University their mentors had included botanist Ron Taylor, author of widely praised books on wildflowers of the region. They had also encountered geologist Scott Babcock at Western and knew of his passion for North Cascades geology and for science education beyond the university classroom. They knew he loved to teach in the field and was good at it. An early recruit was Robert Michael Pyle, whose broad expertise embraced butterflies, about which he had authored the first WA field guide. In 1982 Bob decided he would dedicate his extensive knowledge of conservation, lepidoptera, ecology, and nature interpretation to writing and teaching. The Institute was a great venue for a freelance writer/naturalist/teacher and Bob said, "When NCI came along, it seemed custom made for an approach that one could take to go into the field, connect with plants and animals but also with people who cared about plants and animals."[9] He exemplified the qualities of an ideal Institute instructor.

ADULT FIELD SEMINARS

Instructors like these were the core of programs in the early years of the Institute, most of which were two-day adult field seminars. Saul might, for instance, conceive a seminar on the ecology and wildflowers of the Cascade Crest which he would teach at Harts Pass, the only road access east of the divide to the Cascade Crest not on a main highway. The pass offered expansive views, was accessible by car to a nice campground, and had abundant meadows and trails reaching diverse habitats. The content and locale of the seminar were briefly described in the catalogue and participants could call to reserve a spot. Typically, the group would either meet at a campground in the mountains, or meet somewhere like the Sedro-Woolley office or Mazama store and carpool to the site. If the seminar was an overnight, everyone would come prepared to car-camp in the campground, contribute to a potluck dinner, and bring their other meals. They would be given information prior to the trip about what they might need for the weather and the cooler temperatures of a high mountain place like Harts Pass.

If the group met in Sedro-Wooley they might make a couple of stops at overlooks on the way over the mountains on the North Cascades Highway, where Saul would describe the transition from the marine-influenced (and thus moist) west side of the range to the drier east side. After an exciting passage of aptly named Deadhorse Point on the gravel road up to Harts Pass, the group would pitch camp and head out to explore the subject of the seminar, guided in their inquiry by Saul the field naturalist. A hike up Slate Peak provided an opportunity for a broad overview of the region, its geology, topography, and a bit of history focused on mining and the now-abandoned lookout on the peak. A short hike in nearly any direction led them out to meadows, wildflowers, marmots, and exploration of the many adaptations of life to the high mountain environment.

The evening meal might take a while with everyone contributing, but afterward everyone relaxed and talked around the campfire about what they had learned, what they wished to do tomorrow, and what topics of interest they wanted to investigate. Probing each other's knowledge, the group usually expanded on the lessons of the day. Someone might know a lot about botany, someone else the history of the Methow Valley and its mining industry, and another the history of the wilderness movement and how it played out in the region. The leader, in this case Saul, could bring in more ideas he wanted to share. Social interaction and sharing were essential qualities of these adult field seminars. The group was learning about the content of the seminar conceived by the instructor but also learning about each other, the place they found themselves in, and issues that might be current. The field seminar, brief though it might be, often opened participants to information, ideas, and issues they had not previously encountered. An overnight seminar would wrap up around noon on Sunday and everyone could enjoy the scenic drive back over the North

Cascades Highway. Many participants, having enjoyed their experience, would come back for more and bring friends and family.

Photo by Saul Weisberg

Tom Fleischner and Saul Weisberg relax in 1983 while teaching a three-month Sierra Institute field seminar on the Olympic Peninsula, honing the skills they will later bring to the North Cascades Institute.

One of the goals Tom and Saul shared was to spend as much time teaching this way in the field and as little in the office as possible, but as they realized that they must think of the Institute as a business, they had to admit that running a business inevitably required much office time. Part of this realization came from the necessary tasks of administering the programs, and part from the advice and counsel of participants, Board members, and business people like Brian Scheuch and Chuck Robinson (who ran a very successful independent bookstore in Bellingham with his wife Dee). Saul found that he had a knack for the business side of the enterprise and, while he continued to teach and pursue his passion for natural history, he also enjoyed making the Institute grow. In one Harts Pass class he met a woman who wished to help the still-infant organization. An accountant, she invited Saul to bring her the Institute's rapidly growing account information and she would help him set up a bookkeeping system. He did so. He also attended a workshop on fundraising with Board members. As long as he could get out to do some teaching, office time building this organization was not so bad.

Tom, on the other hand, found the business side of the Institute less interesting. His heart was not in administration. He wanted to teach and was happy to leave the growing business of the Institute to Saul. Taking leave in the spring of 1987, he taught for the Sierra Institute in the canyon country of the southwest and resumed his North Cascades wilderness ranger duties during the summer. That fall, the Association for Experiential Education annual conference was convened at Centrum in Port Townsend, Washington. This conference brought together nearly eight hundred educators to share ideas and practices about teaching through field experience. At the conference Tom met Doug Hulmes, a faculty member at Prescott College in Prescott, Arizona. This small liberal arts college relied heavily on experiential learning models, and Hulmes told Tom they were searching for a faculty member to teach environmental studies and natural history. Tom leapt at the opportunity—the Prescott prospect seemed exactly what he was searching for in his career, a chance to teach through "intensive exploration of wild places . . . helping to facilitate groups of 10-12 people, small tribal units, developing a sense of community as they developed a sense of understanding of place."[10] Tom landed the Prescott position beginning in the fall of 1988 and taught there for nearly thirty years, becoming a leading national advocate for teaching field natural history.

Tom's departure in the fall of 1988 proved a pivotal moment in the early history of the North Cascades Institute. The original Shuksan Institute team had been whittled down to one, Saul Weisberg. All original members of the group were on career paths in which they would find fulfillment and Saul, who had earlier thought he was more interested in becoming a field biologist than an educational entrepreneur, was now the boss. The success and the future of the Institute rode on his shoulders. He and the Board discussed what his title should be; he and Tom had been "program directors." The standard title of leaders of non-profit organizations was, and is, "executive director," but Saul balked at such a "hifalutin" title for such a small outfit. Nonetheless, the Institute was growing and its future seemed bright, so the Board prevailed and he became an executive. Little did he know then what executive challenges were in his immediate future.

So I say to a lot of people if you are worried about power and control quit worrying about it! Back off the control issues and head for opportunities with full knowledge of your shared risks. Go for the opportunity and step back and watch it unfold.

John Reynolds, Superintendent
North Cascades National Park Service Complex, 1985-1988

III | A GROWING MISSION

ONE CHALLENGE FOR SAUL WEISBERG AND THE BOARD was to clarify the organization's mission, and goals that might address that mission. The original mission, "to conserve and restore northwest environments through education", served well. However, the initial optimism that this was an appropriate and achievable mission was tempered as the organization began to examine strategies and tactics. Many questions arose. Were adult field seminars, which so far had been quite successful and launched the Institute, the best or only way to achieve the goal of contributing to the conservation of the North Cascades and surrounding region? Was an adult audience the most appropriate one to focus on? What exactly did it mean to "conserve" a place like this? Was the North Cascades not already national forest, Park, and federally designated wilderness and therefore conserved? What else needed to be done to sustain and further conservation, and how might the Institute contribute to it? What did the National

Park Service, the Institute's principal partner, need to gain from the partnership? What was needed to sustain the partnership over the long term? And of course, what was necessary to sustain the business, to provide a good service and balance the books? The questions seemed to come thicker than deer flies at Cascade Pass in early summer.

Such questions were large and daunting, but by the end of the second season (1987) things were going so well the executive director and the Board were increasingly confident they could meet the challenges. Tom Fleischner's departure made the addition of a staff member necessary and possible. When financial resources allowed staff growth, Saul hired Robyn Dupre in 1988 as his administrative assistant. She proved ideal for the role. She brought an academic background in environmental studies and education to the team, was highly organized, fully understood the mission, and relieved some of the pressure on Saul by carrying part of the day-to-day work. She freed Saul up to think more about the future and how to address the challenges of the many questions just mentioned. Robyn was early in her career, as was Saul—they worked as peers. Tom's and Saul's skills and experiences had a great deal of overlap. With Robyn's hire, the roles of the two staff began to differentiate. Robyn would cover much of the office and daily administrative tasks, freeing Saul to focus on future programs, partnerships, the board, and other executive functions. The Institute staff and board entered a rich period in which ideas flowed, opportunities appeared, and the concept of the Institute began to grow.

One incident in this period is illustrative of a challenge the Institute would face throughout its history: how much to take advantage of "strategic opportunities," as Saul called them, and when to say no. After only two years, the idea of expanding the reach of the Institute to other northwest national parks was floated. In his interactions with other NPS people in the region, John Reynolds was singing the praises of the Institute and its model of educating on the public lands. The park's first Chief of Natural Resources Jon Jarvis said later that he saw the Institute "was taking the public on a deeper dive into understanding issues—and I thought this was a good idea because it was a level of interpretation and education that the National Park Service couldn't provide. We didn't have the time or the resources to take it to that next level."[11] The time might be right to extend the Institute model into national park units across the Pacific Northwest region, an exciting prospect that would enhance education in these other parks. Vigorous discussion of this possibility led to the conclusion that the prospect was flattering, but wildly beyond the capability of the still-infant Institute. It would also take the small Institute staff further away from the field and direct contact with students and instructors. Board members like Russ Dickinson and John Miles counseled caution about overreach; John and Jarvis concurred, recognizing that while the Institute was proving itself in many ways, it was too early to expand. This decision of when and how much to expand and grow was one to be faced by the organization repeatedly in its future.

CAREFUL GROWTH AND EXPANSION

THE DECISION AT THIS POINT WAS NOT TO TOTALLY REJECT geographic expansion but to instead focus on expanding the Institute's audience within the North Cascades Ecosystem in a measured and sustainable way. From the beginning of his Board tenure Brian Scheuch had argued that education of youth should be an Institute priority, but the question of how to do it had not been answered. The modest but essential revenue from fee-for-service adult seminars should continue, and the decision was made to pursue youth education programs, which would have to be subsidized. Funds were raised to bring in an experienced, certified teacher charged with conceiving a program for elementary-level students and writing grants to fund it. That teacher was Wendy Scherrer, an early graduate of Huxley College of Environmental Studies at Western Washington University and a much-revered veteran teacher in Bellingham. She joined the staff for the 1990-91 season. Like Robyn, Wendy enthusiastically embraced the mission of the Institute, was full of ideas, and went to work with a passion that she brought to the Institute for nearly a decade, teaming with Robyn and Saul.

The staff to this point were very modestly paid, the primary sources of revenue being field seminars, in-kind support, donated office space and materials from the NPS, and a few outside donations. If the program was to offer subsidized youth programs, much more revenue was needed, including foundation grants and the support of individual donors. One of the first grants that Wendy and Saul submitted was for a program aimed at fifth graders called Backyard to Backcountry, which evolved into

Mountain School. Outdoor education programs aimed at late elementary students had been offered around the country by school districts for decades. Often these were day camps, or sometimes overnight programs in "school camps" like Clear Creek Camp (established in 1925 by the Los Angeles City Public Schools) and Clear Lake Camp (located in Battle Creek, Michigan in the 1940s). These programs drew on the experiential learning theories of John Dewey and others, and subjects were nature study and science education. They targeted fifth and sixth graders because by this stage students were developing the cognitive skills to understand complex ideas, and soon their curricula in middle school or junior high would divide into discrete and separate subject-oriented classes, making movement beyond the classroom more difficult.

Building on this general outdoor education model, the Mountain School program would transport students into the North Cascades National Park where they would camp for two nights and learn of and from the place. The program would operate out of a Park campground with access to old-growth forests, the Skagit River, and myriad other fascinating natural areas. Partners would be school districts or independent schools, the Park Service, and North Cascades Institute. Instructors would be Institute staff naturalists with support from Park Service Interpretive Rangers.

The proposal to launch Mountain School was initially funded by the Henry M. Jackson Foundation and the program welcomed its first students during the fall of 1990. This funding made possible and necessary the hiring of another staff member to help design the curriculum and implement this program in the field. That brought another experienced teacher, Tracie Johannessen, to the team in 1992. Her title was "Environmental Educator", and her duties involved Mountain School and a wide variety of related projects over time. Working with Wendy, she fleshed out the curriculum, recruited school districts to participate, and trained and led a small staff of Institute teachers and interns who conducted the program. Base camp for the program was the Park Service's Newhalem Campground, one loop of which was dedicated entirely to Mountain School during the spring and fall seasons. For many of the early years the primary Mountain School "facility" was an army surplus MASH tent to provide shelter from the inevitable rain. Mountain School proved to be a strong rebuttal to Ed Grumbine's espoused belief back in the planning days that "you can't teach in the rain."

It might rain, or even snow in the early spring, but the intrepid instructors and plucky students carried on learning. Students, chaperones, and teachers slept in tents provided by the Institute, which also provided other gear including a large array of Coleman gas stoves, tarps, and Rubber Maid tubs full of clothing and teaching materials. Eventually, with support from Washington's National Park Fund, the Park Service would build a covered kitchen and dining area to ease the difficulty of provisioning the program and replace the MASH tent, which was dark and damp in all weather conditions.

Mountain School was hugely significant in the history of the Institute. Ever since it began in 1990 it has been the Institute's signature program, exposing thousands of fifth graders to the North Cascades and giving them a three-day place-based learning experience much different than what they encounter in their daily schooling. Mountain School is hands-on learning in intimate contact with nature, and it is fun. This focus on youth was limited at first, confined to elementary students, but over the decades expanded to more than a dozen programs engaging young people from fifth grade to instructors from the Institute's graduate program, who began instructing as part of their year-long graduate residency in 2002. Some youth programs came and went, as will be seen, but Mountain School has persisted. A major bond has been forged between the Institute and local communities by students, parents, and teachers immersing themselves in the North Cascades through their Mountain School experience. The majority of schools involved over the years have come from Skagit and Whatcom counties, allowing young people from these local communities to literally discover and explore their wild back yard.

Mountain School stimulated growth in several directions. In order to convince school district decision makers to allocate some of their limited time to Mountain School, the Institute had to develop curricula that contributed to and supported the educational goals and essential learning objectives of those schools. They had to sell the program. This curriculum development was a very different challenge than recruiting subject experts to teach adult seminars. If the Mountain School experience was to be integrated with what students were learning in the classroom and be transferred from Mountain School to home, teachers needed to buy in and engage students in pre- and post-Mountain School activities. This challenge connected Tracie and the Institute to teachers and led to an ongoing program of teachers exposing teachers to the opportunities for outdoor and environmental education. Programming expansion toward youth and schools happened over several years so as not to overwhelm the still small Institute staff.

WHEN NORTH CASCADES NATIONAL PARK was established by Congress in 1968, the legislation directed the NPS to do a review of what parts of the park were eligible for designation as wilderness under the Wilderness Act of 1964. The Park Service recommended in the early 1970s that about 516,000 acres be wilderness. No action on this recommendation was taken until 1988, when Washington Senator Dan Evans introduced the Washington Park Wilderness bill to designate more than 1.7 million acres of wilderness in the three Washington National Parks. The idea was politically popular, passed Congress overwhelmingly, and was signed into law on November 16, 1988, giving most of the three Washington parks the highest level of federal protection. The National Park Service regional office in Seattle decided that a workshop for Washington Park Service leaders would be helpful in figuring out what this legislation meant for management of Mount Rainier, Olympic, and North Cascades National Parks, over ninety percent of which were now part of the National Wilderness Preservation System as well as the National Park System.

Indicative of the profile that the Institute had established, the NPS Regional Director invited Saul and Board chair John Miles to meet with officials in the regional office to explore whether the Institute might be able to pull together such a workshop. The result was that in fall 1989, the Institute convened a four-day workshop at Rosemary Lodge in Olympic National Park. Leading experts in wilderness management from the Park Service and Forest Service were recruited to present their ideas, research, and experience to the Park Service officials in attendance. Among presenters were Joe Higgins, David Cole, and Tom Kovalicky from the Forest Service. There was some grumbling that the Forest Service had been brought in to suggest what the Park Service ought to be doing, but at the time the Forest Service was doing the most research on the growing art and science of wilderness management. Backcountry District Ranger Bill Lester from North Cascades and other Washington National Park Service backcountry managers described what they had already been doing in managing the de facto wilderness that was now officially designated part of the National Wilderness

Preservation System. Doug Morris, Chief Ranger at Sequoia/Kings Canyon National Park, and his colleague, Backcountry District Ranger Paul Fodor, shared what they were learning about wilderness management in their park, which was pioneering approaches to such management. The hope was that the discussions of research and best practices in wilderness management would help the National Park Service in Washington State figure out the implications of the wilderness overlay on their park management created by the Washington National Park Wilderness Act.

This episode reveals the reputation the Institute had already established at this point in its young life, at least in the National Park Service Seattle office. The Park Service could certainly have convened their own workshop, but they thought an outside convener would be free to create an approach not overly influenced by the inward-focused NPS culture. If the Park Service had organized the workshop, they might not have brought in a Forest Service researcher like Cole, one of the undisputed leaders in the field of wilderness management, or a veteran wilderness manager like Kovalicky. The two agencies had long been rivals, and both had perspectives to contribute to the workshop. The Forest Service was the lead agency in wilderness research, but the National Park Service had more wilderness to manage after the 1980 Alaska National Interest Land and Conservation Act. The Park Service was working to determine how to carry out its vastly expanded role as a wilderness manager. While the conference organizers from the Institute could not know in any definitive way how much their work influenced the wilderness futures of the parks, positive NPS feedback affirmed the worth of their taking a leap into this world of agency training.

Six years later the Institute mounted another intensive workshop like that aimed at providing the National Park Service insight into their wilderness management challenges. This time the client was the Washington Department of Natural Resources, which managed some three million acres of state trust forest, range, agricultural, and commercial resources. The Commissioner of Public Lands in 1995, Jennifer Belcher, was concerned with the approach the agency was taking to logging. She sought to reorient the agency's thinking about its commercial forest operations from clearcutting to other approaches to forest management being developed at the University of Washington and elsewhere. Miles was serving on the Washington Forest Practices Board at the time and suggested to the commissioner that the North Cascades Institute had some experience facilitating agency self-examinations. She decided to contract the Institute to provide a workshop titled "New Perspectives on Natural Resources Management on State Lands."

As it had done with the Park Service Wilderness workshop, the Institute recruited experts in and practitioners of a range of forest practices and alternatives to the clearcutting approach that the department had long practiced on its forest lands. This time the format was four five-day sessions at the University of Washington's Pack Forest, each session involving 25–30 DNR employees from its divisions involved in logging. While there was resistance from the "old guard" in the agency that Commissioner Belcher was trying to reach with new ideas, the workshop improved with each session as word got around that some of the best people in the forestry field were involved and the time spent on the various topics explored was worthwhile. Since 1995 the agency has moved toward consideration of other resource values on its forest lands such as wildlife and recreation. While it is difficult to assess what impact this workshop might have had, it exposed different circles to the Institute and established some lasting connections with the DNR in its Northwest Regional office. Its manager, Bill Wallace, was impressed with the workshop and became a supporter of and cooperator with the Institute.

Mountain School, the NPS Wilderness Workshop, and the DNR project are examples of the Institute exploring how it might grow and expand its approach to its mission in a careful and measured way. The National Park Service continued to be the Institute's principal partner, but as John Reynolds and others advised, the Institute did not put all of its eggs in the Park Service basket. Memoranda of Understanding were signed with three national forests: Mount Baker-Snoqualmie, Wenatchee, and Okanogan. These agreements authorized Institute programming in the national forests. Mount Baker District Ranger Larry Hudson was supportive of the Institute, attended most Board meetings, and explored how the Institute could assist the Forest Service with USFS and Institute staff. On one notable occasion, Reynolds joined Saul and Board Chair Miles in a meeting with Mount Baker-Snoqualmie Forest Supervisor Doug McWilliams in Seattle. As noted earlier, McWilliams had vociferously objected to the Institute offering any programs that discussed "ecosystem management," a controversial issue in Forest Service management at the time. While not challenging McWilliams, Superintendent Reynolds supported the

Institute's desire to teach about the North Cascades ecosystem as a whole. McWilliams was somewhat mollified, later becoming a solid supporter of the Institute. Ironically, the Forest Service embraced ecosystem management as a guiding policy a few years later. This encounter was part of the education of a forest supervisor.

Reynolds, a rising star in the Park Service, left the North Cascades in 1988 to become the director of the NPS Denver Service Center, and eventually deputy director of the Park Service. He was replaced by John Earnst as superintendent. Earnst continued the Park Service support of the Institute unchanged. During this period, the North Cascades National Park Complex headquarters and the Forest Service Mount Baker Ranger District moved into a shared headquarters office and invited the Institute to join them. This shared office helped to bury old agency antagonisms to the benefit of the Institute, which could comfortably work with both.

At this point, the timber wars in the Pacific Northwest were at their peak, logging had been greatly reduced in the national forests there, and Forest Service budgets were in serious decline in the region. At the same time, the Park Service was not flush by any stretch, but it continued its modest in-kind subsidies of the Institute. The days of the Institute's traveling office were long past. It ultimately moved into an old warehouse behind the FS/NPS offices, which staff modestly renovated to be habitable. This proved to be a good space at this stage of the Institute's growth, throwing the growing staff into one big room. When the new office building housing the Park Service and Forest Service was completed, the Institute moved into part of the west wing of the building, where it remains today.

During its first five years, the North Cascades Institute had firmly established itself in the environmental education community of northwest Washington. Its field seminar instructors were topnotch, drawing on the best expertise on the natural history of the region. Its staff was growing modestly, recruiting experienced educators to conceive and craft new program ideas. Its reputation was growing, as indicated by it being invited to conduct the workshop for a National Park Service in Washington State now charged with increased wilderness management responsibilities. The Institute had proven its commitment to excellence and its strength as a small, non-profit organization working effectively with much larger partners. All of this was about to result in an opportunity beyond the wildest dreams of the small staff and Board of the Institute.

My experience with North Cascades Institute left a positive impression on me that this can be done, should be done elsewhere. These kinds of partnerships enhance our capability and capacity in Parks to do great things and so whatever I can do to develop it, facilitate it, cut through the bureaucracy I will do.

Jon Jarvis, former NOCA Chief of Natural Resources
Former Director, National Park Service

IV | AN UNEXPECTED OPPORTUNITY: CREATION OF THE NORTH CASCADES ENVIRONMENTAL LEARNING CENTER

WHILE THE INSTITUTE WAS PURSUING ITS STRATEGY of slow and careful growth in late 1989, an unexpected opportunity appeared that was to change the Institute in momentous ways. No one in the early days had considered anything on the scale of what was about to happen. A Board meeting was convened in the fall of 1989 at Board member Peg Markworth's home in Seattle. On the way to the meeting, Saul Weisberg and Board Chair John Miles visited Dave Fluharty, president of the North Cascades Conservation Council (NCCC), in his office at the University of Washington. Saul had learned from the Park Service that negotiations were about to begin with Seattle City Light about relicensing its Skagit Hydroelectric Project. Earlier in the twentieth century the Seattle utility had constructed three major dams on the Skagit River: Gorge Dam in 1924,

Diablo Dam in 1930, and Ross Dam in stages between 1940 and 1953. City Light had received a 50-year license for these dams from the Federal Power Commission that had expired in 1977. City Light was required to relicense its hydro project, but criteria had changed since the initial license was granted. The Federal Energy Regulatory Commission (FERC), successor to the Federal Power Commission, required that relicensing proposals contain a plan for mitigation of the continuing environmental impacts of the project during the term of the new license. For a dozen years, City Light had been gathering data about the project's impact. It started negotiations with legal intervenors regarding this mitigation in 1989.

Photo by Paul Davis, Courtesy of NCI

Seattle City Light applied to relicense its Skagit Hydroelectric Project, including three dams (Diablo shown here), which resulted in the creation of the North Cascades Environmental Learning Center in Ross Lake National Recreation Area.

The intervenors included the Park Service, Forest Service, Fish and Wildlife Service, National Oceanic and Atmospheric Administration, Washington Department of Fish and Wildlife, local Indian tribes and First Nations (Upper Skagit Indian Tribe, Sauk-Suiattle Indian Tribe, Swinomish Indian Tribal Community, and Nlaka'pamux Nation), and the North Cascades Conservation Council (NCCC). The Institute had no intervenor standing, but if the NCCC could be convinced to include education as mitigation in their negotiating package, the Institute could provide that education. Fluharty liked the idea and pledged to take it to his board, where it was positively received. After the Fluharty meeting, Saul and Miles took the prospect to the NCI Board meeting, pointing out that the idea was very general at this point and uncertain of outcome. The Institute Board also gave its blessing, authorizing Saul to do whatever was necessary to pursue the opportunity which, at this point, only involved seeking funding to support some of the Institute's programs. Everyone wondered whether City Light and FERC would even consider education as mitigation of the impact of something like the Skagit dams. As far as anyone knew, the idea was breaking new ground.

Even as this idea of education as mitigation was being bandied about, the Park Service was engaged in building a North Cascades National Park Visitor Center east of and above Newhalem Campground. The Institute was hired for two years to work with the NPS Denver Service Center and NPS Interpretation staff on development and research stories for the new Visitor Center. During this time the Park and the Institute began discussing a shared environmental learning center that might be part of the Visitor Center project. Construction of the Center ran into various financial problems that raised its cost, and the environmental learning center was dropped. During the early stages of the FERC negotiations with Seattle City Light, Bill Laitner (the park's interpretive chief and point man on the Visitor Center Project) and Jon Jarvis began casting about for alternatives. Perhaps a learning center could be built elsewhere with other funds than those allocated by the Park Service for the Visitor Center.

Once again, the Institute was the beneficiary of being in the right place at the right time with the right people. One of the park's concessions, Diablo Lake Resort, had failed and was for sale. It consisted of thirty old, mouse-infested, dilapidated cabins and a relatively new restaurant completed in 1975. The "resort" had originally been built decades before to house construction workers building Ross Dam, and when it became a resort, the facilities had been allowed to fall into disrepair. The Park Service wanted to remove the old buildings and leaking gas tanks as part of the mitigation. Jarvis approached Saul with an idea: Though it would take considerable investment, perhaps Diablo Lake Resort could be converted into an environmental learning center operated by North Cascades Institute.

Saul's original proposal in the City Light mitigation negotiations was that the city fund the Institute $50,000 per year for the 25 years of the proposed license. The utility countered with an offer of $5,000 for five years.

The prospect of education as mitigation looked modest at best. Jarvis was the Park Service representative in the negotiations, and Saul regularly rode to license negotiation meetings in Seattle with him. The two talked about how the Park and Institute could collaborate in the negotiations and struck upon the idea of a Diablo Lake environmental learning center. Perhaps the city could buy and renovate the resort as part of its mitigation, and the Institute could run it and provide educational programming. Jarvis and Saul developed the idea in close collaboration with members of the North Cascades Conservation Council, including Dave Fluharty and Joe Miller, and introduced it to the other intervenors. With the support of Superintendent John Earnst, the Park and the NCCC introduced it into the negotiation. Suddenly, education as mitigation became part of an ambitious and attractive public-private partnership proposal. While Jarvis and Saul were privately skeptical that they could sell such a big and innovative idea to City Light, why not go for it?

Negotiations went on for two years, with Saul, Jarvis, and the NCCC working together closely. Jarvis was one key to the success of this initiative, bringing negotiating skill and the weight of the Park Service to the table. Saul could articulate the vision clearly but was still the executive of a small organization working with a couple of Goliaths, the Park Service and the Seattle public utility. The NCCC was a strong advocate, and together they were able to garner stronger support from the Tribes, USFS, and other agencies. In a later interview, Jarvis observed, "The key there in my mind was to put the Institute on sound financial footing, at least in terms of a physical place, so that their primary fundraising could focus on program and content." He added that he felt "that the Institute would put down roots, really deepen the local knowledge of the Cascades and its very complex system, and provide for long-term continuity through transitions that go on in the Park so that successive superintendents and successive chiefs of interpretation might come and go and have different emphasis but the Institute would be there and maintain and grow in terms of its quality programming."[12] The long and arduous negotiations resulted in City Light agreeing to buy the Diablo Lake Resort, tear down all but the relatively new restaurant building (which it would renovate extensively), build an environmental learning center, partially endow its programs, and agree to fund maintenance of the facility. The Park Service would be the landowner, build trails serving the learning center, and contribute to site maintenance. The Institute would develop and offer place-based and experiential educational programs for regional school children and raise funds to do so above and beyond the modest City Light endowment. Ultimately, Seattle City Light became excited about the public education part of the mitigation, as did the other intervenors. The final Settlement Agreements were approved by the City and Intervenors by unanimous consent. The mitigation package went off to the FERC in 1991 and was well received. Dean Shumway, Director of the FERC Office of Hydropower Licensing, informed City Light that he thought the mitigation package was "the most comprehensive set of settlement agreements for the public good ever submitted to FERC."[13] This was encouraging, but would the education part of the package be approved by FERC?

NPS photo, Courtesy of NCI

North Cascades Institute's lasting partnership with the National Park Service was recognized and celebrated in 2011. Left to right: Park Superintendent Chip Jenkins, Saul Weisberg, and National Park Service Director Jon Jarvis.

Laitner and Jarvis were promoted out of North Cascades, both moving on to be superintendents at Craters of the Moon National Monument and then Jarvis to Wrangell-St. Elias National Park. Laitner would serve as superintendent of Olympic National Park and Jarvis would eventually become Director of the National Park Service in the Obama administration after serving in many posts. Earnst was replaced as superintendent by Bill

Paleck, and Tim Manns became chief of interpretation. This high-powered Park Service team continued to support the Institute and hope for a successful outcome of the mitigation package with its environmental learning center. The Skagit River Hydroelectric Project license was approved in 1995 and all the settlement agreements, including the North Cascades Environmental Learning Center, were incorporated into it.

A REMARKABLE "STRATEGIC OPPORTUNITY"

THIS ACHIEVEMENT WAS REMARKABLE IN SEVERAL ways. Saul has said often that the Institute team were "strategic opportunists" who aimed to do nothing less than "save the world," and doing that would require some risk and imagination. The bid to have education be considered environmental mitigation seemed a long shot, yet at the same time it seemed reasonable, though measuring the mitigation effect of education would be difficult. Nevertheless, the Learning Center had the potential to greatly extend the Institute's reach, to bring more people young and old, but especially young, into contact with the natural world in the Upper Skagit Valley and surroundings and introduce them to public lands and a national park. Believing that if someone does not know a place or even have an awareness of the natural world, they will not care for them, Saul and Jarvis convinced the intervenors and ultimately City Light to embrace the potential of education as mitigation.

Also remarkable was the willingness of the Park Service and Seattle City Light to reach out to an educational partner. Both could have argued that relying on a small non-profit to operate and program the Learning Center was too risky. The National Park Service, after all, had been at this work for seventy years, the Institute for only five. Yet they embraced the idea of a partnership, for reasons expressed by John Reynolds and Jarvis. They saw the partnership as long term, and they embraced the Institute as an equal and independent collaborator. Independence was crucial, for while government agencies have had many partners, they generally try to control them. In this case Jarvis and his colleagues knew that the Institute did not just educate in and about the park. Its mission was to teach about the entire North Cascades ecosystem, which included National Forests, British Columbia's parks, and private lands in the

Nooksack, Skagit, and Methow River Watersheds. Reynolds had from the beginning recognized this and promoted it. "Part of Saul and Tom's idea that I did not initially have was that this [program] should be eco-system based and not Park based. Which was brilliant. Absolutely brilliant." John saw that Saul and Tom understood, from their education as biologists, that "natural resources don't only exist within the boundaries of a park and one can't understand all of the pressures and opportunities in an ecosystem if you don't include the whole ecosystem."[14] Entering an agreement on the scale of the Environmental Learning Center cemented the deep partnership between the Park Service and the Institute and was a very strong endorsement of the Institute's mission. The Park Service wanted a long-term partner and entering into this learning center agree-ment seemed one way to ensure this outcome. It also began a new, unique public/private partnership between a federal agency (the National Park Service), a city government (Seattle City Light) and a private nonprofit educational organization (North Cascades Institute).

Also remarkable was eventual support for the environmental learning center idea from Seattle City Light. The unprecedented nature of the idea could have been used as an excuse by City Light negotiators to block it. They might have argued that it was outside their charge as a public utility to be engaged in environmental education, but they didn't. Lead City Light negotiators Toby Thaler and Keith Kurko were strong environmentalists in the agency's Conservation Division and found themselves in difficult positions across the negotiating table from the other negotiators who sup-ported the idea. They challenged Saul, Jarvis, and the others, but eventu-ally came to support the radical notion of providing the region and North Cascades National Park with an environmental learning center. Their sup-port was, in the end, critical to its inclusion in the mitigation proposal.

In 1995 the licensing agreement was approved, and it was a block-buster for the Institute and for education as mitigation. It revealed how remarkably effective Saul, Jarvis, and their colleagues at the NCCC had been in their negotiations. At the time the agreement was written in 1991 and the negotiations were completed, the location of the North Cascades Environmental Learning Center (NCELC) was undecided with two locations in the running—the Diablo Lake Resort and the Visitor Center above Newhalem Campground. Wherever it would be, City Light would construct a center that would accommodate an initial capacity of

40 students and 12 faculty/staff, and be so constructed that it could expand to accommodate 60 students and 18 staff. It was to include dorms, as well as a main service building with offices, classrooms, a library, and a laboratory. A cafeteria, covered shelter, outdoor amphitheater, rec area, outdoor "rooms" for small learning groups, parking, staff housing, and trails would also be constructed. The facility would, of course, be handicap-accessible, and on-site recycling facilities would be included. Of these the agreement stated: "Environmental conservation such as on-site recycling facilities will be included in the NCELC facilities design ... [that] would illustrate the possibilities for development that integrate and balance everyday human needs with those of the natural environment."[15] Even at the negotiation stage Saul and Jarvis understood that one of the opportunities and challenges of designing and programming an environmental learning center would be to do so in a way that would encourage visitors to transfer what they learned there back home. With remarkable foresight, they had this written into the agreement with reference to recycling, and when the ELC became a reality many years later, this theme of transfer of learning from Learning Center to students' home communities became central to its programs. The decision was made that all of these provisions could be met best at the site of the former Diablo Lake Resort.

Even more remarkable were the provisions involving programs. "Educational seminars, covering a broad variety of topics, generally will last from one day to several weeks. The programming will be directed toward many different age groups, including seniors." This granted the operators of the ELC broad latitude in the content of programs, and a mandate to program for a diverse range of participants. But the agreement didn't stop there. It laid out what the City of Seattle would provide, including electricity (reasonable enough for a hydroelectric utility) and facility maintenance. City Light would also financially guarantee the start-up of the Learning Center, allocating $100,000 in the first two years, then it would endow ongoing NCELC programs and staffing up to $4,150,000 over the course of the license. A schedule of disbursement of this endowment was specified. The agreement even stipulated three vans would be provided to transport program participants, and operating costs would be subsidized up to $10,000 for the first ten years of the NCELC operation. The agreement stated, "The city will begin preparation for construction of the learning center facilities as soon as a new Project license is issued and accepted." The projection, wildly optimistic as it turned out, was that the Learning Center would be completed in 3-5 years, "by the third June of the new licensing agreement."

PLANNING THE NORTH CASCADES ENVIRONMENTAL LEARNING CENTER

Institute response to the news that the agreement for the North Cascades Environmental Learning Center had been approved was at once elation and trepidation. At first the idea of working under the umbrella of the NCCC to propose education as mitigation had seemed a long shot. When Jarvis (representing the North Cascades National Park) suggested that the partnership with the Institute propose a learning center as mitigation, the prospect was still a dream, at least to many Institute staff and Board members. If the Institute were to operate a facility, what would that mean to the organization? It would mean a huge leap in operational scale. It would require learning many new skills, hiring facility maintenance, kitchen, and housekeeping staff, and revising strategic and operational goals. It would require a major leap forward in fundraising and marketing. The prospect was daunting, but the decision had been made back in 1990 to take the leap, to grasp the opportunity knowing there would be risks and challenges no one in the Institute could even foresee. Now the real work began.

Design of any educational facility should be driven by program, but few facilities run by outdoor and environmental education organizations have enjoyed the luxury of designing their facility from scratch. Often the facility is recycled and adapted to the programmatic needs of their new operators. One of the great and daunting challenges of the NCELC was to figure out what programs might be offered there, what design considerations they might require, and how they would be staffed and funded. The process of facility design would involve brainstorming by the Institute about programs and design considerations, notification of architects of the design opportunity and requests for qualifications by Seattle City Light, selection of an architecture firm, formation of a design team involving the three partners in the project, and meetings of the team with the architect to create a program description of all the elements that would be in the design. This design process would take several years. The role of executive director that Saul had resisted a decade earlier grew exponentially with the approval of the NCELC.

Two years elapsed before an architect was chosen through a process driven by City Light. While the wheels slowly turned toward this decision, the Institute staff and Board worked to identify design considerations that they would bring to the design team meetings. The first question to address was what programs might be staged at the facility. One would certainly be Mountain School, so what design elements would be necessary for that program to flourish at the Learning Center site on Diablo Lake? What would be needed to service adult programs? A flock of new questions arose, and staff queried and visited colleagues at other residential learning centers around the country to learn what they should consider. They collected ideas about what operators of these other facilities would seek if they had the opportunity to build their facility from scratch.

The search for an architect resulted in one of the great strokes of luck that propelled the Institute successfully into this new phase. Among the firms interested in the project was the Henry Klein Partnership, which had an office in Mount Vernon, Washington in the Skagit Valley. David Hall was a partner in the firm and worked out of the Mount Vernon office. He knew the North Cascades, had hiked, backpacked and fished in them for more than a decade, and consequently had a unique perspective on the potential of the Center from someone who knew the place intimately. He had also worked on the design of the restaurant at the failed Diablo Lake Resort and included plein air watercolor drawings and sketches he had done in his North Cascades backcountry travels in his firm's Environmental Learning Center proposal. All of this, and the firm's solid reputation, won the project for Klein and Hall, and an award-winning design of the Learning Center was to be the result.

Hall's first challenge was to meet with a design committee comprised of two representatives from the Institute, two from the Park Service, and two from City Light to create the program description of the Learning Center, which would include all the elements prescribed in the licensing agreement and other considerations brought up by the parties. Hall commented later about this process, "We had a three-headed client which was pretty unusual and I have to be honest and say that they had to come together to learn to work with each other in the beginning." He characterized his role as "the mediator to bring together the design and ideas."[16]

Over the next few years Hall and his staff succeeded in this difficult role, visiting Institute classes like Mountain School to see what they required and studying existing learning centers. He commented later on his Mountain School visit at Newhalem Campground, "I remember that one clearly because it was just raining like hell and it was like 'How do these people do this?', but it was interesting." His deep, on-the-ground research into the nature of the Institute and what it was trying to do gave him insight into the challenges and potentials of the facility he would be designing.

City Light ultimately demolished all the resort cabins, leaving only the restaurant. The Center had to be 200 feet from the lakeshore, could not encroach on Deer Creek to the east, and had to stay out of the Sourdough Creek washout to the west. This required the campus to be narrow and built up the site between these boundaries. Since the site was in the national park, as many trees as possible were to be saved and the impact on the site minimized. This ultimately required changes in the design described in the licensing agreement, which specified a single large building for offices, classrooms, lab, and library. To minimize impact and step the campus up the narrow site, the large building had to be broken into several separate ones, ultimately resulting in an office building, two lab/classroom buildings, and a library. Above these were the dormitories and above them, the staff housing, while the cafeteria and maintenance facilities were closer to the lake.

All of this was to be tucked into the trees on the north shore of Diablo Lake, barely visible from the lake and invisible from Highway 20, which passed above the lake to the south and east. Since each level of the tiered campus above the dining hall would be looking down on the one below, the buildings would be low profile with attractive roofs. Aesthetics were paramount in building design, and the buildings would be modern but appropriate to the park setting. Hall's design was influenced by his love of the wild creeks he knew in the North Cascades, and he said of walking the main "canopy" between the administration and lab/classroom buildings, "It's kind of like you're almost enclosed in a forest with light coming through and the walls are like rock walls, reflecting sound and light." Hall proved to have an understanding of the place and the aesthetic vision that resulted in a remarkably beautiful and appropriate design.

Weather and a remote and rugged site made construction of the North Cascades Environmental Learning Center a challenge, but progress was being made in 2003.

Another set of design considerations involved sustainability—the Park and Institute hoped they could use the facility to teach about energy conservation, recycling, minimum impact, and other sustainable lifestyle concepts. To achieve this the design specified that construction would use environmentally friendly materials, recycled materials, sustainably harvested wood, and heating systems and insulated buildings above code. These were written into the contract. Hall was guided by a mantra that said, "Let no one say, all was beauty here before you came." The result was that the campus was Silver LEED certified (Leadership in Energy and Design) at a time when LEED certification was in its early stages, and the beauty of the place was protected and enhanced from its resort period. Achieving the certification in such a remote setting was quite an accomplishment.

The licensing agreement had stipulated that the Learning Center would be "in operable condition by the third June of the new licensing agreement," but this was not to be. Two years passed before the design phase could even begin. The projection then was that design would be completed and construction begun in 2000/2001, but complications in City Light's public bidding of the construction contract delayed awarding it until 2002. The winning contractor was from Colorado and did not know the area, and the result was disastrous. Many problems plagued the project including washouts and landslides, work stoppages, complications with contracting and construction, and ultimately bankruptcy by the contractor.

With all the delays, the cost of the project grew significantly, and after the contractor bankruptcy promising more expensive delays, Seattle City Light decided it was too costly. The two engineers overseeing the project for City Light were instructed to inform the Institute and Park that they would cap the cost by returning to the original idea of including classrooms, lab, and office in one building. The foundations for the classroom buildings were in, but they would not be completed. Needless to say, this was unacceptable to the Park Service and the Institute. Negotiations ensued, facilitated by Superintendent Bill Palleck, the upshot of which was that the buildings would be finished as designed but the Institute would have to raise several million dollars to furnish and equip the facilities, pave paths as planned in high-traffic areas, and landscape the site. The Park was already contracted to build the Learning Center's trails and grow the plants for revegetation of the site. The Institute Board agreed to this challenge and met it, and a Bellingham contractor completed the buildings under a new contract with the City. Construction had stretched over four years. A story in the *Seattle Times* newspaper about the architecture of the Learning Center observed that "the buildings say that civilization has come to the forest, but they have come in peace."

A remarkable aspect of the NCELC story is what a marathon it turned out to be. The idea for education as mitigation was first considered late in 1989. Two years of negotiations were completed in 1992. The license was granted in 1995. Ground was broken in 2001, and the facility was opened in the summer of 2005. Over these sixteen years the Institute had to sustain its programs, design the Learning Center, and keep to its mission in a period of uncertainty, for no one knew what challenges having a facility, and a large one at that, would pose. The Learning Center would occupy a 20-acre site and consist of sixteen buildings, with 38,582 square feet of space. It would be one and half hours from the office in Sedro Woolley, and quite removed from many of the communities it would serve. So, as will be seen, it is remarkable that everyone at the Institute kept their eye on the mission while running this long race.

Mountain School is a loving, caring place to experience nature.
Mountain School is COOL!

1995 Mountain School student

V | THE BEAT GOES ON

Throughout the two-year negotiation, the four-year wait for an FERC decision, and the long and slow design and construction phases of the Learning Center, Institute programs continued to evolve and expand. Foremost among them was Mountain School. While Wendy Scherrer had conceived the program, Tracie Johannessen was the lead on its implementation. Buses pulled into Newhalem Campground on Monday or Wednesday morning and programming began at lunch. Twenty to thirty students, teachers, and parent chaperones settled into tents provided by the Institute and set up ready for occupancy. Students brought their own sleeping bags if they had them, and if they didn't, the Institute would provide them. Many fifth graders from low-income families in Seattle, Mount Vernon, or other communities did not have everything they needed, and the Institute was committed to providing the tools for safety, comfort, and a productive learning experience. After lunch at picnic tables, prepared on camp stoves, the students were led in learning activities by staff and interns. Learning activities continued until late morning on day three, when students gathered in a large circle around a campfire and shared an observation about their experience. Tired and happy, they boarded their buses and headed home.

This Mountain School format has continued, as of this writing, for more than 30 years. In the beginning, the camping-based operation was pretty challenging. Teaching in the rain became an Institute motif and tradition. "There is no such thing as bad weather, only inappropriate clothing" became the motto. Programming went on whether conditions were sleet, rain, or sunshine, and Institute staff did everything they could to make the Mountain Schoolers comfortable in sometimes challenging conditions. A positive experience was essential to encouraging participants to carry away with them an appreciation for the beauty and wonder of a natural place like North Cascades National Park. The hope was that at least some would want more and bring their families to North Cascades National Park and other northwest natural places. Eventually the Park Service built an enclosed kitchen and a covered meeting and dining area in the campground loop, retiring the MASH tent. When the Learning Center opened in the fifteenth year of Mountain School, it operated out of relatively luxurious accommodations there.

Mountain School's curriculum was designed from the beginning to adhere and contribute to Washington State K-12 learning standards, particularly those in science. If school districts were to be convinced that their students should spend three of their mandated 180 days of schooling at Mountain School, they had to understand how the experience would contribute to their curriculum objectives. Specific Mountain School learning objectives aligned with the state standards accomplished this. A core theme of all Institute programs was that its teaching would be at "the convergence of natural and cultural history, science, humanities and the arts." Learning activities would often involve inquiry, and would be hands-on, mostly in small groups, and fun. Trails wound through the forest and out to the bank of the Skagit River and a large sandbar. Learning occurred in deep immersion in the nature of the place, examining how Indigenous People lived in the area for millennia, and what happened when the white settlers arrived. Park Service interpreters contributed in many ways, and for the first time many fifth graders encountered and explored the idea of public land.

The Institute and Park Service erected a MASH tent and tarp-covered shelters to allow students and instructors to escape the elements in the early days of Mountain School at Newhalem Campground.

Mountain School was offered in the fall and spring. Tracie spent the rest of the year recruiting schools to participate, helping to raise funds to support Mountain School, staffing the program, and refining the curriculum. Fundraising in these early days was especially the province of the executive director. Most of the schools participating received significant financial aid. The Institute was committed to raising funds to supplement what the schools could provide, and later what districts could contribute. The eventual shift from individual school to school district attendance at Mountain School proved key to increasing equity but continued to require significant support from the Institute's fundraising. Early in the history of Mountain School, funding was received from the Skagit Environmental Endowment Commission (SEEC). The SEEC was established by treaty between Canada and the United States in 1984 to resolve the issue of raising Ross Dam, which would flood part of the Skagit Valley in British Columbia among other impacts. City Light agreed not to raise the dam for 80 years in exchange for power purchased at rates equivalent to what would have resulted from raising the dam.[17] The treaty committed the SEEC to, among other duties, administer an endowment fund of $5 million. It solicited annual applications and would make grants from interest and other funds it might receive. Initially most grants were made to fund recreation infrastructure on Ross Lake and scientific research. The Institute operated Mountain School in the Upper Skagit Valley, below Ross Lake, but decided to submit a proposal making the case that education would contribute to the conservation goals of the SEEC. They received funding and, with support from the National Park Service, began a partnership with the SEEC that continues to this day. As Mountain School grew, funding needs did also, and the fundraising net was thrown far and wide. Need for funds rose to the point that the Institute hired a staff member, Gale Sterrett, to coordinate a growing and ever-more-sophisticated fundraising effort in 1993. Mountain School was very much the driver of much of the development work at this stage of Institute history.

OTHER PROJECTS: SKAGIT WATERSHED EDUCATION PROJECT

MOUNTAIN SCHOOL WAS NOT THE ONLY ATTRACTION during these years; adult seminars continued to be popular, offering a venue for many excellent instructors. Mountain Camp was launched in 1992, a summer camp aimed at middle- and high-school age students—more on this later. Mountain Camp and Mountain School began what would grow into a major focus on youth programming, expanded further in 1993 with the launch of the Skagit Watershed Education Project (SWEP). As noted earlier with reference to the argument over "ecosystem management" in the Forest Service, by the early 1990s conservationists, resource managers, and environmental educators had become aware of the necessity to understand whole systems, not just parts separately. In a river system like the Skagit, for instance, degrading the environment with activities here and there could create a negative cumulative effect on the watershed. It became imperative for environmental educators to teach that "Everyone lives in a watershed." This provided a terrific organizing metaphor to explore human effects on nature and how those effects might impact watershed inhabitants, human and otherwise. Many Institute programs focused on parts of the Skagit River Watershed, so Institute staff wrote a proposal to fund a school- and field-based program to teach every child in the area about their watershed.

SWEP was a huge undertaking, ultimately involving seven school districts, forty schools, preparation and dissemination of pre- and post-field elements, field activities, and sharing results with the watershed community. It was aimed at fourth, fifth, and sixth graders. The 1993 catalogue stated that the goal was "to enable elementary students to understand issues and activities that affect water quality and quantity within the river basin. Each class will study their local drainage basin through Institute led field trips, classroom presentations, and ongoing projects throughout the year." SWEP turned into a community effort involving schools, local environmental organizations, land and natural resource agencies, local Tribes, and businesses. Tracie was tapped to lead the project in 1994, with Christie Fairchild taking responsibility for Mountain School. Tracie would oversee the complicated coordination of many partners until she replaced Wendy as Program Director and Jeff Giesen took over as SWEP coordinator in 1999.

SWEP integrated science, math, art, music, social studies, and language arts in its approach. Field trips aimed to make "watershed" more than an abstraction, with students experiencing how a stream might be healthy or not, how they benefited from the watershed, and how water quality and quantity could be protected. The project culminated in an annual Watershed Festival at the Skagit County Fairgrounds and a "Skagit Awareness Day" at the Cascades Mall where students could present what they had learned to the community. The ambitious and multi-faceted program began with a contract from the Puget Sound Water Quality Authority Public Education and Involvement Fund, with the additional support of grants from the Forest Service Challenge Cost Share and the Skagit Environmental Endowment Commission. The program involved many volunteers and Institute interns.

STEWARDSHIP PROGRAMS

IN THE EARLY 1990s THE INSTITUTE also began partnering with the Forest Service on "stewardship programs." The Mount Baker District had been harvesting a lot of timber since the late 1940s, and by the late 1980s timber resources had been depleted and the timber base significantly reduced by harvest and wilderness legislation. The timber "war" over old growth and dependent species like the northern spotted owl also reduced harvest, and thus revenue, especially when the Clinton Forest Plan to address the spotted owl issue cut the timber harvest in the Mount Baker-Snoqualmie National Forest to virtually nothing. Consequently, the Forest Service budget was stretched ever thinner, and while the budget shrank, the management responsibilities did not. Forest Service budgets were tied to timber harvests, so less harvest meant less money at the Forest and District levels. Maybe the Institute could help.

The first stewardship partnership with the Forest Service was called Eagle Watchers. Congress passed the National Wild and Scenic Rivers Act in 1968, and a decade later a portion of the Skagit and its tributaries were designated part of the Wild and Scenic River System. Fifty-four miles of the middle Skagit River were designated a scenic river and the Forest Service was charged with "managing" it and the wild river sections of its tributaries. This was a complex and demanding task because the Skagit scenic river ran through much private land, and in some stretches right beside the main highway up the Skagit Valley. One management challenge involved bald eagles, which gathered in large numbers in late fall and early winter to feed on spawning salmon. From Highway 20 it was possible to see dozens of these magnificent birds perched in trees along the river or standing on gravel bars feeding on spawned-out fish. People would stop along the highway to watch them or float the river to get even closer. Problems of safety on the highway and concerns about the impact on feeding birds by boaters led to calls for action by the Washington Department of Transportation, the State Patrol, and the Department of Fish and Wildlife. The solution, they thought, was regulation of watchers and boaters. The Forest Service agreed, but enforcement of regulation would be difficult. Forest Service River Ranger Jim Chu asked the Institute if education might be a way to help with these problems.

The solution the Institute suggested was to educate a cadre of volunteers about the eagles, train them on eagle natural history, and station them at spots along the highway where eagles could be seen at peak eagle watching times such as December and January weekends. The program publicized the joys of eagle watching and invited people to come to specific spots to see the birds, thus concentrating public impact to safe locations along Highway 20. The volunteers would share binoculars and spotting scopes for watching the birds, as well as tarps to keep the watchers dry (this was really teaching in the rain at this wettest time of the year). Watchers would thus be educated, relatively comfortable, and more manageable, to the benefit of motorists, eagles, watchers, and the Forest Service. Volunteers were successfully recruited and eagle watching became a staple of winter recreation in the upper Skagit Valley. The eagle attraction eventually spawned an annual Eagle Festival in the small community of Rockport. While it did not solve all the problems, Eagle Watchers reduced the need for regulation and created another vehicle for education. The volunteers were the "stewards" of the eagles during the birds' approximately four-month feast on Skagit salmon.

The Forest Service liked this volunteer steward approach, and modestly funded the Institute to create other such programs. Another problem they had was the impact of visitors to Mount Baker, a popular destination for climbers, hikers and sightseers. Two areas on the mountain were relatively accessible and heavily impacted. Schreibers Meadow trailhead on the south side was a popular access to the Railroad Grade, a lateral moraine of the Easton Glacier that allowed terrific views of the mountain for hikers and access to routes for climbers. Even more popular was the only west side access for drivers to the subalpine region of these mountains, the road beyond the Mount Baker Ski Area that led to a large parking lot at Artist Point, three miles above the ski area and seven miles north of Mount Baker. During summer, especially on weekends, the parking lot would be full as hikers wandered the east face of Table Mountain or climbed a trail to its broad top. When the road to Artist Point was cleared of snow, usually in late June or early July, thousands of motorists would drive up and take short hikes or simply sunbathe and take in the spectacular views of Mount Shuksan and Mount Baker. The parking lot often took on a party atmosphere on warm, sunny days.

Institute and Mount Baker Ranger District staff provided a training session to volunteer Mountain Stewards that included visits to the sites where they would serve, Schreibers Meadows and Artist Point. Volunteers could see the problems they were helping to address and were then assigned to weekend stints of visitor contact and information at these sites. Their training included some natural history and suggestions on how to approach visitors in non-threatening ways and offer help on how to reduce their impact. They could make suggestions on where visitors might go without damaging the fragile subalpine vegetation. The program proved popular with volunteers and continues after many years. The Institute helped get it going and the Forest Service eventually took it over.

Other stewardship programs emerged, including a teacher training called Celebrating Wildflowers and a citizen science project to monitor conditions in the Skagit River called Skagit River Stewards. Many of these programs developed lives of their own; in many cases, after the Institute established the program and created the training materials, the program was returned to the Forest Service for continued administration. The Institute was learning that it did not have to do everything alone.

Many programs like these launched during the early 1990s flourished, but were seasonal, tied to the school calendar, and of short duration. This was a continuing staffing challenge because core staff needed year-round employment to make a living. Staff were on a constant search to find projects to fill time in between the busy summer, when there was lots of access to the mountains, and winter, when it rained in the lowlands and the mountains were blanketed deep in snow. Mountain School ended in November and started up again in March. The Watershed Education season depended on good weather in early fall or late spring. Eagle Watchers was a winter program, but small and of short duration. Winter was a time to tweak programs to improve them, write grants to fund them, and do "indoor work" like writing curricula. During this time the Park Service tapped Institute staff expertise to help design educational elements of the North Cascades Visitor Center.

ADULT FIELD SEMINARS

NEW ADULT FIELD PROGRAMS EMERGED during this time, as the Institute waited on the Learning Center decision, and popular adult programs continued. The strong faculty of instructors for these programs broadened to include more artists, photographers, and writers as well as field naturalists. While in the initial stages of Institute history most adult programs had been one- or two-day weekend outings, over time new program formats were tried. A few multi-day backpacks were offered that introduced participants to the back country and focused on wilderness and natural history literature. Multi-day writing workshops were convened in facilities rented in the Methow Valley and as far south as Leavenworth, with teams of authors teaching writing and offering critiques and students sharing each other's work. The team might have been Tim McNulty, Art

Kruckeberg, Libby Mills, and Robert Michael Pyle, or have included nationally prominent writers like nature writer Ann Zwinger and novelist Barbara Kingsolver.

Most adult seminars in the beginning focused on natural history, but a core theme that emerged as the Institute grew was that it would strive to "teach at the convergence of natural and cultural history, science, humanities and the arts."[18] Saul and Tom had been reading poets Gary Snyder and Wendell Berry since their days at Antioch College, and Saul was an aspiring poet. They knew of the rich literary history of the North Cascades. Writers and poets Snyder, Jack Kerouac, and Philip Whalen had served as fire lookouts in the 1950s and been inspired by the place. As they pondered how to teach about connections to nature and wilderness and reach both the hearts and minds of those who experienced Institute programs, they concluded that simply sharing facts about the place would not be enough. They had to reach the whole person somehow to encourage participants to care about nature and become conservationists. Experiential learning in the field with instructors who loved the place and could share that love through their teaching was the way. They knew of Rachel Carson's belief, expressed in her essay *The Sense of Wonder,* that "if facts are the seeds that later produce knowledge and wisdom, then the emotions and impressions of the senses are the fertile soil in which the seeds must grow."[19] Carson was writing of young children, but most of her work directed at all readers reflected this. Carson, in turn, had been inspired by Henry Beston who, in his classic *The Outermost House*, had observed, "Poetry is as necessary to comprehension as science. It is as impossible to live without reverence as it is without joy."[20] Institute leaders knew these writers, and began to work more at the confluence of art and natural history in the 1990s.

The instructor who best exemplified and believed in, as he put it, "walking the high ridge" between science and literature was Robert Michael "Bob" Pyle, literary naturalist. He had a serious scientific side, earning a Bachelor's degree from the University of Washington in Nature Perception and Protection, a Master's degree in Nature Interpretation, and a Ph.D. from Yale University, where he wrote a dissertation titled *The Eco-Geographic Basis for Lepidoptera Conservation*. Bob was a lepidopterist, or scholarly student of butterflies, but had decided he would be a writer first and a lepidopterist second. Bob cast his lot as a freelance writer, but to supplement the unreliable income of that calling, he was a teacher with the National Wildlife Federation and other conservation organizations. A natural teacher, he brought deep knowledge, energy, and enthusiasm to his classes. In a literary sketch contributed to Bob's book *Walking the High Ridge: Life as Field Trip,* literary scholar Scott Slovic wrote, "Naturalists in general may be a breed apart, especially in this day and age. But Pyle is a breed apart from most naturalists, so cheerful can he be even amidst the damp gray that so well suits the name of his Gray's River home . . . To say, sincerely, that the coastal Northwest's ever-present winter fog is 'more palliative than pall' takes special affection . . . some would say gall."[21] This being so, Bob proved to be the ideal instructor for the Institute. If it was too wet or cold for butterflies, he could always find something else to share with his group.

In a 2011 interview, Bob reflected, "When I think back to early days with NCI, butterflies and writing classes at Goat Wall, a house rented for classes perfectly situated beneath cliffs in the Methow . . . it was always catch as catch can where we could find lodging, eat potlucks." He captured the adaptive spirit of those pre-learning center days when he and other instructors like Libby Mills, Art Kruckeberg, and Dennis Paulson would lead forays during the day and come together in a campground, a rented farmhouse, or the Sun Mountain Lodge in the evening, "a community of discovery and curiosity, coming back together in evenings and bringing it all in." In his typically direct way, Bob said what he and his colleagues were doing was "rubbing people's noses in the dirt." The goal was to get people to say, "Wow! I'd like to know more, and know that this particular group of organisms has a future." The instructors hoped they had "created someone who is a naturalist AND a conservationist."[22]

Another instructor at the confluence was Libby Mills who, like Bob, has now instructed for the Institute for over a quarter-century. A long-time seasonal National Park Service ranger and naturalist, Libby lived near the mouth of the Skagit River, working as a freelance naturalist, artist, and photographer. When she heard of the Institute, she approached Saul and said she would like to teach. She was delighted when Saul said, "So, make a proposal." She did, having become an expert on the natural history of Skagit bald eagles. This was her first field seminar, and she has now taught it for decades. If the Eagle Watchers wanted more understanding of the eagles they saw on a drippy December afternoon, they could take Libby's class. Her approach to this and other natural history topics used art and journaling as a means to get close to the subject, along with the information she could share. Her field journals use images and words to describe what her close observation of nature reveals to her, and to express her feelings about the experience. She teaches observation and sketching skills and in doing so brings her students close to their subjects in a very intimate and personal way.

So, even as the Institute waited for the decision on the proposed Environmental Learning Center, they continued to grow in other directions. Most seminars were in the mountains, but some ventured farther afield. This waiting period was the heyday of adult field seminars. The Methow Valley on the east side of the range offered myriad opportunities, and the weather was often better there. In winter, when the closed North Cascade Highway blocked access to the Methow, the lower Skagit Valley offered spectacular encounters with birds. Tens of thousands of snow geese migrating from Alaska gathered to winter on the Skagit Flats, along with thousands of trumpeter swans that had migrated all the way from Wrangell Island north of Siberia. "White Birds of Winter" was a popular offering. Even after all the work that had come before, the Institute could not bank on the approval of a Learning Center for the future. While they knew its approval would change the organization in many ways, they continued to explore how to better address their mission and to take advantage of other strategic opportunities.

The 1994 Institute catalogue provides a window into the wealth and breadth of field seminars offered at this time. A sample of natural history offerings included: "Coming to Know the Land: the Natural History of Puget Sound Country," taught by the leading expert and author on the subject, Art Kruckeberg; "Butterflies of the South Cascades," taught by Bob Pyle; "Wings Over the Methow: Birds and Butterflies from Sagebrush to Snow," offered by Libby Mills and Saul Weisberg; "From Stream to Sea: The Story of the Northwest Salmon," taught by Peter Capen; and "A Natural History Backpack in the Glacier Peak Wilderness Area," five days of instruction with author Daniel Matthews, who wrote the natural history guidebook to the area. Seminars also examined marine mammals, North Cascades geology, wildflowers, grizzly and wolf biology, and other topics. The same catalogue offered a rich menu of cultural and aesthetic seminars. Among the cultural offerings were: "Island Ethnobiology by Kayak" with Ryan Drum; "Columbia River Indians and Their Land" with James Selan and Eugene Hunn; "Okanogan Archaeology" with Mark DeLeon; and "Lummi Basketry" with Anna Jefferson of the Lummi people. The 1994 year was especially rich with offerings focused on aesthetics.

CORE BELIEFS DRIVE PROGRAMMING

The ideas reflected in that first catalogue back in 1986 had been fleshed out over the years. Early on the Institute had subscribed to a set of beliefs that governed programming: (1) powerful, place-based learning experiences inspire environmental and community stewardship; (2) hands-on learning about the environment begins in childhood and continues throughout life; (3) intimate, informed contact with the natural world helps people lead healthy, well-balanced lives; and (4) fun is an essential part of learning, engagement, and health. The Institute experimented with how to incorporate these ideas, staying focused on the broad North Cascades region from the Puget Sound Basin to the Methow Valley. It went beyond providing informative seminars and outings to offering opportunities for people to practice stewardship in the region, especially with the Forest Service. The learning process it used was always hands on and experiential, involving field experiences as much as possible and striving to offer them to learners from fifth graders to people enrolled in Elderhostels. It sought ways to target various age groups, espousing a strong belief in lifelong learning. Always there was intimate contact with nature, and teachers and leaders were encouraged to make the experience as enjoyable as possible, regardless of the occasionally harsh mountain weather.

Programs also addressed what the Institute called "core themes": (1) we teach at the convergence of natural and cultural history, science, humanities, and the arts; (2) we value the importance of public lands for education, recreation, and renewal; (3) we inspire and support broad participation in informed civic engagement; and (4) we commit to quality education, effective community engagement, sound business practices, and a clear sense of purpose. The curriculum of the Institute demonstrated adherence to all these themes. Anyone perusing the catalogue could see that the Institute was not just about natural history, but was providing opportunities to explore the convergence of various ways to understand, study, and describe a place. Most programs were in the National Park or Forest, and participants learned the histories of the places they were enjoying and how and why they became public land. An underlying message in all programs was that everyone needed to care for these places, and they should be engaged in decision-making about them. Everyone needed to practice conservation in some way. Finally, staff recruited the best instructors and leaders, asked constantly for feedback from participants, and worked to be efficient and responsive in running the whole operation. Commitment to guiding beliefs and themes never faltered.

Courtesy of NCI

Expert instructors like Libby Mills (left) and Robert Michael Pyle (right) have taught in many Institute venues for years, here identifying a butterfly in the field.

EXPLORING NEW PROGRAM FORMATS

EXPERIMENTATION WITH PROGRAM FORMATS WAS EXTENSIVE as this period of planning, design, and ultimately construction of the Learning Center crept along. Early on in the Institute's life programs were mostly confined to weekends—one- and two-day forays into the field. As the years passed and staff grew, longer program formats were introduced. The

Spring Naturalist Retreat at Sun Mountain Lodge, a four-day immersion in the natural history of the Methow Valley, was launched in 1992 and continued into the 2000s. A team of naturalists would host and teach over four days at the luxurious lodge perched high above the valley. In 1993 the Institute joined the national Elderhostel program, hosting senior citizens from around the country for a five-day exploration of the natural history of the Puget Sound region. This was hosted at Warm Beach, a facility on Whidbey Island. That same year, "Environmental Education in the Classroom and Field: A Workshop for Teachers" was offered. This five-day workshop was an attempt to help teachers see how they could incorporate teaching about the environment into their curriculum.

The Institute also experimented with expanding its season. Most of its programming was in summer for the obvious reason that late fall, winter, and early spring in the Cascades region featured inclement weather. Institute staff, however, needed year-round work; while they might take on special projects like curriculum development and planning for the peak summer season, more winter work was needed. The 1994 catalogue offered "Spring Ornithology," four lectures at the Whatcom Museum in Bellingham by ornithologists Don Burgess and David Drummond and four field trips. A few years later, in 1997, a winter catalogue featured seminars on "Bald Eagles of the Upper Skagit," "Water Birds of Bellingham Bay," and "Winter Ethnobotany of the Island Landscape," among others. While the mountains might have been inaccessible, the Puget Lowlands offered rich opportunities, so the decision was made to try and lure participants from their warm, dry homes. This initiative was successful, and the seminar season henceforth became year-round.

One seminar launched in 1998 was "People of the Upper Skagit," offered by North Cascades National Park archaeologist Bob Mierendorf and "Captain" Gerry Cook, a Park Service staffer of many skills and responsibilities. Participants were treated to a day cruising Ross Lake on the Park Service *Ross Mule*, a work boat that became a floating classroom for Mierendorf and Cook, both of whom knew the Ross Lake region intimately. The *Mule* would cruise slowly up the lake with Cook at the wheel while Mierendorf taught the archaeology of the area. Cook would nose the *Mule* to shore and drop its bow grate on a convenient rock or bank, and everyone would scramble to a site of historical or archaeological interest. Cook, who had been with the park since its beginning, would regale everyone with stories from its history while they gazed up at the fern-covered walls and waterfalls of streams dropping into the lake. This seminar became a perennial favorite.

A remarkable offering in 1999 was a four-day "Nature Writer's Retreat" at the Sleeping Lady resort at Leavenworth on the east side of the mountains. The teachers were a nationally prominent cast of popular novelist Barbara Kingsolver, prolific nature writer Ann Zwinger, regular Institute instructor and poet Tim McNulty, and, of course, Bob Pyle. This retreat signified two developments in Institute history. One was a growing national recognition that something special was going on in North Cascades National Park, and the other was the use of facilities in the region, partly in anticipation of facility-based programming to come with the Environmental Learning Center.

During the 1990s many Institute programs were staged out of facilities including Sun Mountain Lodge, Sleeping Lady Resort, Brown's Farm in the Methow Valley, Warm Beach, Cornet Bay Environmental Learning Center, and Four Winds Camp in the Puget Lowlands and San Juan Islands. Many seminars still involved camping and there were numerous thematic, multi-day backpacks, but the Institute was also programming for people not interested in or able to camp, like the elders who attended Elderhostels. Some facilities were on the luxurious side, others not so much. A comfortable boat trip out of Bellingham, operated by retired Huxley College marine biologist Bert Webber and his biologist wife Sue, offered forays onto what Dr. Webber was striving, with ultimate success, to have designated the Salish Sea. Bert and Sue Webber shared deep knowledge of the natural history of the marine environment.

STAFF GROWTH

ONE FINAL ASPECT OF THE DECADE-LONG anticipation of the Environmental Learning Center was staff growth. The emergence of Mountain School, the Watershed Education Program, and an ever-expanding menu of seminars required more planning, more funding, and more staff. The design phase of the Environmental Learning Center was very demanding. During the 1990s the staff grew from four to sixteen. Saul Weisberg, Robyn Dupre, Wendy Scherrer, and Sally Hewitt were on staff in 1991. Tracie Johannessen came in 1992 as an environmental educator, as did Christie Fairchild and Chuck Luckmann in 1993; Kirsten Tain became a registrar and office manager in 1994, followed by Gail Sterrett and Ruthy Porter in 1995. Sterrett was the institute's first development coordinator. Someone was needed to care full time for the needs of the "moneyshed," as financial development came to be called, playing on the word "watershed". Porter, a very capable artist, would shepherd the catalogue and eventually become the natural history seminar coordinator. Don Burgess came on as an environmental education center coordinator in 1998. Jeff Giesen became an environmental educator in 1999 along with Jeff Muse, who became SWEP coordinator and would become the Learning Center's first director when it neared completion. By 1999 everyone was optimistic that the facility on Diablo Lake would soon be a reality, and the Institute was actively preparing for the new challenges such a facility would pose. All involved thought the construction phase might be two years, but the facility, it turned out, was still six years from opening.

I learned a lot about the world and my place in it. I have now been part of a community of inspired and inspiring naturalists. After this I know I can make a difference in the world . . . This is the most meaningful learning community I have ever been a part of.

CeCe Bowerman, graduate student, Cohort 10

VI | INTO THE NEW MILLENNIUM

R EFLECTING OPTIMISM THAT THE NORTH CASCADES Environmental
Education Center (as it was called at this point) would be coming
soon, the 1998 catalogue presented a nice illustration of the center and stated, "The North Cascades Environmental Education Center is scheduled to
open in two years. As we enter the year 2000, new site-specific programs
will complement current NCI learning adventures throughout the region."
It continued, "The North Cascades Environmental Education Center will
be a place of discovery, exploration, reflection and shared learning in one
of the most spectacular wild areas of North America—a place where ra-
vens dance and rivers sing." The 1999 catalogue pushed the opening date
to 2001, and the 2000 catalogue optimistically projected Fall 2001. By this
time the name was officially the North Cascades Environmental Learning
Center, and the introduction of the Center mentioned a new program idea
that was emerging. "In partnership with Western Washington University,

a new Institute *graduate program in environmental education* will combine on-campus academic study with professional residency at the Center." This new program would accept its first students in 2001.

For many years the Institute had offered an internship program for aspiring environmental educators, and young people had come from afar to learn what they could at the Institute. Most were undergraduate students, some were graduates, and many expressed a desire for more than they could learn in a brief internship. At the same time at Western Washington University's Huxley College of Environmental Studies, a small, campus-based graduate program in environmental education was being offered. Students in it often wished they could have more field experience through which they could learn and practice skills as environmental educators. John Miles, long-time Institute Board member and coordinator of the program at Huxley, sat down with Saul Weisberg over coffee one 1998 morning in Bellingham's Fairhaven district and sketched out ideas on napkins for a cooperative graduate program bringing the University and Institute together. A committee was formed representing both partners, and brainstorming began. The core idea was to take advantage of the soon-to-be-opened Environmental Learning Center for the experiential part of the program. Students would live up there for a year, helping teach Mountain School and other programs and bringing to them the academic background they would have gained from two quarters of work at Western Washington University.

For the next two years the committee explored the possibilities and designed a program, with professors John Miles and Gene Myers representing Huxley and Don Burgess and Tracie Johannessen taking the lead for the Institute. Saul participated whenever his burgeoning responsibilities allowed. The idea faced many hurdles, mostly from the University side. Where, for instance, would the program reside academically? This was resolved by placing what were called the on- and off-campus options in the Master of Education in the Science Education program offered by the University. If students had to take science education courses for that program, what environmental education courses might be squeezed in before the students went to the Learning Center for their residency? How long should the residency be? Answers to such questions were worked out, and Miles and Myers shepherded the idea through the Huxley faculty and obtained necessary approval from other committees at the University.

These obstacles were hurdled, and the plan was for the first graduate group to enroll in 2001, spending their first two quarters at Western and moving into the Environmental Learning Center for their internship in the spring of 2002.

Issues for the Institute involved what to charge students for the internship, which was called the "residency," and how to house and feed them. The University was concerned that students in a remote location like Diablo Lake would not have access to the library or proper academic oversight. How would that be achieved? The team explored how emerging digital technology promised access to university resources. Miles agreed to teach courses at the Learning Center, Saul became an adjunct professor at Huxley College, and the University's qualms were somewhat calmed. The Institute would house grad students in the staff housing planned for the Learning Center, and overflow might be accommodated in Seattle City Light housing in the company town of Diablo, only a mile away. None of the obstacles to the program seemed unsurmountable, so it was advertised and the first cohort of students were selected. They would enroll at Western in the fall of 2001.

Don Burgess served as point man on design and construction oversight for the Learning Center and became the Institute's Graduate Program Coordinator. His life, and those of everyone else involved in the graduate program, grew more complicated when it became clear that there was no way the Learning Center would open in the spring of 2001 as planned. Thus, the graduate student residency for the first cohort would not be at the new facility. The contractor selected, as noted earlier, ran into unforeseen difficulty with the project and eventually went bankrupt. The remoteness of the Learning Center created problems recruiting and keeping a construction crew and work had to cease for winter rain and snow. The final blow to the contractor was the huge rock avalanche on Highway 20, the only access to the site, that stopped all work for six months in the winter of 2003-2004.

Even prior to all these difficulties it was clear that the Learning Center would not be available for the first graduate cohort, so what to do? Students were committed and enrolled, but their internship could not be "residential" in the way envisioned. Seattle City Light would help to house them in Diablo, some could stay in Marblemount, and they would teach Mountain School at its Newhalem Campground location. Various projects could be conceived, coordinated, and supervised by the Institute office in Sedro-Woolley. Miles could teach his courses in Sedro-Woolley and there would be a facility for the next cohort—or would there? Optimism prevailed, and the decision was made to recruit the next group with some assurance that they would have a facility to move to in the spring of 2004.

THE GRAD PROGRAM BEGINS

The graduate program began in summer and introduced the students to the place where they would be studying and teaching. Some time was spent at the University in Bellingham, and many field trips gave this initial group of graduate students, who came from all over the country, a basic understanding of the place. This included its natural and cultural histories, which would form the core of what they would be teaching to Mountain School fifth graders and other participants during their residency. They then enrolled in courses at Western Washington University for two quarters and began their year-long residency in the spring. Mountain School was operating out of the facility in Newhalem Campground with students living in tents. Everyone ate at picnic tables in an open-air space out of the rain (and sometimes even sleet and a little snow) attached to the covered kitchen. Raincoats lined the east wall of the dining area, and when weather was not cooperating some parts of the program could be delivered in this shelter. Most of the time, even when it was cold and sleeting in early spring, lessons continued along the trail system that connected the campground and the river. The Park Visitor Center was an easy hike from camp and could offer some refuge from the weather and rich indoor learning resources.

The second graduate cohort arrived in the summer of 2002 and were assured they would inaugurate the Environmental Learning Center in the spring of 2003. After their summer orientation to the North Cascades (which culminated in a 75-mile, ten-day backpack from the west side of the mountains up the Suiattle River, over Suiattle Pass, and eventually finishing over Cascade Pass), they went to Western for the coursework there. The first cohort, who were living in Marblemount and Diablo, continued working on projects in the field. They graduated at Western in March of 2003.

The "Passing of the Paddle" from one graduate cohort to the next became a ritual at the graduation ceremony held at the Environmental Learning Center. Here, Brandi Stewart of Cohort 8 passes the ceremonial paddle to Cohort 9 as they meet in the big canoes on Diablo Lake.

Cohort Two finished their first two quarters at Western and began their time in the field in the spring, teaching Mountain School. Over the summer they worked on educational programs with adults and youth groups, returning to work with Mountain School when public schools opened in the fall. Then came the tremendous storm of October 2003 that dumped prodigious amounts of rain over parts of the mountains. The huge rock avalanche that stopped construction on the Learning Center was triggered just north of Newhalem, burying the highway under millions of tons of rock and isolating the town of Diablo. Graduate students living there were trapped and eventually flown out by helicopter. They were temporarily housed in various places down the Skagit Valley and would graduate in March 2004 after a final quarter at Western, well before the road was cleared.

Once the North Cascades Environmental Learning Center opened in summer 2005, the fifth cohort of graduate students enjoyed the residency as it was originally envisioned, a living/learning experience in the North Cascades. Students in the first four cohorts earned an M.Ed. in Science Education. Beginning with the fifth cohort and residency at the Learning Center, the degree earned was an M.Ed. in Environmental Education. All responsibility for instruction shifted from the Science Education faculty to Huxley and the Institute instructors.

At this time a clear distinction was being made in the field of environmental education between "formal" environmental education, and that which was "non-formal." The former took place in the K-12 classroom, delivered as part of a school curriculum taught by certified teachers, while the latter was outside the formal curriculum and usually literally outside the classroom. Students who applied to Huxley's M.Ed. program generally sought preparation for working in the non-profit and government sectors which served populations outside formal schooling, as in adult programs and non-school-based youth programs. Their Masters degrees would not lead to teacher certification, though some might go on to seek that later. Supplemented by academic content provided by Huxley College faculty, the opportunity to serve a residency at the Environmental Learning Center, where they could experience teaching outdoor curricula to enrich formal schooling and teach other populations, promised to build a strong tool kit for careers in environmental education.

EXPERIENTIAL LEARNING AT THE CORE OF THE GRADUATE PROGRAM

CENTRAL TO THE RESIDENCY PROGRAM, and in contrast to another M.Ed. option offered on campus at Western, was experiential learning, the hallmark of all Institute programs. In early discussions of the program the idea of a residency analogous to a medical residency was brought up. While not entirely apt, this analogy captured the idea of a living-and-learning, deep immersion experience where practice of skills and experimentation with theory could occur. Experiential learning in conventional teacher training was called "practice teaching," so the idea for the residency was certainly not unique. However, the depth, breadth, and duration of the residency was quite exceptional and certainly unique among the degree offerings at Western.

While the residency program was radically more experiential than more conventional campus-based programs, it involved a mix of learning processes: practice of teaching skills, reflection on the process, and critical analysis of outcomes; critique and mentoring of practice by professional staff; and classroom sessions involving presentation and discussion of learning theory, curriculum design, non-profit administration, leadership, and many other topics. There was a lot of reading, but no textbooks. One goal of the program, for instance, was probing a "sense of place" and how it might be encouraged based on the idea that to care for a place, one must know it and come to love it. The field experience of the first summer aimed to introduce the incoming cohort to the North Cascades and its natural and human history by taking them into the field to engage with it, to be immersed in wilderness and public land. The North Cascades region was seen as a microcosm of the larger world, and reflecting on how they experienced it, learned about it, and came to care for it would give the graduate students insights into how they could help others learn to care in whatever places their careers might take them. They were encouraged to reflect on how their program design contributed to this and other goals.

A core experiential learning concept was immersion in place, in this case the physical environment of the North Cascades region reaching from the Puget Sound Basin to the high North Cascade mountains. Students read *The Natural History of the Puget Sound Country* by naturalist and University of Washington Botany Professor Art Kruckeberg, but deep understanding of the forests described in the book came from hiking through the lowland forests of Thunder Creek or the alpine trail to Yellow Aster Buttes and identifying the plant communities they had read about. Insights into how plants adapted to the severe conditions in the subalpine zone came from observing the plants and the environment they lived in—high winds, extreme temperatures, drought, and poor soils. Reading about a glacier and visiting one produced dramatically different levels of understanding. The power of experiential learning was reinforced again and again.

Many of the graduate students had already served as instructors, often seasonally, in nature centers, camps, and other programs. They hoped their M.Ed. would help them advance to leadership and administration of such programs. To this end, one of the required courses (nearly all courses in the program were required) was Saul's course on "Nonprofit Leadership and Administration." This course, which was spread over the four quarters of the residency, incorporated Saul's experience in creating and growing the Institute. At the core was the understanding that not-for-profit organizations melded ideas, strategies, and operations from many sources, including the for-profit business world and government agencies. Mission and money were both important and had to be measured and managed. Saul encouraged senior Institute staff as well as local nonprofit business and agency leaders to work with the graduate students. The leaders shared their personal and professional experiences with both startups and established organizations in the areas of budgeting and finance, fundraising, marketing, communications, strategic planning, partnerships, and program development and evaluation. Students used North Cascades Institute programs and its business model as a living case study of what succeeded, and learned lessons from the inevitable failures.

Building experiential learning into the process of learning non-profit administration, students worked in small groups to develop their own proposals for a non-profit environmental education organization, complete with boards of directors, staffing models, programs, and budgets. This culminated in a grant proposal to a "foundation board" that would grill them on the details. In this and other ways, including investigation and reflection on many other organizations, the students would gain practical as well as theoretical knowledge and experience in the fundamentals of non-profit leadership and administration.

The fifth cohort were finally able to spend their residency at the long-delayed Environmental Learning Center and inaugurated a different approach than that of their predecessors. They began with eight weeks in the summer introducing the program and the North Cascades as place, then moved into the Learning Center and began their first teaching of Mountain School after several weeks of training. They would be at the Center for four quarters and finish with two quarters at Western. The program concept was flipped, from emphasis on theory and background preparation to then be applied and tested in the residency, to a field experience followed by reflection on that residency, what they had learned from it, and questions it raised for them. This was a major change in program structure and was a response to student desires to jump right into their residency and do the classroom work at the university later.

This cohort also initiated a revised Mountain School curriculum at the Learning Center. When Mountain School was based in Newhalem Campground, learning resources included the banks of the Skagit River, a late seral stage forest, the National Park Visitor Center, a rock shelter used by Indigenous People, and a set of trails. At the Learning

Center, resources included Diablo Lake, plus various trails and strategically placed shelters built under the leadership of Gerry Cook and the National Park Service. The Learning Center trail system offered access to more and different forest communities than had been available at the Newhalem Campground. The Learning Center also featured classrooms and library facilities and an impressive array of equipment and materials that had not been available before. Additionally, there was much less outside intrusion by park visitors than in the heavily used campground. The camping-based situation of early Mountain School had worked well, but in the new facility, the logistics of feeding and housing elementary-school students were easier and their living/learning experience was quite different. A wealth of new learning activities could now be introduced into the Mountain School curriculum.

John Miles photo

Field study in the wilderness classroom, often guided by the graduate students themselves, was a hallmark of the experientially oriented graduate program. Here, atop Tiffany Mountain, Chris Kiser Girard of Cohort 10 leads discussion of the life cycle and impact of the pine bark beetle.

The graduate program ran for eighteen years, attracting many excellent students from various academic backgrounds and from across the United States (and a few from Canada). Cohort sizes varied, ranging from a low of four to a high of sixteen. The goal was to recruit a group of twelve, but that was hard to achieve. Sometimes the applicant pool was simply too small to reach that optimal size. At times with a big pool, the trick was to select a few more than twelve with the expectation that some would decide not to enter the program; when they all accepted admission, the group would be large. Part of the rationale for a group size of twelve was that it is an ideal size for group interaction, and part was that the size of a group allowed to travel together in designated wilderness was limited to twelve. Much of the "outdoor classroom" surrounding the Learning Center was wilderness—the Park's Stephen Mather Wilderness, and the Pasayten, Glacier Peak, and Chelan Sawtooth Wilderness areas in the national forests. Various workarounds were needed for the wilderness travel components of the program into these areas when students and leaders exceeded a dozen. Several times, one group backpacked over War Creek Pass from the Twisp River to Stehekin while the other traveled over Cascade Pass, the groups meeting and camping together in Stehekin. After some good food, camaraderie, and exploration of the history of this unique village, each group backpacked out the trail the other had taken in.

CHALLENGES AND OPPORTUNITIES
OF THE GRADUATE PROGRAM

THE INSTITUTE HAD TO STAFF THE LEARNING CENTER and the grad program, and ideally a graduate program coordinator would live in staff housing at the ELC to be easily accessible to the resident students. After a shaky start with the first resident coordinator, who couldn't adapt to living in such a remote place surrounded by energetic young people, three successful grad coordinators taught, mentored, critiqued, and counseled the students over the next dozen years: Tanya Anderson, Stephanie Bennett, and Joshua Porter. The grad coordinator's job was a demanding one in many ways—emotionally, intellectually, and physically. While not in the same living quarters as the students, they were constantly close and available to them. They were the on-site facilitators of all the graduate student learning, helping them process their experiences, serving as liaisons with other staff at the ELC and in Sedro Woolley, and counseling and cajoling when students needed it for one reason or another. While other staff handled Learning Center operation and maintenance, booking of schools into

Mountain School, and facilitating a range of other programs, the graduate coordinator oversaw graduate student schedules, planned field excursions, and instructed them in various ways. Their role often involved critiquing the work being done by students, which made for strained relations on occasion, but professionals like Anderson, Bennett, and Porter reminded them that all critiques were intended to be constructive and the students came around most of the time.

A challenge for many working at the Learning Center, whether staff or student, was its remote location and the long, dark period from November to March. As long as Mountain School was in session everyone was busy, but by early November weather ended the routines of teaching. The program involved more classroom work, often conducted by John Miles and Saul, who traveled from Bellingham. After a long holiday break, students returned for more classwork, a few field excursions to connect with other programs "outside," and preparation for the spring session of Mountain School, which began in early March. Nights were long, days short, and isolation sometimes exacerbated by avalanches on Highway 20, torrential rain, or deep snow at the Learning Center. Difficulties in coping with such conditions were to be expected but knowing this did not make things easier. During these periods the burdens on the grad coordinator and all staff increased, but generally the staff and graduate students formed a cohesive group.

Eventually the rain would subside, the sun would occasionally rise above Colonial and Pyramid Peaks, snow would melt, and Mountain Schoolers would return with the spring migratory birds. Moods would improve, and outdoor life would resume. One spring, as the snow melted, staff and students living in the duplexes at the top of the ELC campus noticed a strong, unpleasant odor. A search for the cause revealed a deer carcass not far from the residences: prey killed and partially eaten by a mountain lion, then buried as cats do in anticipation of a return to the kill. This was a sobering realization for those who had been coming and going all winter not far from the kill site. The presence of mountain lions was known, accepted, and appreciated, but having one as a close neighbor was motivation to keep a sharp lookout when moving about the Learning Center campus, especially at night.

Staff and students reveled in the wildlife encountered at the ELC. Mountain lions and black bears were the most common charismatic megafauna, but the trails and even the campus offered ample opportunity for wildlife watching. On one occasion a black bear cub climbed onto the railing of the dining hall porch, thrilling the Mountain Schoolers inside. Not so thrilling was an occasion when a group of fifth graders watched a bear stalk and kill a deer fawn on the Learning Center campus. Ornithologist Don Burgess was a master at finding owls, whose calls he could mimic beautifully. Often an unplanned teachable moment would occur as instructors led Mountain School groups, such as when a bald eagle would fly up or down the Skagit near the Newhalem Mountain School or a family of mergansers would drift by on the current. Large groups of youngsters did not make for ideal wildlife watchers, but quiet moments (planned or not) with students encouraged to look and listen often revealed birds and other critters. Myriad stories could be told of the learning adventures that Mountain Schoolers and their graduate student mentors enjoyed over the years.

John Miles photo

Graduate students who completed their year of field study at the Institute and coursework at Western Washington University earned an M.Ed. degree and could participate in Commencement.

Several changes to the Institute resulted from launching the graduate program. One big one was that it involved a commitment to teach learners over a much longer time span than any other program. The longest programs prior to the launching of the graduate program had run for a week.

With the grad program, the Institute was contracting to provide an educational experience and room and board to clients for a year. It was embarking on a complex relationship with another big institutional partner, Western Washington University. Other environmental education graduate programs with residencies had credit-granting arrangements with universities, such as the Teton Science Schools with the University of Wyoming, but those programs did not commit to a degree with cooperating institutions. The NCI/WWU partnership promised that an advanced degree would be granted to students who completed the requirements of both partners. This was a new, unique, and risky model in the field, requiring trust and good faith by both partners.

The graduate program would, over the years, bring many challenges to the Institute. One that stretched over much of the eighteen-year history of the program involved graduate student housing. When the Learning Center was designed, housing on the campus was planned to accommodate staff in duplexes. With the graduate program came an annual unpredictable number of students as well as additional challenges unanticipated during the Center's design, such as new kitchen, maintenance, and housekeeping needs, and the need to create the new position of graduate coordinator. From the very beginning the Learning Center could not house everyone, and some grad students and staff lived in Diablo through agreement with Seattle City Light. This was fine, as the Diablo housing was a mere walk from the Learning Center. However, City Light constantly changed the availability of Diablo housing as they struggled to maintain the buildings, ultimately making it necessary for the Institute to purchase housing for graduate students down near Marblemount. One purchase was the "Blue House," which proved an ideal location for graduate student housing and offered an opportunity to work with the Skagit Land Trust on a conservation easement to protect land of significance to the Tribes at the mouth of Diobsud Creek.

Housing was just one of the logistical challenges involving the graduate program. Another involved both Institute and National Park Service culture. Prior to grad students appearing, all Institute staff were paid professionals, be they contract instructors, full-time professionals, or seasonal instructors hired to teach Mountain School. The status of grad students, who initially replaced most of the seasonal Mountain School instructors, was a bit of a puzzle for both regular staff and the students.

Graduate students needed instruction and training to teach Mountain School, which added to the burdens of regular staff. Legitimate questions arose in some minds as to whether graduate students, some of whom had limited backgrounds in teaching and environmental education, could deliver programs to the high standards the Institute had held from its beginning. Such questions were answered by the excellent training offered to incoming graduate students by Education Director Tracie Johannessen and other professional staff. Still, having to train many beginners was an added burden.

On the National Park Service side, there was a feeling of resentment in some agency professionals of the Institute itself. North Cascades National Park superintendents from John Reynolds through Chip Jenkins, and National Park Service leaders like Jon Jarvis and long-time Chief of Interpretation Tim Manns, recognized the added educational value the Institute brought to the park and fully supported Institute contributions. They saw the graduate program as an opportunity to recruit young people with solid training and leadership skills to the field of environmental education, and even to the ranks of the agency. Still, the Park Service's cultural belief was that in the parks, the professionals wearing the green and gray ought to deliver the educational programming. The model that not only involved a private, non-profit partner but relied on students to deliver programs raised some eyebrows among the Park Service professionals.

On the plus side, the graduate program created new opportunities. Curricula needed to be developed, something the students were required to study and practice. Graduate students were also required to study the nature of the place, from the macro scale of the region to the micro scale of the environs of Mountain School. They had to do so in some depth and could, in some cases, develop a greater depth of knowledge of these places to apply to their teaching than a revolving group of seasonal instructors. They were required to inquire into the nature of the Institute as an organization and to ask questions about it, which could be clarifying not only to them but to the Institute at large. Many of the students went well beyond what they were required to do, pitching in to help with Learning Center operations. They brought a sustained youthful energy to the organization.

Amy Brown, a member of Cohort Four, was an example of all of this.

Part of Amy's solid background was exceptional skill and achievement in whitewater sports, especially kayaking. She had boundless energy and enthusiasm for her sport, and when required to develop a curriculum as part of the program's curriculum course, decided to build on a summer program the Institute was offering on Ross Lake called "Canoe Camp." The Institute sought to serve all age groups, and it was developing a group of "Summer Wilderness Adventures" aimed to give middle- and high-school youth an opportunity to learn skills in wilderness travel, minimum impact camping, and team building in the outdoor classroom of the North Cascades. Other programs aimed at this age group were "Mountain Camp" and "Girls on Ice." Recruiting for Canoe Camp was proving difficult, so Amy developed a curriculum that focused on a more local, diverse, and underserved audience. Amy's leadership as a student, and later as Youth Leadership Adventures manager, would ramp up youth programming that flourishes to this day. Amy and others could in this way use their backgrounds, growing knowledge, and leadership skills to create and enhance Institute programs in many ways.

GRADUATE PROGRAM ENDS

After eighteen cohorts, the graduate program unexpectedly ended in 2019 when the Western Washington University part of the program unilaterally decided not to accept students for the coming year. The faculty wanted to make significant changes in the program and wanted a "hiatus" in accepting students to give them time to develop their revisions. Unfortunately, the Institute could not support this decision for several reasons. The Western faculty sought to reduce their graduate program workload to a maximum of eight students in a cohort. This level of enrollment was not financially sustainable for the Institute, which aimed for cohorts of twelve to fifteen students. Saul wrote to the chair of the department at Western housing the M.Ed. to explain that at the fifteen-student level, the Institute's graduate program budget had been $482,000, including $35,000 in NCI scholarships and an annual subsidy of $115,000 provided by the Institute. In the three years prior to the Western faculty's 2018 decision, Saul pointed out, the Institute had invested more than $1 million in housing for grad students, including the purchase, construction, and renovation of three houses in Marblemount to house fifteen graduate students. With this level of investment, which had grown over eighteen years of building the program, the Institute could not simply "pause" and wait for Western faculty to decide if they wished to continue partnering with the Institute. The Western faculty involved refused to negotiate and, despite the efforts of many program supporters, the program ended with Cohort Eighteen, which graduated in March 2020. Over the years, 166 students had successfully completed the residency program.

As mentioned earlier, the Institute had entered into several major partnerships, the success of which depended on mutual consultation, negotiation, and trust. In the grad program's case, these necessary qualities in the WWU-NCI partnership had been present during the first fifteen years of the program. This had been in part because the University end of the program had been nurtured by John Miles, who had originally come up with the program idea with Saul. When Miles retired from Western in 2014, young faculty were hired who did not have the commitment to or understanding of the program from the Western side of the partnership. The world was changing, and they thought the program should have new elements and emphases, with their interests and focus moving toward urban settings. The Institute agreed that urban programs would serve new audiences but had hoped that the successful partnership would not be jettisoned entirely. Indeed, graduate applications had never been higher. Some aspects of the program, such as the cohort size and the residency component at the Learning Center, were core components for the Institute. The Western faculty would not negotiate to find an alternative that would work for both partners, and the partnership ended. This was unfortunately a rancorous conclusion to what, for most of its life, had been a very productive and positive partnership.

Perhaps one of the most important sustainable features of the Learning Center is to help visitors learn about sustainability by participating in it.

NCI Catalogue

VII | A FACILITY CHANGES NEARLY EVERYTHING

THE OPENING OF THE NORTH CASCADES Environmental Learning Center in the summer of 2005 changed everything. Prior to the Learning Center, programs had been offered across the North Cascades Ecosystem in venues as far away from the Skagit Valley as Leavenworth in the Wenatchee Valley, the Puget Sound Basin, and the Methow Valley and surrounding high country of the east slope of the North Cascades. While programming across the ecosystem continued, the Institute's focus naturally shifted to the Upper Skagit Valley and the immediate surroundings of North Cascades National Park when the Learning Center opened its doors. Managing a facility brought challenges and opportunities, and greatly increased the Institute's budget and fundraising needs. Most of these costs were borne by the Institute, with some in-kind and financial support from Seattle City Light. The Park continued its significant in-kind support for programs. Within a short period of time, the costs of full-time residential programming (and the associated need for increased staffing) became apparent. New types of programs could be offered at the facility, with its relatively luxurious accommodations compared to camping-based programs. New audiences could now be served, including families with young children and others unable or unwilling to sleep on the ground. The rental facilities used before the opening of the Learning Center were good locations with varying amenities but posed scheduling challenges. Costs varied and had to be incorporated into program prices, booking them could be an involved process, and many of them required long drives from the Puget Sound Basin where most participants lived.

While managing a facility safely, efficiently, and in a financially sustainable way was complex and challenging, running a majority of programs from a fixed base also had advantages. A small fleet of vans was purchased to simplify transportation. The logistics of feeding groups during multiday programs were reduced by having a dining hall, a good chef and kitchen staff, and an efficient system of cleanup and composting. Rather than camping, program participants could enjoy a day in the field and return to a good meal, a soft bed, and a shower. The Learning Center shifted the programming focus more onto the Upper Skagit region and opened up many new programming opportunities there. Also, since the facility was in the North Cascades National Park Complex, the presence and role of the Park Service increased and the overall Forest Service presence was lessened. The Mount Baker-Snoqualmie and Okanogan-Wenatchee National Forests continued to be the sites of programs, but the opening of the Environmental Learning Center resulted in the Institute becoming even more connected to the National Park Service.

The 2005 catalogue featured the Learning Center as "a hub of discovery within wildlands" and introduced its campus of sixteen buildings, including multimedia classrooms, a research library, aquatic and terrestrial labs, overnight lodging, a dining hall, an amphitheater, and outdoor learning shelters. Also featured were a dock on Diablo Lake for paddling adventures, as well as ADA accessibility for the facilities and the paths along the lakeshore and Deer Creek bordering the east side of the campus. The menu of programs continued as before with the exception that some of them were located at the Learning Center. Among these were the North Cascades Naturalist Retreat (which had previously been held at Sun

Mountain Lodge and other locations), canoeing-oriented adventures on Diablo Lake, and art, literature, and writing seminars.

NEW PROGRAM OPPORTUNITIES AT THE LEARNING CENTER

The Learning Center facilities inspired a new program idea first advertised in the 2005 catalogue for Fourth of July weekend called "Family Getaways." Here is the program description:

> *Looking for something different this Fourth of July? Celebrate our American heritage of wilderness by bringing the whole family to North Cascades Environmental Learning Center. Hike in towering forests and explore rambling streams, canoe Diablo Lake, or search for owls and bats on a night hike. Whether you're an adult or a child, you'll find something you'll like at this program, including free time for family exploration. Mothers and daughters, fathers and sons, families of all shapes and sizes—all are welcome. Children under the age of five are the responsibility of the parents throughout the program.*

Three weekend sessions were offered this first year and were so successful in 2006 that in 2007, four three-day sessions were offered and two four-day sessions were added. Activities included hikes and paddle adventures such as "I'm Lichen Hikin'" and "The Big Canoe and You," games, arts and crafts, and inquiries using microscopes and hand lenses encouraging explorations by budding young naturalists. Family Getaways was a big programming step, extending the range of Institute clientele to younger children and extended families and introducing less structured program formats than had been the rule. Learning Center staff and resident graduate students offered the programs. Chef Charles Claassen and his staff prepared wonderful meals.

Programs like Family Getaways reveal the scope of operational capabilities that had to be developed and implemented by the Learning Center director and staff. Safety, comfort, and quality environmental education were core operational goals. A fleet of standard canoes and one large voyageur-style canoe illustrate the safety challenges faced by staff when the Learning Center opened. Staff had to be trained in canoe rescue, and a rescue boat and procedures were put in place to ensure that all programs on the lake were safe. The weather on Diablo Lake could be an issue, with winds blowing predictably up the Skagit Gorge on warm summer afternoons, so strict guidelines had to be in place about when to go and when to stay on shore. On the comfort side, plumbing, heating, and electrical systems had to operate reliably, and facilities had to be cleaned and serviced by maintenance and housekeeping staff. This operational stuff was new to the Institute; Jeff Muse, Eric Dean, Charles Claassen, and their staffs were learning on the job. Things didn't always go smoothly at the start, but they improved quickly.

Quality educational programming was the Institute's strength and the Learning Center allowed exciting and creative initiatives, so much so that two seasons were advertised in two catalogues in 2006. The Spring/Summer catalogue offered free "Learning Center Day Trips" including Saturday afternoon forest hikes and Sunday morning canoeing from June through August: a good way to introduce the Learning Center to everyone, especially the people of the Upper Skagit Valley. A "Sourdough Speaker Series" of one-night events was launched featuring northwest artists, writers, and naturalists with a "fireside" presentation following a gourmet dinner and overnight accommodations. Many field seminars were based out of the Learning Center, especially art-oriented sessions like "North Cascades Landscape Watercolors" with Molly Hashimoto and "Drawing the Details" with Libby Mills. Previously, instructors of such seminars often had to worry about logistics while in the field, which detracted somewhat from their concentration on their instructional duties. The Learning Center allowed for more teaching and fewer headaches for instructors along with accommodations and good food for everyone.

Just before the Learning Center opened to the public, the Institute had the opportunity to invite a small group of artists, scientists, writers, and staff to the Center to test the facilities. This gathering allowed the cooks and maintenance staff to work out some of the early bugs in their systems. During one of these evenings, watching all the people in the dining hall animatedly talking, drinking wine, and planning for the future after dinner, Development Director Kris Molesworth turned to Saul and said, "We have a clubhouse!" That realization, that the Center was more than just a school in the woods, was recognition of an important moment in Institute history. It was now a home for a growing community with a "clubhouse" at its center.

The Institute pitched the Learning Center as a *community*, inviting everyone to join in celebrating the beauties of the place, experiencing its wonders, and probing its mysteries. Here is how they described the "Learning Center Experience" in the 2007 catalogue:

> *The Learning Center is a community—of people, plants, wildlife, and more—and you'll quickly feel a part of things once you arrive. In fact, we're counting on it.*
>
> *The feeling starts as you walk onto campus, when your gaze lifts skyward to steep, snow-riven mountains rising more than a mile above the Skagit Valley. Located in the heart of North Cascades National Park, the Learning Center sits along Diablo Lake between Colonial and Pyramid Peaks and meadow-topped Sourdough Mountain, where poets such as Gary Snyder and our own Tim McNulty worked as fire lookouts in years past. Few places feel as wild and welcoming at the same time.*
>
> *The feeling deepens when you hit the trail or grab a paddle, hiking through the vine maples along Deer Creek or meandering a canoe down the shoreline. Raven calls, the scent of sun-warmed evergreens, a rustling breeze across the lake—the sights and sounds and smells of the neighborhood embrace you like a good friend. You begin to feel at home here thanks to little things that invite the senses. By dinnertime, everything falls into place—you're part of the community.*
>
> *At North Cascades Institute, we believe that how we learn is as important as what we learn. That's why everyone you meet at the Learning Center is dedicated to the idea that community life inspires stewardship. From our naturalist Ned Corkran and chef Charles Claassen, mountain boys with skinned knuckles and tall tales of climbers, to Minnesota-born graduate resident Lansia Jipson and her talented cohort of peers, we are a community. All that's missing is you.*

An entirely new element of Institute programming involved opportunities only a facility could provide, one of which involved dining. Meals in the dining hall were a highly social experience with visitors mixing at tables and relaxing before and after on the long porch overlooking Diablo Lake.

Exploring how it could extend environmental education to the dining experience, staff came up with the Foodshed Project, an extension of the watershed metaphor. In 2004, anticipating this opportunity the Learning Center would provide, the Institute convened local farmers, business people, community members, and Institute staff and grad students to consider how they might best address their goals. These were (1) offering appealing, wholesome food choices, (2) serving organic and sustainably produced food, (3) purchasing locally grown, seasonally appropriate food, (4) minimizing waste, and (5) educating others about the power of food choice. Partnerships were established with local producers such as Blue Heron Farm in the nearby village of Rockport, Skagit Valley Farm in Concrete, and Breadfarm in Bow. Displays on the walls of the dining hall and brief presentations around meals provided the opportunity to explain the flow of food to the dining tables and what values were being served with the meals. The 2007 catalogue declared, "Real food, real people, real close—together, we increase food awareness and inspire healthy choices for our bodies and the planet."

Courtesy of NCI

Facilities at the Environmental Learning Center allowed new programming. Here, families gather for instruction and sharing.

This initiative extended to Mountain School because all Mountain School participants ate five meals in the dining hall. One idea, for instance, was to identify dining "teams" and see which teams had the least waste. Extending over several meals, the waste could be calculated in various ways and the winning team recognized for their achievement. Whatever method was employed to address food sustainability, the goal was to have diners of any age think about how food could be responsibly and sustainably sourced and consumed and waste minimized.

A recycling center was part of the Learning Center, located on the edge of the campus because part of it was composting food waste that could on occasion become quite fragrant—the farther away from the centers of action, the less its odiferous impact. Composting was part of the sustainability dimension of the Learning Center experience. The system used involved earth tubs which churned, heated, and sterilized the waste to make the process more rapid and hopefully less fragrant than conventional methods of composting. The physical campus itself offered examples of sustainability such as the architecture, which was designed so the facilities would have the least possible impact on the already disturbed site of the former Diablo Lake Resort. As noted earlier, the Park Service dictated that the site be as "natural" as possible. To this end, every tree that could be saved was protected and 20,000 plants were grown from seeds taken from the site before construction began, nurtured for five years at the Park Service greenhouse in Marblemount before being planted by volunteers and the Park Service to restore disturbed parts of the site. Erin Schneider, a graduate student with a strong background and interest in botany, focused her curriculum project on making the site restoration an educational process. She coordinated the site restoration project, explaining and demonstrating the process and importance of environmental restoration to volunteers.

Sustainability was also served in sourcing the building materials, with as much as possible acquired within a one-hundred-mile radius of the site to reduce the energy used in transport of materials. Lumber used in the buildings was certified by the Forest Stewardship Council. In 2007, in recognition of its sustainable design, the Learning Center was awarded silver certification by the U.S. Green Building Council's Leadership in Energy and Environmental Design (LEED) Green Building Rating System. Earth Day weekend 2007 was celebrated with a seminar titled "Environmental Architecture: Green Building Design and Operation." This was offered by David Hall and Russ Weiser of the Henry Klein Partnership (architects for the Learning Center), Center Director Jeff Muse, and Eric Dean, the first overseer of maintenance and operations.

NEW INSTRUCTIONAL CAPABILITIES AT THE LEARNING CENTER

Other assets the Learning Center brought to the instructional efforts of the Institute were the facilities and a site that offered new instructional capabilities, especially to the Mountain School program. The essential goal of Mountain School was to give students a different, exciting, fun, and immersive outdoor learning experience. It was to be as different from everyday school as possible (despite the "school" in the name) while at the same time complementing and enriching what was being taught in the conventional classroom. While there were now classrooms, labs, and a library at the Learning Center, how might these be integrated into the learning process without detracting from the essential outdoor part of the program? Hall, a veteran of many forays into the North Cascades, was well aware of how often and how hard it could rain up there, so his design included a core campus which would allow somewhat protected movement between the office building, classrooms (two of which were the "labs"), and the Wild Ginger Library. If the weather was too inclement for prolonged outdoor work, classes could retreat to the warm and dry classrooms or library. They could process outdoor lessons in the indoor settings, perhaps examine specimens from the various collections of mammals, birds, and insects, or look more deeply into the objects of their interest through microscopes. If they needed to do a bit of research into the trees and plants they were studying, they could dip into the Wild Ginger Library.

The Learning Center was the hub of an extensive trail system constructed by the National Park Service, guided by the curriculum ideas of the Institute's educators and Park Service interpretive staff. One trail looped out onto the peninsula reaching into Diablo Lake from the Salmonberry Dining Hall. Another wound uphill above the campus to Sourdough Creek. Yet another traveled along Deer Creek. All trails allowed for slow walks to sites incorporated into the various learning experiences of Mountain School or other Learning Center-based programs. Strategically located along the trails were beautiful, rustic, and artistically designed shelters into which groups could go as they studied and observed the forest, journaled, painted, or drew what they saw around them. Gerry Cook had lovingly designed and constructed these shelters, named Fawn Shelter, Sourdough Creek Shelter, and Deer Creek Shelter. A fourth, larger shelter near the core campus was Lily Shelter, where a campfire or night program could be held. Night walks could be safely conducted along trails close to the central campus.

Courtesy of NCI

When driven indoors by wild weather or curiosity, Mountain School students could use the resources of the Learning Center's labs with their equipment and collections in warm and dry comfort.

The site itself offered many new opportunities for teaching and learning. At Newhalem Campground, students could study and experience the Skagit River. At the Learning Center, the river was in a reservoir which offered new perspectives on rivers and what society does with them. Students could consider the impact of dams and how humans have changed natural systems like rivers on a large scale. The trails allowed access to creeks and opportunities for the study of aquatic and riparian life. The composition of the forest on the site varied considerably and inquiries into why these forest communities differed were developed. Field experience was supplemented and enhanced by presentations accessing technology that had not been available at the Marblemount site except in the Visitor Center (and access to that had been limited).

Teachers and parent chaperones accompanied Mountain School students on their learning adventure, and it was less challenging for these adults, who might not be outdoor enthusiasts, to come to a facility like the Learning Center than to a camping-based situation. Parents of Mountain School students became some of the most enthusiastic boosters of the Institute and its programs, many becoming Institute ambassadors back home in the communities of Mount Vernon, Bellingham, and other school districts in the region.

A core task for any organization working with the public, and especially working with children and youth outdoors, is risk management. This is especially true when public schools are involved because they are held to the highest standard in this regard, and school administrators must be highly confident that when their students go off campus they are in competent hands regarding the issue of risk. Institute staff recognized this from the very beginning, whether the clients involved were adults in field seminars or fifth graders in Mountain School. Risks were assessed from the conceptualization of each field seminar and involved factors such as the experience and preparation of the instructors, transportation, best safety practices in the field, and first aid and emergency response procedures. The Institute was remarkably successful in managing risk over the years.

When the Learning Center came online it brought with it new and complex risk assessment, management, and emergency response challenges. It was a backcountry facility, more than one hour from definitive medical care. Paramedics could reach the facility in 70 minutes from Concrete, and it would take an hour and a half to reach the hospital in Sedro-Woolley. Prevention was paramount, but thorough preparation for any incidents was essential. An Incident Command System that followed a nationally recognized protocol for managing emergency incidents was established for the Learning Center to respond to emergencies. It includes, as listed in the *2021 Emergency Response Procedures,* "medical, fire, severe weather, road closure, hazmat spills, law enforcement, search and rescue, campus-wide evacuation, earthquake, or dam emergencies." This list indicates the scope of the incidents for which Institute staff at the Learning Center needed to be prepared.

Stephanie Friesen photo, Courtesy of NCI

The National Park Service built a trail system at the Environmental Learning Center. Gerry Cook designed and supervised the building of three shelters along the trails that could offer an instructional refuge out of the weather: Deer Creek, Fawn Creek, and Whispering Pines.

Other risk factors appeared at this time because the Learning Center was on Diablo Lake and would include the lake in its programming. As will be described in the next chapter, youth programs grew to involve canoeing and backcountry travel, so the risks of such activities needed to be assessed and managed. All staff who would work with canoe programs were trained in canoe rescue procedures. A fast rescue boat was stationed at the Learning Center dock; staff were trained in its use and it was ready to go if needed when canoe programs were under way. Jeff Muse oversaw the development of emergency response procedures in his role as facility manager, followed by Kristofer Gilje in his years in this key role. The Institute's *Risk Tolerance Statement* recognizes that NCI "acknowledges that there are inherent and other risks associated with our programs, with the Learning Center location, and with all outdoor activities. We further acknowledge that taking risk is necessary, appropriate, and beneficial in fulfilling our mission." The statement specifies that a risk management plan must be created and approved for any new program and "will be evaluated annually by NCI leadership for effectiveness and relevance." It concludes with the assertion, "An acceptable risk is one that is well managed and leads directly to mission fulfillment." One measure taken was to require all instructors and graduate students to be certified in first aid as Wilderness First Responders. Some staff were certified as Emergency Medical Technicians. The aim was to provide the highest level of care possible should an incident occur before paramedics could arrive on the scene. Fortunately, such incidents were very rare.

The Learning Center had large buildings with steep roofs. The design of the largest, the administrative building, recognized that winter snow could be considerable on the roof and would slide off, posing a hazard to anyone below. Bars were installed toward the bottom of the roof to reduce slide risk, but this measure proved entirely inadequate. Mitigation of the risk of "roofalanches" threatening visitors on walkways was alleviated by closing threatened walkways and rerouting visitors during the winter. A "winter walkways" map was drawn up to ensure safe passage between buildings. This is an example of the new dimensions of risk management that were required with the opening of the Learning Center. After the first major snowstorm, the risk was recognized and measures taken to eliminate it. Overall, the Institute has compiled an excellent record of assessing and managing risk and handling the few emergencies that have occurred over the years. Anything less would have jeopardized the entire organization.

The North Cascades Environmental Learning Center did not change the mission of the North Cascades Institute, but it surely broadened opportunities to address that mission. The Institute crew were naturalists and environmental educators not versed in the arts of hospitality and facility management, but they rose to the challenge quickly. Over the years they ran a smooth operation in the face of storms, rockslides, avalanches, and even wildfires in a remote location. Running a food service operation in such a location was difficult but provided opportunities like the Foodshed Project, contributing to local producers, offering farm-fresh food much of the time, and educating all the while about good and responsible food consumption. A particularly important set of opportunities that arose from the Learning Center as base camp involved youth programs, which expanded significantly and broadened the reach of the Institute considerably.

A crowd of enthusiastic supporters gathered at the Environmental Learning Center to mark its opening in 2005. Many celebratory remarks were offered, but a note from nationally prominent and award-winning writer Barbara Kingsolver, who had taught at an Institute writer's retreat and become a strong supporter, captured the significance of the moment:

> *The very least you can do in your life is to figure out what you hope for. And the most you can do is live inside that hope. Not admire it from a distance, but live right in it, under its roof. What I want is so simple I almost can't say it: elemental kindness. Enough to eat, enough to go around. The possibility that kids might one day grow up to be neither the destroyers nor the destroyed. That's about it. Right now I'm living in that hope, running down its hallway and touching the walls on both sides.*
>
> *Today, as the North Cascades Institute opens the Learning Center, I feel I'm being given a gift of hope. In future years, people will come here to learn about the environment that shelters and sustains us— the natural systems that we do not own but to which we, as a species, belong—and those people will grow up to be neither the destroyers nor the destroyed, but responsible citizens of a habitat, a food web, and a planet. I would like to express my gratitude to all the people who've worked hard to reach this point. Thanks to your work, past and future, and with the support of everyone here, we have this chance to live inside our hope, running down its hallway, touching the walls on both sides.*

Once I viewed the beauty of the North Cascades, I realized something. I actually want to help preserve this captivating place for many future generations.

Bianca, North Cascades Wild student

VIII | THE YOUTH MOVEMENT

Brian Scheuch, who challenged Saul Weisberg to think of the Institute as a business and run it on sound business principles, joined the Board and issued another challenge in the late 1980s. As a frequent participant in natural history field seminars, he opined that the adult programming was great, but wondered if it was not a bit self-serving. Everyone was enjoying themselves but the real work of advancing conservation through education, he thought, would be to extend programs to young people. He wanted to "catch the next generation" and provide programs for them; then the Institute would really be doing significant work. The problem was (and as a businessman, Brian knew this perhaps more than any of his colleagues) that to this point in its history the Institute was running mostly on fee-for-service, and the principal service was quality programming for adults. How would youth education be financed? Youth programs would likely need subsidies. Nudged into action by Brian's urging, and agreeing with him, Saul and the Board members who could get away attended a fundraising workshop in Seattle to explore the possibilities of funding youth programs. A new stage in the Institute's growth was launched.

Brian recognized, as he noted in an interview with Christian Martin two decades later, that young people were not getting out into nature like he had growing up in the 40s and 50s. "I don't see enough young people following us and I'm concerned." Though "nature deficit disorder," as Richard Louv would call it in his 2005 book *Last Child in the Woods*, had yet to be described and the digital age was just beginning, the need to find ways to connect children with nature was clear to Brian and the rest of the Institute community. Doing so became an Institute goal, donations were solicited, and staff were brought on board to draft an approach and find a way to fund it. Mountain School opened in 1990, the beginning of programming directed at young people.

In his 1993 book *The Thunder Tree*, Bob Pyle wrote, "People who care conserve; people who don't know don't care. What is the extinction of the condor to a child who has never known a wren?" There is no more succinct or powerful rationale for what Brian advocated for and the Institute set out to do. Description of the Institute's youth programming must be divided into two parts—school programs and youth programs. The former included Mountain School, the Skagit Watershed Education Project and, more recently, Mount Baker Snow School and Forest School. Youth programming was a longer list: Mountain Camp, Ross Lake Canoe Camp, North Cascades Wild, Parks Climate Challenge, Cascade Climate Challenge, and Youth Leadership Adventures. Another category that has involved youth is Community Programming such as the Kulshan Creek Neighborhood Youth Program and Concrete Summer Learning Adventure. Family-oriented programming like Family Getaways also involved young people. Youth programs of various length and focus have sought to help children to "know a wren" and are the subject of this chapter in Institute history.

Less artfully than Bob, writers today describe a "shifting baseline" and "ecological amnesia," elaborating on what he was saying. One part of the task embraced by youth programming was to literally enable the child to hear a wren, a loon, an owl, or a warbler; to see a butterfly up close, probe for life in a mountain stream, and think about the weather and climate they are experiencing. It is to provide opportunities to encounter wildlife and experience an ancient forest and wild places. The new baseline is the experience of a modern, impoverished natural world as "normal," as opposed to what it might have been in the past, and to have no sense of what has been lost or of what might be restored. The "amnesia" part of this is that the younger generation does not miss what has been lost if they do not know of it. Many children grow up with little contact with nature, living lives of programmed activities entirely in human-built environments. Youth programs set out to introduce them to the natural world, to encourage them to explore that world and to care for it.

MOUNTAIN CAMP

WITH MOUNTAIN SCHOOL UNDER WAY during the fall and spring for fifth graders, the next youth initiative was directed at older youth in summer. A hallowed approach to offering summer activities in the outdoors, the summer camp, suggested how the Institute might offer opportunities to older kids. Mountain Camp was first offered in the summer of 1991. It would be camping-based at walk-in sites of the Colonial Creek Campground, using the same tents, rain jackets, and other gear that had been acquired for Mountain School. Four sessions were offered, targeting youngsters ages 10-12, 12-14, and 14-18. Wendy Scherrer organized the camps, which advertised "natural history day hikes and science exploration in different habitats and life zones throughout North Cascades National Park under the supervision of gifted teachers and naturalists." Each session would have twelve campers and four full-time staff. The price of each session was $295 and covered food and most of the gear campers would need. The campground provided water, restrooms, and other amenities for everyone. Excursions could be made right out of the campground up Thunder Creek through old-growth forests and up to the 3,600-foot Fourth of July Pass. Campers would attend evening presentations by Park Service interpreters in the Colonial Creek Amphitheater.

The first year was a success and the program continued in 1992 with campers venturing farther afield. The catalogue promised varied learning experiences: "visit high mountain passes and lush meadows," "slide down snowbanks in the middle of summer," and "lie beneath a canopy of stars and listen to Indian legends." Campers could ponder the source of the icy cold Thunder Creek high in the mountain cirques above their camp, water flowing from beneath some of the North Cascades' largest glaciers and laden with glacial silt that drained into Diablo Lake, where it colored the water a deep aqua blue-green. They could try to comprehend the size and age of stands of Douglas fir and western redcedar that lived just upstream from camp. The Institute recruited resource people from its pool of biologists, geologists, musicians, artists, and an archaeologist for the program. Park rangers explained what they did, described what constituted a national park, and offered some history of their park. The campers, most of junior-high age, enjoyed a rich menu of experiences.

The program in 1993 was much like that of the previous year, with the price a bit higher at $325, and offered some scholarship aid to help needy campers afford the experience. In 1994 two of the Mountain Camp sessions were offered at Rockport State Park down the Skagit Valley, more narrowly focused on stream and forest natural history and conservation. One session was "Stream Scene," which offered hands-on explorations of stream ecology. Camp was in the ancient forest of the state park with excursions to nearby streams, wetlands, and the Skagit River. Campers tied flies and tried their hands at flyfishing, explored life in the waters, and discussed what could be done to protect the aquatic areas they visited. The other session at Rockport State Park was "Cedar Summer," where campers examined the nature of forests and how they had been and were being used and sometimes conserved. Scientists, they learned, probe the mysteries of forest ecology while artists carve, paint, draw, and photograph as they seek the essences of these stands of towering trees. They learned how Indigenous People had used these forests in various ways, as well as early settlers of the Upper Skagit Valley. Campers were immersed in the Rockport State Park Forest, listening to the croak of ravens and songs of unseen birds in the canopy. Perhaps they heard the long, melodic song of the Pacific wren, fulfilling the hopes expressed by Bob Pyle. The other two sessions of Mountain Camp were back at Colonial Creek Campground, conducted much as they had been for the previous two years. One new experience was introduced in 1994, "Return to Mountain Camp," responding to interest by campers from previous years who wanted more.

Mountain Camp continued to expand over the next couple of years, offering programs titled "Wet and Wild," "Fire and Ice," and in 1995, "Birds,

Bugs and Load-bearing Llamas." Led by field biologists Dana Visalli and Lanette Smith, this was a seven-day backpack in the Pasayten Wilderness, targeted to an older 14-17 age group. Youth programming was slowly experimenting with more extended outings, with their logistical and risk-management challenges, while continuing their now standard camp programs. The 1995 catalogue featured a testimonial to Mountain Camp by William Van Almkerk, a grandfather who described what he got out of sending his grandson to Mountain Camp:

> *Grandpas can make a difference! When your grandson shares with you the excitement, the joy and pleasure of his fellowship with new friends at Mountain Camp as mine has, you know you have made a worthwhile contribution to his summer! You've also helped make a lifelong memory for the two of you to share. I find I look forward to sending my grandson to camp as much as he enjoys going. I hope to meet some new grandparents next year when I take him to camp.*

In 1996, six sessions of Mountain Camp were offered, one of which was a session of Stream Scene for women and girls to attend together. The two sessions of Stream Scene received scholarship support from a fly-fishing store in Seattle, along with gear from another supporter.

Institute program designers were challenged to come up with program ideas that would appeal to teens, an age group that had great potential for exploration, discovery, and adventure, yet was at a stage of personal development with more concern about fitting in to their peer group than younger children. As psychologist Stephen Kellert has written, "Most children at this age also engage in daring, expansive, and challenging activities testing the physical limits of the natural world. In doing so, they often nurture self-confidence, self-esteem, and an increased sense of identity. Opportunities for this kind of experience of nature in modern society often occur through participating in outdoor programs involving considerable challenge in relatively undisturbed and unfamiliar settings."[23] Outward Bound schools have famously recognized this, emphasizing the challenge and the personal development side of the experience. The Institute sought to contribute to personal growth, but not exclusively, as did programs like Outward Bound. They wanted youth in their programs to have adventures but also to learn about the natural and human histories of the North Cascades. They hoped to plant seeds that might grow into an ethic of caring for the North Cascades and other such places.

So, in working to appeal to this age group, youth programs began to involve activities that were more challenging than hiking out of a national park campground and that reached farther into the North Cascades. They would involve a bit more challenge and require developing skills most likely new to them. The programs would immerse participants more in the wilderness classroom while delving, as all Institute programs did, into the history of the place. Starting in 2001, they called the youth program North Cascades Discovery, billed as "Summer Wilderness Adventures for Youth." The first two programs were Discovery Canoe Camp and Girls on Ice.

DISCOVERY CANOE CAMP

AS DESCRIBED EARLIER, THE ONCE FREE-FLOWING Skagit River was dammed by Seattle City Light for hydropower. Two of the three dams created spectacular and accessible mountain reservoirs, Diablo and Ross Lakes, which became part of the North Cascades National Park Complex in Ross Lake National Recreation Area in 1968. Some of the Institute leadership, especially Saul as executive director, were avid canoeists and thought it a shame that Institute programs were not taking advantage of these assets. In one sense, of course, the Institute had taken great advantage of the reservoirs by participating in the relicensing negotiations for City Light's Skagit Hydro Project, which ultimately resulted in the Environmental Learning Center, but Institute youth programming had yet to do so. The Learning Center would open canoeing on Diablo Lake eventually, but in the meantime needed other ways to take advantage of the lakes. The Institute began to do so in the summer of 1998 using a modification of its Mountain Camp approach in Canoe Camp.

Ross Lake reaches 23 miles south to north from the dam into Canada's Skagit Valley and is spectacularly scenic, rimmed as it is by the North Cascades peaks. Since there is no road access to the south end of the lake, canoeing on Ross requires a short paddle from Colonial Creek Campground across the north end of Diablo Lake to a dock in the gorge just below Ross Dam. Canoeists and canoes can be portaged by truck around the dam to another dock just above the dam on Ross Lake. These docks served the clients of Ross Lake Resort, popular as a retreat and a base for fishing and boating on the lake. The resort operated a shuttle service for their clients and other canoeists and kayakers who prearranged to be taken around the dam. For Canoe Camp, the Institute arranged to have its small fleet of canoes based at the resort. Campers could hike down a short trail from Highway 20 to be shuttled to the resort, from which to launch their adventure up the lake.

Six lightweight and stable fiberglass Clipper canoes were purchased, and Christie Fairchild and other Institute staff literally launched this new program from the dock at Ross Lake Resort. After some basic instruction in paddling around the resort, canoes were loaded with food and other gear and supplies for six days. Boys and girls ages 12-16 set off up the lake, gazing up at Sourdough Mountain over their left shoulders and at Jack Mountain towering 7,000 feet above them to their right. All group gear, and of course canoes and life jackets, were provided by the Institute, and scholarships were offered to defer some of the $395 cost for those who needed it. The destination the first day was Big Beaver Camp near where Big Beaver Creek entered the lake. Here, instruction in camping skills began. A short hike up Big Beaver Trail brought the group to a stand of immense western red cedar, among the largest and oldest trees in the North Cascades. After dinner back at camp, stories were shared around the campfire of how Indigenous People traveled through and used this country as campers watched alpineglow light up Jack Mountain. If the weather was challenging, as it often was, tricks on how to be comfortable in such mountain weather were taught and put to immediate use. There was some challenge in that.

One challenge of canoeing a mountain lake is wind, which can raise whitecaps and pose problems especially for novice paddlers. One set of lessons the campers learned involved judging when it was safe to travel on the lake, the instructors explaining their decision-making as to whether to paddle or not. Winds on Ross Lake were fairly predictable, so an early-morning start and early landfall were often good ideas. Lessons about how to assess weather and topography as part of making trip decisions would be part of the day's adventure. Campsites maintained by the Park Service dot the east bank of the lake: May Creek, Devil's Junction,

Tenmile, Lightning Creek, and others. The flotilla could go ashore at any of these camps if necessary.

One stop on the trip up lake was always Devil's Creek, where canoes could poke into a deep gorge through which the creek entered the Lake. A quarter mile into the gorge, maidenhair fern draped the overhanging walls and progress upstream was stopped by a logjam. Here was an ideal spot to raft up and talk about the plants the group was seeing, where the logjam came from and why, and other natural history of this unique spot. Swallows and other birds could often be seen skimming for insects, and keeping still might reveal schools of minnows and the occasional trout in the clear water. A moment of quiet contemplation was part of the visit to this remarkable feature of the lakeshore. Paddling back out onto the lake, campers might see bald eagles and the occasional osprey and spot their nests high in trees along the shore, which provided more rich opportunities to raft up and talk about these marvelous birds. "Nature moments" could come at any time when a glacier on Jack Mountain appeared, a loon or mergansers were spotted, or avalanche tracks and burns on the mountainsides were part of the scene. Staff were always ready to take advantage of any such moments. Since the lake is a reservoir, trip leaders asked paddlers to consider what was hidden beneath the lake's surface, along with the costs and benefits of damming the Skagit River to form the lake they were enjoying.

As with Mountain Camp, the staff was often supplemented by other resource people. This was obviously more difficult to arrange on the lake than at Colonial Creek, but Park Service rangers regularly patrolled and would stop by to talk about the park and wilderness, and the special challenges and opportunities of managing the uses of such a large reservoir. Gerry Cook would stop by, piloting the Park Service work boat *Ross Mule* up and down the lake to service crews working on campsites, trails, and other projects. As an unofficial park historian with an encyclopedic knowledge of the history of the lake and the park, he would join the group and tell some tales, adding another dimension to their understanding of the place. A great storyteller, Gerry, like Brian Scheuch, was a strong proponent of youth programs Whenever his duties allowed, he contributed in any way he could.

The 2002 catalogue advertised North Cascades Discovery for ages 10-19 as follows:

North Cascades Discovery programs are exciting summer adven-
tures for young people who love the outdoors. Each session builds
skills in minimum-impact wilderness travel—from hiking, back-
packing and canoeing to first aid, camping and backcountry cooking.
Team-building exercises foster confidence and respect for yourself,
your peers, and the environment, while daily instruction in natural
and cultural history capture your imagination. Find out for yourself
the difference a wilderness experience can make in your life.

Personal growth, skill development, and learning about nature and
culture are all balanced in this description, evidence of the way Institute
staff integrated the elements appropriate for this age group. While the catalogue terminology might change ("North Cascades Discovery" yielded to
"Summer Youth Programs" after a few years), the approaches and formats
of Mountain School and Canoe Camp persisted until programming shifted sharply to the Learning Center in 2005. These programs did not end at
that point but would change as programming incorporated the Learning
Center into its menu of offerings.

GIRLS ON ICE

JOINING MOUNTAIN CAMP AND CANOE CAMP in the 2001 North Cascades
Discovery was a program exclusively for girls that took youth programs to new
levels of adventure and inquiry. "Girls on Ice" was taught by two University of
Washington PhD glaciologists who had extensive experience studying glaciers
across the world. They were also mountaineers, and their program involved
backpacking, mountaineering, and deep wilderness travel to the remote
South Cascade Glacier in the Glacier Peak Wilderness. This was the most
studied glacier in the extensively glaciated North Cascade Range and the U.S.
Geological Survey had established a research station there. Using the station
as base camp, seven girls aged 15-18 and their two instructors, Erin Pettit and
Michele Koppes, would "conduct geological research focusing on glaciers as
indicators of climate change, as water reservoirs, and as erosive forces in alpine terrain." To do this, students would need to learn basic mountaineering
skills like roped climbing, self-arrest, and safe glacial travel. Just reaching the
research station required some serious bushwhacking and stamina.

Ross Lake was an ideal classroom, visited by adventurous young people via canoe in Canoe Camp, North Cascades Wild, Cascade Climate Challenge, and Youth Leadership Adventures programs.

The seven-day trip was very successful in 2001, and the next year Girls on Ice expanded to two sessions, one a ten-day expedition to South Cascade Glacier for girls entering grades 10-12, the other for women grade 12 through college sophomore who would spend six days studying the more accessible Easton Glacier on the south side of Mount Baker. The Easton Glacier session would add exploration of the relationship between volcanoes and glaciers to the curriculum. In 2003 one session was again offered on Easton Glacier, and in 2004 it moved to Mount Rainier for a "research expedition" to Emmons Glacier. A participant wrote of her experience, "To be with a group of girls who are serious about science is awesome! Using real equipment and doing real projects with an instructor like Erin made me believe I can pursue my dream of being a geologist. Thank you for offering such an amazing opportunity." Mounting a program this sophisticated with complex logistical and risk management challenges depended on highly specialized knowledge and became increasingly expensive for participants. After 2004, Pettit and her students (who now focused their field time on Mount Baker) continued to work with the Institute to use the Learning Center as a site for crunching the data they gathered and presented information to park visitors at Newhalem Campground. The program was eventually hosted at the University of Alaska when Pettit took a faculty position there, and finally morphed many years later into its own nonprofit—Inspiring Girls Expeditions, which runs programs all over the world today.

NORTH CASCADES WILD

THESE YOUTH PROGRAMS WERE WONDERFUL FOR the participants, but they initially served a well-to-do population, those who could afford the tuition. Few had a grandfather like William Van Almkerk who could or would send them to camp. Limited scholarship support was available, but not enough for large numbers of "underserved" young people to be able to participate. Another problem was that only a slice of the population even heard about the opportunities, those who knew someone who had attended an Institute program or who came across a catalogue or online description of what the Institute was offering. Institute staff developed strong relationships with teachers and school counselors from Whatcom and Skagit Counties and south to Seattle, and began recruiting in schools throughout the region. The National Park Service was trying to diversify park visitation nationally, working to find ways to introduce minority communities to their parks, and encouraged the Institute to do what it could to contribute to this effort.

An opportunity to do this fortuitously appeared in the winter of 2006. The Arthur Carhart Wilderness Training Center in Missoula, Montana is a federal interagency center that trains wilderness stewards in land management agencies and advances wilderness education in various ways. The Institute learned that in 2006, the Center had funding to support a wilderness education program for underserved youth in the national park system, but had not been able to find an organization willing to take on the project. Funding had been made available late and most park-affiliated organizations that might mount such a program could not do so on short notice. The North Cascades Institute, on the other hand, was primed and ready. They met with the Center director and convinced her that they could do the job. The Institute already had wilderness-based programs that could be modified to meet the goals of providing leadership development and wilderness conservation awareness and knowledge to underserved youth. It was seeking a way to satisfy the Park Service's push to serve them, and graduate student Amy Brown, soon to graduate, had prepared program ideas in her curriculum project that began necessary modifications to Canoe Camp. A big challenge on short notice was recruiting participants who fit the profile required in the program, but that was overcome, and a diverse group of young people enjoyed an eye-opening experience in the North Cascades.

North Cascades Wild marked a shift in youth programs that continues to this day. They became more socially, economically, and racially inclusive, drawing more participants from the urban centers of Seattle and Tacoma as well as Skagit and Whatcom counties. Many of the young people recruited from urban areas into North Cascades Wild were barely aware of the North Cascades, if at all, let alone that there was a wilderness national park there in their own backyard. Perhaps they could see Mount Rainier in the distance from Seattle and Tacoma and knew it was in a national park, but they knew little about what a park was, why it was a park, or anything about the ideas and history behind conservation of places like Mount Rainier, the Olympic Mountains, or the North Cascades. These were urban youth, many of whom had some inkling that there was something out there beyond the city limits that they didn't know the name of yet, and they were ready to embrace it. If they could be recruited to spend ten days in the backcountry, paddling canoes, sleeping under the stars, and sharing the experiences with peers, they would enjoy a great adventure and might recruit others into the ranks of those, as Bob Pyle said, who care.

The other shift in programming for older youth was not an insignificant one—from primarily tuition-based to subsidized programs. Underserved youth needed tuition subsidies because they came from poor communities without the means to provide them with the advantages and amenities of more wealthy neighbors. The families in those communities, often struggling to make ends meet, might aspire to enjoy the outdoors and nature, but were constrained in providing enrichment programs like a wilderness experience for their young people. The values were there; the means were not. The Institute and its partners would need to raise the money to finance such programs. The Carhart grant was seed money to begin a new initiative for youth programming.

Amy was hired to fast-track North Cascades Wild into existence and, with her abundant energy and the help of other Institute staff, the program was launched in the Clipper canoes on Ross Lake. Most of the participants in North Cascades Wild had little or no outdoor experience and had never been in a canoe. The basics of safety and comfort in a canoe and in camp were taught at the beginning of each program. Many of the hikes, lessons, and activities of past Canoe Camps were the same, but a greater emphasis on leadership, service, and communicating their experiences was crucially added. Previous campers were paying to have a great adventure, to have a lot of fun, and to learn in the process, but North Cascades Wilders took advantage of a larger, more inclusive opportunity. Part of their experience was service—they would give back to the park, the wilderness, and their sponsors. Under the guidance of Cook and others in the Park Service, projects were identified that would contribute to the restoration of areas along Ross Lake that had been impacted by heavy use and other disturbances. They might also build things to enhance campsites and in other ways help with the big challenges of managing this heavily used area of the North Cascades National Park Complex. All of this advanced their understanding of public lands and what was needed to keep these lands in good shape for the "publics," including the wild beings, that used them.

Another theme of the North Cascades Wild experience was leadership. Woven into discussions throughout the ten days were inquiries into what constituted leadership, what the many styles of leadership were, whether leaders were born or they could be made, and if they could be made, how that might happen. Who were the leaders in the communities from which they came, and what were their qualities? As the expedition proceeded, participants were given leadership responsibilities, helping the group make decisions. Institute staff could step in as facilitators if necessary, to manage risks and help the group process any issues that might arise, but practice of leadership skills was built into the process. All the students from the summer's programs would be convened in the fall at the new Learning Center for a follow-up conference focused on further exploration of leadership. Many of these young people had not thought of themselves as leaders or even possessing the potential to be leaders. The goal was to grow their sense of self-efficacy, their power to affect the world around them.

Youth programs that included canoeing on Ross Lake such as North Cascades Wild used service projects to improve and restore recreation resources in the heavily used Ross Lake National Recreation Area. This group is under the leadership of Institute staff Amy Brown and Michael Parelskin.

One challenge of all programs that removed learners from their community to a place like the North Cascades, so different from their homes, was the transfer of what they learned back to those communities. Could a ten-day experience generate understandings and insights that participants could take back with them and apply in their home settings? What might help achieve such a transfer of learning? These were questions Amy and others wrestled with in designing the program. One way to increase the likelihood of some transfer was to bring the group back together for reflection and sharing about how the experience had enhanced their understandings of themselves, of the world beyond their usual boundaries, and especially of leadership. All Institute youth programs, from Mountain School to North Cascades Wild and beyond, have from their beginning sought to assess whether transfer was happening, and to do follow-ups to field experiences to help students reflect and connect their field experiences to their lives back home. Follow-up conferences would become a feature of North Cascades Wild, which would continue in the basic format Amy established until it merged with Cascade Climate Challenge to become Youth Leadership Adventures in 2013.

PARKS CLIMATE CHALLENGE

A UNIQUE PROGRAM FOR HIGH-SCHOOL STUDENTS from across the United States called Parks Climate Challenge was offered by the Institute in 2009. A warming global climate was becoming of increasing concern to the National Park Service. Jon Jarvis had risen through the ranks of the Service since leaving his position as chief of natural resources at North Cascades National Park. He was now Director of the Park Service in the Obama administration and had long been advocating for greater attention to climate change threats in general, and especially those posed to parks by a warming climate. They were impacting national parks in various ways, not least in the recession of glaciers in parks like Glacier National Park and the North Cascades.

The National Parks Foundation, with funding from corporate sponsors, proposed a youth program dedicated strictly to climate change in a park being affected by the warming climate and approached several parks to conduct such a program. All replied that they could not mount a program on short notice. North Cascades Superintendent Chip Jenkins got a call in January from the Foundation inquiring whether his park could. He responded that the Park Service could not itself do it under the circumstances, but its partner, the Institute, probably could. It had proven its ability to respond to such situations earlier when it created North Cascades Wild in short order. He would ask whether they were interested. Seeing another strategic opportunity, the Institute said it could rise to the challenge. The Foundation would support a 30-day workshop for 20 high school students from around the country. The goals would be to show the students how climate change was affecting national parks with North Cascades National Park as a prime example, engage them in examination of the nature of climate change and possible responses to it, and encourage them to return home and do something to combat it.

Two graduates of the Institute/Huxley College M.Ed. program, Megan McGinty and Aneka Sweeney, were hired and charged with creating and leading the program. Both brought solid science backgrounds as well as training and experience in environmental education to the task, and both knew the North Cascades, the Institute, and the climate change issue well and could get right to work. The Foundation selected the cities from which high-school students would be recruited and applicants were screened and chosen by the Institute, the Park Service, and the Foundation. Megan and Aneka would design the program, set up all the itineraries for field experiences, recruit experts from the Park Service and elsewhere, and organize the logistics. All of this was accomplished in less than six months. Students traveled from metropolitan areas in Chicago, Washington D.C., Denver, Seattle, and California's Napa Valley. They settled into the Learning Center and set out to take advantage of an exceptional learning opportunity.

Parks Climate Challenge had three phases: first, the experience in North Cascades National Park; second, a trip to Washington, DC to meet legislators, land management agency leaders, and legislators; and third back home, where they would create a project to address the challenge of climate change in their urban areas. As Megan told writer Elizabeth Keating, "We weren't necessarily looking for students who are interested in careers in the environment. What's most important is that they demonstrate leadership potential and that they return to their urban communities as 'climate change ambassadors' that the community will respond to."[24] During the thirty days with the Institute the students examined, among other topics, what was known about how climate change was a factor in wildfire, glacial retreat, and forest and stream ecology and its impacts on wildlife. They took a field trip with park glaciologist Jon Riedel to the Railroad Grade on the south side of Mount Baker. From the moraine they could see how the glacier had receded several miles and was continuing to do so. These students had never enjoyed such a close view of a glacier before (most had never seen one). Gazing up the mountain at the glacier, then down into the trough up which it had retreated, the reality of climate change was clear. Riedel explained what they were seeing, exploring the changes a warming climate was bringing to the glaciers and why that was important to the human community.

The Learning Center was, of course, on a reservoir created by damming the Skagit River to provide electricity to the city of Seattle. Hydro-electric power generation uses a renewable resource to meet the energy needs of the city, and the students learned about this with Seattle City Light personnel. They learned that City Light was concerned about climate change because it would affect precipitation patterns, threatening the reliability of power generation from the Skagit Hydro Project. Warmer weather, more rain rather than snow, and faster melt and runoff of water stored in the snowpack (which, as one City Light presenter explained, acts like a storage battery) all threatened to reduce the capacity of the reservoirs to supply their share of Seattle's energy throughout the year. They learned that salmon required adequate instream flow to ensure the viability of their spawning, which again might be threatened by too much rain in the winter and too little in summer, both projected consequences of climate change. The lessons went on and on.

Courtesy of NCI

Glaciers in North Cascades National Park are retreating. Here, glaciologist Jon Riedel explains to Parks Climate Challenge students what is happening on the lateral moraine of Easton Glacier on Mount Baker's south side.

After this intensive summer, the students traveled to Washington, DC, where they met with various politicians and legislators and made presentations on what they had learned and what they were thinking of doing for their projects back home. At their presentation, the twenty students sat at one end of a large conference table with the various bigwigs from the Park Service, the Forest Service, and other agencies at the other end. The students were enthusiastic and eloquent, and many in the audience of government bureaucrats took notes as the students presented some of what they had learned. Asked to introduce themselves and explain what their agencies were doing to address the climate change issue, the agency people didn't have much to share. One explained that they were addressing the threat to polar bears, to which one young man from Chicago responded that he hoped they were thinking of the people in the cities as well. The students were no doubt impressed by the opportunity to speak to leaders at the seat of government, but as the Chicago student's question revealed, they were not intimidated. Their presentations and the responses demonstrated that, indeed, the group were the potential leaders that Megan and the rest of the team behind Parks Climate Challenge were hoping to encourage.

After all the work that went into the program to develop and implement Parks Climate Challenge, Institute and park staff expected it to continue for many years, but that was not to be. The National Parks Foundation decided that providing an intensive experience in a park for a small group was not the best way to address their goals to educate youth about climate change, and instead funded an approach using media that they projected could reach thousands of young people. Technology that was captivating youth would be, they thought, a better way to go. In the view of the Institute, this was a "mile wide and inch deep" approach to climate change education, but the program they had conducted at North Cascades National Park had been very successful. Thus, the Institute and Park staffs decided to do their own program. The contradiction in flying youth from all over the country to participate in a climate change education program was not lost on them, so they decided they would focus on high-school students from Washington and Oregon and thus significantly reduce the carbon footprint of the students involved. Using much that had worked well for Parks Climate Challenge in 2009, Cascade Climate Challenge was launched under the leadership of North Cascades Institute and North Cascades National Park.

CASCADE CLIMATE CHALLENGE

WHEN THEY LEARNED THAT THE NATIONAL Parks Foundation had other plans, the Institute immediately submitted grant proposals to a wide range of funders to continue the program. The Paul Allen Family Foundation stepped up and provided funding for two years of Cascade Climate Challenge, two 22-day sessions each summer with high-school students recruited from Washington and Oregon. Aneka, Megan, and other staff hit the road to recruit participants, traveling all over western Oregon and Washington making presentations about the new program as well as North Cascades Wild. Aneka reported in late May that youth programs were full, with diverse students from 35 high schools and 12 counties in the two states. On June 29, 19 eager young people arrived at the rendezvous at Sea-Tac Airport and traveled to the Learning Center. Institute staff and grad students had been busy over the previous months packing food, preparing the curriculum, calling students, and organizing and finalizing lessons. Everyone was excited to get started.

In the first few days the students ran through some basic camping skills they would need in the field, practiced with the audio and video equipment they would use to document their experience, got their equipment into shape, and explored trails around the Learning Center. They were oriented to the program by Megan and Aneka and met some North Cascades National Park scientists and rangers who introduced them to the park and began focusing their attention on climate change. Mike Brondi, a North Cascades National Park maintenance worker with wide knowledge and skills, gave them an introduction to concepts of forest ecology, which he could do out of the Learning Center. Park Wildlife Biologist Anne Braaten introduced them to bear biology and behavior, exploring how climate change might impact the bears and other wildlife in the park. One student commented after that session, "My favorite day was where we learned about bears and the effect of climate change on bear habitat. I didn't know the bears we have were endangered, I thought it was all about polar bears."

Megan and Aneka kept the group busy. They hiked up Sauk Mountain with naturalist Don Burgess, enjoying the view and studying the mountain's abundant wildflowers. They gazed down the Skagit Valley, the perfect place to talk about Pleistocene glaciation, and enjoyed a raven's-eye view of the confluence of the Skagit and Sauk rivers. The Sauk, laden with glacial flour, was gray, and they could see a clear line in the Skagit where the Sauk joined the clear water of the larger river. Why, they asked, were the rivers so different? This generated more discussion of glacial melt, the impacts of dams on rivers, and other topics. Camped at Baker Lake, the participants split into two groups, one examining amphibian ecology on Baker River and the East Bank Trail, the other trekking up to the Railroad Grade and Easton Glacier on Mount Baker with Jon Riedel. Then it was on to Ross Lake with a fisheries biologist and a cruise with Gerry Cook on the *Ross Mule*, during which they snorkeled in the icy water, gazed at some of the fish, and discussed how climate change might be affecting the lake and the life in it. They hiked to Boston Basin and Cascade Pass and canoed on Ross Lake, from which they made the strenuous hike up Desolation Peak. One student wrote, "Canoeing away after we had climbed Desolation Peak—I looked back and saw how far we had climbed and it felt amazing."[25]

A service project was also built into the program, and students did a little restoration work or whatever projects Cook and his colleagues thought they could do in the short time available for such work, but their days were certainly not all work and no play. Hiking and canoeing were just good fun, and swims in the lake were great on hot summer days after a strenuous hike. Keating quoted another student exclaiming, "Remember how we held hands and ran the last few yards up to Desolation Peak? I couldn't believe we made it." This hike tested even veteran hikers' stamina, and this was just one example of students doing things they thought beyond them before they were infected with the enthusiasm and spirit of their fellows in the program. Another student commented to Keating, "Watching meteor showers from a dock on Ross Lake—we were all on the dock laughing and talking but there were a few moments of complete silence. People find themselves and realize what's important looking up at the stars." These students learned much, not just about climate change but about themselves and a universe of nature they had not experienced that reached to the stars.

The expectation of Parks Climate Challenge that participants take home what they had learned and apply it was carried over to Cascade Climate Challenge. They would make a group presentation to Park visitors at the end of the program and come up with a plan to teach elementary-school children back home about climate change. They pondered this charge as they enjoyed their three-week intensive exposure to the way climate change was affecting the natural world in the Pacific Northwest, and the consequences of such for people there. After a session with two Park Service interpreters at the North Cascades Visitor Center toward the end of their adventure, they brainstormed what their projects might be and did some preliminary planning with helpful critiques from the rangers and from Aneka and Megan. Afterward they gathered around the campfire, as they had often throughout the summer, for sharing and reflection. A student was appointed "Camp Philosopher" to share a quotation that would spark reflection. At the campfire after the brainstorm, a student named Savannah read a proverb that reminds her both what she has learned, and the way that the class will impart knowledge to younger students:

> *Tell me, and I'll listen.*
> *Show me, and I'll understand.*
> *Involve me, and I'll learn.*

SAVANNAH'S CHOICE OF THIS PROVERB TESTIFIED to the fact that she understood the approach to learning underlying her experience of the previous three weeks. She was sharing this insight with her fellow students so that they would keep it in mind as they created learning experiences for the younger students back home. This young philosopher expressed in her choice the very essence of the approach the Institute has taken to youth programming throughout its history.

Cascade Climate Challenge continued for three summers and was then merged with North Cascades Wild into Youth Leadership Adventures. The decision was made to consolidate the youth programs, which were highly successful but expensive to run. In November 2010 the Institute partnered with North Cascades National Park and the Mount Baker-Snoqualmie National Forest to offer the "North Cascades Youth Leadership Conference, A Confluence of Young Leaders" at the Learning Center. Organized by Institute staff and grad students, with help from agency partners, the conference invited high-school students who had participated in a program on public lands such as Cascade Climate Challenge, North Cascades Wild, International District Housing Alliance Wild, or the Youth Conservation Corps. The group of 48 students included first-generation Americans from Bhutan, Cameroon, Eritrea, Ethiopia, India, Mexico, Nepal, the Philippines, and Somalia, a culturally rich and diverse group of young people united by their experiences in the North Cascades.

One of the conference organizers and facilitators was Institute graduate student Kate Rinder, who wrote an eloquent blog about the event. She was inspired by all she saw at the conference. There was time for some canoeing and hiking, but these fun activities had to be squeezed in between a full schedule of activities. The keynote on Saturday was presented by brothers Benjie Howard and Maketa Wilborn of the New Wilderness Project, who delivered "a powerful interactive message on race, identity, and the natural world through spoken word poetry, songs, storytelling, video and still imagery" to what Rinder described as a spellbound audience. Then came breakout sessions on leadership styles, college admissions, job interviewing, and public speaking led by Western Washington University and Washington Conservation Corps staffs. This was in turn followed by the Opportunity Fair at which students could talk about job, internship, and volunteer opportunities with representatives from the Park Service, Forest Service, Earthcorps, Student Conservation Association, and other public lands organizations. The day was capped off in an evening session by filmmakers Benj Drummond and Sara Joy Steele on "Facing Climate Change." They explained how documentary films and other media could be used to change people's attitudes, behaviors, and policies.

On Sunday morning the conferees worked to finalize their personal action plans and held an "Open Space Discussion" in which students suggested topics and led round table discussion on such topics as "Stress Management," "Overpopulation and Consumption of Resources," "Group Dynamics," and "The Philosophy of Climate Change and the Environment," all weighty topics indeed. A closing ceremony was a staple of all Institute youth programs, usually in big sharing circles. At the conference closing ceremony Grace Bogne, a North Cascades Wild alumna and North Cascades National Park summer seasonal staff member, reflected, "My involvement in the North Cascades has totally changed my life. I'm grateful there's a place like this where we can all come together and be in nature, and be free." Rinder commented in her blog that "this sentiment was shared by youth and adults alike."[26]

PATH FOR YOUTH INITIATIVE

THE YEAR 2010 WAS A BIG ONE for youth programming and initiated a decade of youth backcountry adventures, youth leadership conferences, and introductions to public lands, environmental issues, and the natural world for hundreds of diverse and underserved young people. Taken together, all these programs became part of the Path for Youth Initiative, a conceptual partnership between the Institute, the National Park Service, and the Forest Service. Over 25 years the Institute had found ways to reach its goal of serving youth of all ages, from elementary students to university graduate students. At a retreat of Institute staff, Board members, graduate students, and Park and Forest Service supporters at the Learning Center, the realization dawned that what had been created was a continuum of opportunity for youth that might lead some to lifelong commitments to conservation and environmental stewardship. Discussion of this, with enthusiastic participation by Superintendent Jenkins, led to the concept of considering youth programs holistically. They could metaphorically provide a Path for Youth which did not necessarily involve more programs, but was a comprehensive way of thinking about and describing the suite of programs that were already being implemented.

In an article for *Clearing: A Resource Journal of Environmental and Place-based Education*, graduate student Mollie Behn wrote, "The strength of the Path for Youth Initiative lies in the creation of a continuum of intentional interconnected experiences. For example, a student who participates in a 3-day ecosystem studies program in fifth grade could return again in the eleventh grade for a course in wilderness stewardship and leadership development. With guidance and mentorship, that student could return as a young adult intern for a national park or local conservation non-profit. This continuum of experiences, or pathway, ensures students have follow-up, repeated connections that build on prior experiences, and ongoing opportunities to stay engaged."[27] From Mountain School to North Cascades Wild to work as a seasonal Park Service employee, the path Grace Bogne had followed, some young people could move toward possible careers in conservation. Superintendent Jenkins was particularly excited by this program narrative, arguing that it might very well lead to recruitment of young leaders into public land agency careers.

Over the next decade the idea of a Path for Youth Initiative was re-alized. Mountain School expanded and Youth Leadership Adventures offered eight-day Outdoor Leadership courses for 14-16-year-olds, and 16-day science and sustainability courses for those 16-18 years old. Year-round mentorships were offered to alumni, and youth leadership confer-ences, summits, and alumni reunions continued. Several courses were all girls, and a program called Youth Ambassadors was launched. This was a school-year extension of summer programs that engaged Institute students and alumni from Whatcom and Skagit Counties in outdoor adventure, service work, and preparation for college. The Ambassadors would meet as a group twice a month for an excursion into nearby public lands or a visit to a local college or university. The goal was to continue the participants' education about environmental and public land stew-ardship, and to help them prepare for college.

Here is the story in the words of one girl who followed the Pathway for Youth, told in the 2017 Youth Leadership annual report:

My name is Mia. I'm a small-town girl and member of the Swinomish Tribe. My dad taught me how to hunt before I could walk, and I had the record for the third-largest elk taken out of Western Washington. Since 2015, I've participated in a Youth Leadership Adventures Trip, the Summit, and Ambassadors. Before YLA I had a closed-minded view on people. My first thoughts when I arrived were: this place is beautiful, and what did I get myself into? The woods aren't new to me, but these activities with nine strangers felt awkward.

During our trip, we hiked over 90 miles, completed stewardship projects, studied wildlife and glaciology, and helped each other grow. I pushed myself and came to know myself in a new way. After my trip, the Youth Ambassador program taught me useful college skills.

These programs shaped my environmental consciousness by shaping my actions. I used to not think twice about the ground I walked on. Now, I've seen the effects on an environmental area when we complete a project together. Even more, YLA shaped the way I view people. I realized that we all share commonalities. I formed connections with peers who are now my friends, with National Park Service mentors, and most of all, with people who care about me. Thanks to people at North Cascades Institute, I know that I'll always have someone in my corner.

Today I'm at Skagit Valley College, working toward a degree in environmental conservation. I am pursuing my dream job to be a wildlife biologist, so that I can preserve our wildlife for future generations to come.

Mia's account describes the many ways the Path for Youth helps young people grow. She, and many others, are testimony to the success of youth programs the Institute has mounted for decades.

If facts are the seeds that later produce knowledge and wisdom, then the emotions and the impressions of the senses are the fertile soil in which the seeds must grow.

Rachel Carson, *The Sense of Wonder*

IX | COMMUNITY AND
OTHER SCHOOL PROGRAMS

THERE HAVE BEEN SO MANY DIMENSIONS to the work of the North Cascades Institute over 35 years that it is difficult to fit descriptions of them into neat categories. The "youth movement" has been so extensive and impressive that much attention has been devoted to it here, from the story of early Mountain School to the more recent Youth Ambassador program. There is overlap in categories like youth leadership programs, community programs, and school programs, all of which involve young people. The targeted audiences may be the same, but the goals of the programs differ, as do some of the locations. The Kulshan Creek Neighborhood Program is a prime example. There are and have been adult-oriented programs as well that serve other needs like those of elders, teachers, and tourists visiting North Cascades National Park and the Mount Baker-Snoqualmie National Forest. Teacher workshops, Elderhostels, and retail stores have all addressed important clients.

Over the years the Institute has mounted what it calls "community programs," based not at the Learning Center but in population centers within or close to the North Cascades. The Kulshan Creek Neighborhood Youth Program, launched in 2007 with the Forest Service's Mount Baker Ranger District, involved partnerships between the Institute, the Forest Service, North Cascades National Park, the Mount Vernon Police Department, and Catholic Housing Services of Washington. Initially aimed at young people from the Kulshan Creek Neighborhood, it grew to involve the Mount Vernon communities of Casa de San Jose and the Harrison apartments. In the 1990s the Kulshan Creek Neighborhood housed largely Hispanic families, many of them migrant agricultural workers, and was considered one of the city's highest-crime neighborhoods. Their parents working, children were often unsupervised after school and there was increasing gang activity. In response, a police station was opened in the neighborhood and an effort made to find ways beyond policing to address problems there. Out of this need came the Kulshan Creek Neighborhood Project.

KULSHAN CREEK NEIGHBORHOOD PROJECT

Every month throughout the year Kulshan Creek youngsters take field trips to learn about the natural and cultural history of the Skagit Valley. They have joined the Skagit Fisheries Enhancement Group to plant trees at Cornet Bay to stabilize shorelines and provide shade for fish. During the winter they go eagle watching on the upper Skagit River. They attend the Migratory Bird Festival at Fort Casey on Whidbey Island in the spring and join North Cascades Wild on Baker Lake to do stewardship work on a campground and learn about future opportunities. Most of these youngsters have few opportunities to visit these places, to see a mountain goat or learn about the natural world around them. They cannot experience their watershed, a concept to which they are introduced in school. The Kulshan Creek Project provides such opportunities and broadens the participants' perspectives of their home.

Leaders on these outings include agency staff, a Mount Vernon police officer, and Institute staff and graduate students. In 2016, for instance, the program adopted the Skagit River as a theme and the group took a field trip to Rasar State Park to explore how such a dominant and important natural feature of the children's home ground connected to everything else in the ecosystem. The session there was led by M.Ed. graduate student Sasha Savoian, who facilitated discussion of salmon biology, life cycle, and habitat, about which the students had been taught in school. Sasha organized the fun and active Salmon Run Game in which everyone played various roles that illustrated the amazing journey salmon make returning to their birthplace to spawn. M.Ed. graduate Lee Whitford volunteered on many Kulshan Creek field trips. On one, she was attempting to get the youngsters interested in natural history on the banks of the Baker River above Baker Lake and wasn't making much progress. Finally, she let them entertain themselves by throwing rocks into the river, something universally enjoyed by kids but not previously possible for many of the youngsters in the Kulshan Creek Neighborhood. Whitford believed that just having fun along the river might plant a seed that would grow into appreciation and understanding of what the natural world had to offer them.

This community program (funded by the Institute, the Forest Service and other partners) exposed participants to ideas about natural resources, public lands, and stewardship of the environment. Activities were aimed at helping them build self-esteem and foster community pride. On many field trips, they contributed to the Skagit Valley community by doing a bit of service work. They were exposed to positive, diverse role models like agency and Institute staff, young people in North Cascades Wild, and graduate students. One goal statement for the program was, "Provide a pathway for students to continue their engagement through next step opportunities including Youth Leadership Adventures and exposure to internships and to careers in natural resources, community services, and environmental education." Over the years, more than 500 young people have participated in this program. While it is small, it offers a wonderful example of another way to reach out and help youngsters from local communities who would otherwise be stuck in their neighborhoods, limited in their ability to explore the world around them. The Institute led coordination of the program for five years, then the Forest Service took over the coordination and the Institute contributed as lead fiscal agent. It provides educational staff, curricula, risk management, liability release forms, and coordination assistance to this day.

The Institute partnered with the U.S. Forest Service and others to create the Kulshan Creek program for youth from Mount Vernon, Washington. This involved them in many activities like restoring impacted recreation sites, as this youngster is doing here.

CONCRETE SUMMER LEARNING ADVENTURE

ANOTHER COMMUNITY PROGRAM IS THE CONCRETE Summer Learning Adventure, a day camp for Concrete Elementary School students. Concrete is the closest school district to the Learning Center. This began as a four-week summer camp in 2013 as a partnership and collaboration between United General Hospital's Community Health Outreach Program, the Concrete School District, North Cascades National Park, and the North Cascades Institute. Campers are first through fifth graders from rural areas around Concrete and the program offers them fun, interactive enrichment activities along with two healthy meals per day during the camp season. In 2015 the camp was expanded to five weeks and four days per week. In her 2016 Institute *Program Overview,* Education Director Tracie Johannessen reported, "The program is now led by United General Hospital VISTA volunteers, a National Park/Institute VISTA volunteer and an Institute graduate student. Concrete School District para-educators and food service staff, Western Washington University interns, Concrete High School Interns, and North Cascades National Park staff and volunteers serve as staff for the camp."[28] Through its leadership and example, the Institute inspired many others to step up to meet environmental education needs and opportunities in the Upper Skagit Valley.

The Institute was of course only one of many partners in these community programs. In many cases the Institute, with its environmental education expertise, commitment to providing programs for young people in the Skagit Valley, and extensive resource of trained staff and graduate students, took on a critical early leading role. Without this, these programs would have been very difficult to start and sustain. Here as in many other cases, the Institute served as a catalyst to start these programs and to provide services and resources after primary responsibility for the programs moved to others. Throughout its history the Institute has sought ways to support the Skagit Valley Community, sourcing resources from it when possible and providing programs that meet specific needs in the Valley.

On one occasion prior to completion of the Learning Center, the Skagit Environmental Endowment Commission (of which the author was then a member) was meeting in Park Service facilities in Newhalem. Before the meeting convened, Saul Weisberg went into the Newhalem store and was cornered by a City Light employee who had serious questions about the wisdom of spending Seattle City Light money to build a facility for environmental education, of all things. She could think of many better things on which to spend it. After a spirited exchange in which Saul patiently explained how a Learning Center was being funded through a mandated partnership with the Park Service and City Light, and how he thought it would bring many good things to the Upper Skagit community, he escaped to the SEEC meeting. This anecdote illustrates a belief on the part of some upriver residents that the Learning Center was unnecessary and would not benefit them. It also suggests that residents should have been more involved in planning for the Learning Center, or at least kept informed throughout negotiations of what was being considered. From that day forward, Saul and his staff were dedicated to proving the skeptics wrong and to involving the Valley community in programs. The Kulshan Creek and Concrete programs, among the many others described in this history, indicate that they succeeded.

SCHOOL PROGRAMS BEYOND MOUNTAIN SCHOOL

ANOTHER CATEGORY OF PROGRAMS IS SCHOOL PROGRAMS, defined by their direct interaction with school curricula. The biggest of these, of course, is Mountain School, which continues to this day, albeit with many changes due to the COVID-19 pandemic. During this period (2020-2022) Institute staff created "Mountain School at Home" lessons (more on them later in the discussion of how the Institute has adapted to the COVID-19 situation). Two recent school programs are Snow School and Forest School. The Mount Baker Ski Area is 55 miles up state highway 542 from Bellingham. Its annual snowfall is among the highest in the United States as storms roll in off the North Pacific and often dump several feet in a single event that can grow a snowpack to fifteen or twenty feet over a winter. The Ski Area receives an average of fifty feet of snow annually and this snowpack, along with steep terrain, heavy winds, and a wide temperature range, makes the area prime for avalanches. It is the perfect place to study snow and its role in the ecology of the high country. The Ski Area began a pilot program for schools in the winter of 2014, serving a small number of local middle schools from rural Whatcom County including the Lummi Nation Tribal School. When the pilot proved a success, the Ski Area partnered with the Northwest Avalanche Center, Mount Baker-Snoqualmie National Forest, and Winter Wildlands Alliance in 2015 to continue the program, and approached the Institute to become the lead education program partner to operate and staff it.

Snow school was in session every Friday from January through March in 2016, part of a national program established by the Winter Wildlands Alliance that took place in more than sixty locations in the western United States. Abbey Sussman, a veteran outdoorswoman, writer, and youth program leader, was hired by the Institute as coordinator of the program. Writing in *Cascadia Weekly* in 2017, she explains what might happen on a winter field trip:

When Jeff Hambleton, NWAC [Northwest Avalanche Center] ambassador and professional observer, invites students into a freshly dug snow profile pit and guides them through a hand hardness test he is not only demonstrating skills needed to produce avalanche forecasts, but he is also introducing how we might predict summertime Nooksack River flows.

When undergrads from Robin Kodner's biology lab at Western Washington University model how to properly collect samples for snow algae and bacteria research, they are not only illustrating how microbial communities impact our watersheds, but also that science takes place outside institutional walls.

When volunteer instructors ask students to describe the cloud cover or observe shapes of snow crystals, they are not only teaching about weather and snow morphology, but also about how to pay attention to the natural world.

When teachers help load students onto a bus as far away as Bow or as close as Deming, they are not only displaying a willingness to provide new opportunities, but they are also exemplifying the idea that learning takes place everywhere, at every age, in every community.

Abbey's summary of what students were doing and learning, most tromping around on snowshoes for the first time, paints a great picture of what goes on in Snow School. One of the key elements underlying Snow School is that a large majority of the kids in the school districts around the mountain have never been up to Mount Baker Ski Area or the high country. There is no public transportation to the ski area or to trailheads, skiing is an expensive sport, and even hiking the mountain in summer requires Forest Service fees for day use and parking. As with other youth programs, Snow School extends horizons for students who otherwise would not experience them because their families could not afford them.

The program format involves a pre-field trip classroom visit by in-structors to introduce students to weather monitoring, public lands, and what constitutes a healthy watershed—in this case the Nooksack River watershed. Then students go into the field for a day, doing what Abbey describes. The program outcomes, described by the Institute, were: (1) applied science learning of watersheds, weather, and climate; (2) increased access to public lands for local kids and families; (3) encouragement of healthy lifestyles through winter recreation; (4) increase in observation and inquiry skills; (5) fostering of a greater sense of place and connection to community; and (6) exposure to STEM education and career pathways. Another approach was piloted in in 2018 with Mount Baker Jr. High students who conducted a "real life lab from start to finish, preparing them for success in high school science. Western Washington University interns and Northwest Avalanche Center scientists visited classes after trips to help students analyze data and draw conclusions. Students presented findings to peers, parents, and the Mount Baker community at a symposium." Eric Henry, a Mount Baker Jr. High science teacher, commented on this approach, "Students took what they'd learned in the classroom to a deeper level—analyzing specimens under a microscope (many for the first time) and thinking about organisms in novel ways." In 2018, 556 youth from sixteen schools participated in Snow School.

Another aspect of this program is that it requires training of the volunteer instructors who teach the students in the field. This training is conducted by Institute staff like Abbey, but also by experts from the NWAC and students from Western Washington University. Volunteer instructors in 2019 came from the University, the NW Indian College, the Washington Conservation Corps, the NWAC, the Mount Baker Ski Area, and nearby communities. As with many programs, learning occurring at Snow School has a multiplier effect—volunteers who learn in turn teach students. The Institute's 2019 report on the program records that 515 youth, 105 teachers and parents, and 26 volunteer and intern instructors were involved. This is not just youth education but adult and community education as well. Some of the outcomes described above go well beyond the students. Schools paid $10 per student; philanthropic support enabled the Institute to subsidize fees by $39,000 in 2019.

FOREST SCHOOL

THE OTHER SCHOOL PROGRAM WHICH STARTED IN 2019, only to be stopped by the pandemic, was Forest School. The Bellingham School District, which had long been sending its fifth graders to Mountain School, asked the Institute to develop a curriculum for a third-grade unit on the local forest ecosystem to be conducted at the Gordon Carter Environmental Education Site on the south end of Lake Whatcom. The program would be a one-day field trip to the site, integrated with classroom work and aligned with the Washington State Science Learning Standards and the Next Generation Science Standards guiding Bellingham district's curriculum at this grade level. Specifically, the learning standards (which used to be called "learning objectives") were: (1) construct an argument that some animals form groups that help other members survive; (2) construct an argument with evidence that in a particular habitat some organisms can survive well, some survive less well, and some cannot survive at all; and (3) make a claim about the merit of a solution to a problem caused when the environment changes and the types of plants and animals that live there change. The Institute's long and successful work to align a curriculum with the current learning standards in Mountain School were undoubtedly a reason the Bellingham School District asked them to create and implement the curriculum for this new program. The Institute's willingness to consult with teachers and curriculum staff at school districts to align programs with their learning standards was another factor in districts having confidence in their work.

Courtesy of NCI

A Snow School instructor explains to curious students what can be learned from the examination of snow layers revealed in a snow pit he has dug.

Bellingham Public Schools acquired the 120-acre land that would become the Gordon Carter Environmental Education Site in 1954. Beginning in 1972, they ran a program there as part of a unit on Washington state history. Lack of funding led to the end of that program in 2008, but in 2013 voters approved a bond for a feasibility study to consider construction of an educational facility there, and ultimately this led to the idea of Forest School. As with Snow School, the program would involve students from Western Washington University and volunteer instructors under the coordination and leadership of Institute staff. These instructors would help the children with inquiries about habitat, adaptation, and interactions between plants and animals. Unfortunately, there is not much yet to report about Forest School since it was canceled by the pandemic in 2020 and 2021, but the expectation is that it will resume when it is safe to get back to in-person school.

School programs are labor intensive in many ways and involve extensive persuasive and diplomatic effort to recruit school districts as partners. One would think districts would leap at the opportunity for curriculum enrichment offered by the Institute's school programs, but they are understandably cautious about trusting even a small portion of their mandated school days to an outside provider. Teachers may view three days at Mountain School as disruptive or unnecessary, involving more work. While the Institute provides financial support for schools that cannot foot the bill for programs like Mountain School, school districts still need to provide some financial support, even if it is just bus transportation. Administrators are sometimes reluctant to commit to what they view as "risky" outdoor environmental education, and some educators do not think environmental education is important enough to be part of what they see as an already overloaded curriculum. Given all of these obstacles, it took hard work by a series of Institute staff beginning with Wendy Scherrer and running through Tracie Johannessen, Christie Fairchild, Jeff Giesen, and Codi Hamblin to do the outreach essential to recruiting schools and districts into the programs. Over decades the Institute has established a reputation for quality that has convinced schools that, when they have the resources, they should invest some of them in environmental education with the North Cascades Institute.

TEACHER EDUCATION

Support for these programs and the realization that the Institute could not carry this load on their own led to a focus on teacher education. "Environmental education" did not appear in the educational lexicon until 1970, and while outdoor education had been around for a long time, it was a methodology rarely taught in conventional teacher education programs. Only a small portion of the teacher population had any knowledge of or interest in environmental education when the North Cascades Institute appeared on the scene. Back when they were conceiving the idea of a Shuksan Institute, the founders thought teaching teachers would be a central part of their work but were rebuffed by the educational bureaucracy. Soon after the North Cascades Institute started, Wendy and Tracie, teachers who knew environmental education and embraced it in their teaching, pushed for teacher education to become part of the Institute's mission. Mountain School brought public schools and teachers into the field, and the next step was to train the teachers to begin doing this on their own closer to home. Saul, Wendy, and Tracie all began to work on this challenge, creating the curriculum and, with the start of Mountain School, working with teachers to persuade them of the importance of environmental education.

One obvious way the Institute contributed to increasing the awareness of and knowledge about environmental education in teachers was interacting with them around Mountain School. This was an indirect approach in which some, but not all, teachers whose classes went to Mountain School absorbed what the Institute was trying to do with their students and how they went about it. Some teachers, like Mount Baker Jr. High's Eric Henry, were themselves advocates, practitioners, and innovators of environmental education in their teaching. But for most, exposure to what the Institute was doing with Mountain School advanced their understanding of environmental education. Some were inspired to incorporate it into the curriculum back in the classroom.

Another way to reach teachers was to encourage them to take adult field seminars as a way to advance themselves professionally. Teachers might take a wildflower course with Art Kruckeberg, a butterfly course with Bob Pyle, or a three-day course on alpine ecology with Shelley Weisberg and earn either credit or clock hours they could apply toward their continuing teacher certification, salary advancement, or both. However, this was a scattershot approach that depended on enough willingness on the teacher's part to enroll, pay the tuition, and spend the time. Over thirty-five years it has probably contributed to the environmental education of a lot of educators, but it was not a very effective way to target the teacher population.

A more targeted approach was to offer teacher workshops, which the Institute did occasionally in the 1990s and more often in the early 2000s. These were advertised as "balancing content-specific learning with activities and resources that can help you share what you learn with your students." For several years, for instance, a workshop on forest ecology, (titled "From the Ground Up in the Wind River Canopy Crane" in 2002 and "Treetop Science" in 2003) attracted teacher interest. University of Washington forest ecologists had erected a 250-foot crane to lift them into the forest canopy to study what was going on up there. They and other scientists were making some remarkable discoveries about tree canopy ecology. Teachers could literally, as the catalogue text explained, "examine an old-growth temperate rainforest from the ground up." The two-day workshop in the Gifford Pinchot National Forest introduced them to forest canopy science, research technology, and insect ecology. Other workshops explored "Native Plants of the Eastslope Cascades," and "Drawing from Nature: Blending Art and Science in the Classroom."

Some workshops introduced teachers to curriculum materials developed by Institute staff. The principal curriculum writing team included Wendy, Tracie, Saul, and Chuck Luckmann. Park glaciologist Jon Riedel joined Saul, Wendy, and Tracie to write *Sharing the Skagit: An Educator's Guide to the Skagit River Basin* (1993); Wendy joined Tracie to create *Celebrating Wildflowers: Educator's Guide to the Appreciation and Conservation of Native Plants* (1996); and Wendy and Saul collaborated on *Living with Mountains: A Guide for Learning and Teaching about Mountain Landscapes* (1991) and *Teaching for Wilderness: A Guide for Teaching about Wilderness and Wildlands* (1991). Tracie wrote several curricula, including *An Educator's Guide to the Samish and Padilla Bay Watersheds* (1999) and *Skagit Watershed Education Project Teacher Handbook* (1998). All of these were for grades 4-8, and Luckmann contributed to a grade 6-12 audience with his *Voices Along the Skagit: Teaching the History of the First People in the Skagit Watershed* (1998). The Institute published these curriculum resources and sold them to interested teachers, or teachers could sign up for a workshop focused on a curriculum resource and receive a copy.

These were all great resources for teachers in the region and gave staff projects to work on during the winter off season, but as the Institute grew, planning revved up for the Learning Center, and teacher interest in such material was less than overwhelming, priorities led staff in other directions. After 2003, teacher workshops disappeared from annual catalogues. The investment of time and energy in reaching out to teachers did not produce enough of a response to merit continuing when other initiatives such as youth programs, a growing Mountain School, and various new projects like the graduate program arose with the opening of the Learning Center. Nonetheless, in the many ways the Institute managed to connect with teachers, it made a significant contribution to their understanding of the nature and importance of regionally focused environmental education.

The great work of the twenty-first century will be to reconnect to the natural world as a source of meaning.

Richard Louv, *The Nature Principle*

X | ADULT EDUCATION

ANOTHER GOAL OF THE INSTITUTE IN THE 1990S was to provide opportunities for lifelong learning, and as youth programs grew and adult field seminars were thriving, the question of how best to serve adults and an older, senior audience arose. Seniors were adults of course, but perhaps not as capable of sleeping on the ground and spending long days in the field, or as inclined to do so. There was as yet no Learning Center and this demographic had expectations of comfortable lodging on their educational adventures. What might the Institute provide for this group? A program flourishing nationally for seniors at this time was Elderhostel (renamed Road Scholars in 2010), a not-for-profit organization headquartered in Boston offering noncredit classes and lodging for retired people who would travel from anywhere to a site for a week-long course. The program's founders had created it in response to what they saw as ageism in American society and offered learning experiences intended to help older adults stay sharp and interested in adventure.

The Institute proposed to the Elderhostel office in Boston that they offer courses in their service area and established another partnership. The Institute would design and staff the courses; Elderhostel would advertise them nationally and enroll participants from across the United States. For a decade this was one way the Institute programmed for this population. In the 2000-2001 catalogue, for instance, Elderhostel courses included: "Eagles, Swans, Seals & You: An Outdoor Adventure on a Northwest Shore" taught by David Drummond and Ann Eisinger out of the La Conner Country Inn; "Spring in the Cascades: The Natural and Cultural History of the Methow Valley" instructed by Libby Mills, Dana Visalli, and Shelley Weisberg with housing at the Sun Mountain Lodge; and "Song of the Sea: Marine and Tidal Ecology" with Rusty Kuntze and David Drummond at the Warm Beach Conference Center on Port Susan Bay. These were week-long courses requiring a lot of arrangements and preparation. This partnership lasted for nearly a decade, and in some ways was doomed by its success. Elderhostel was growing rapidly nationwide, and with increased competition from other Elderhostel programs throughout the Pacific Northwest and Elderhostel's requirement that their partners not cancel programs even if enrollment was only a small percentage of capacity, it became financially untenable for the Institute to continue in the partnership. In addition, the Institute's mission had long been to focus on a northwest rather than a national audience to be more in line with its conservation mission.

Throughout its history the Institute often had opportunities to offer programs for clientele outside what it considered its Pacific Northwest service area, but resisted the temptation. The idea of advertising field seminars and retreats nationally was discussed periodically, but Institute leaders were skeptical of whether this would be successful and were especially wary of suffering mission creep and overextension. With the growing success of programs in the North Cascades, John Reynolds suggested that perhaps the model of national park education the Institute was pioneering could be exported to Mount Rainier and other national park units, such as John Day Fossil Beds National Monument in Oregon. Complimented at first and excited by the possibilities, Institute leaders came to their senses and realized the infant organization was in no shape to contemplate such expansion. This began a series of realistic assessments of capabilities and definitions of the mission that allowed the Institute to do what it had set out to do on a modest and manageable scale. Time would prove the wisdom of such decisions, and this was one factor in deciding to end programming with Elderhostel.

RETREATS

Another need identified was for more in-depth learning experiences that would immerse participants in topics more than was possible in a typical field seminar lasting a few days. Might teams of excellent instructors offering short-format, weekend seminars and field instruction be brought together in teams so participants could learn from interactions with multiple instructors? This would require more time and be more expensive, but there seemed to be interest, so why not try a longer format? The Institute aspired to attract even greater expertise and prominence in its instructors than it already had, and if such people were to be recruited it would require a program longer than a weekend. This led to the decision to offer retreats, which were longer than field seminars and much more intensive. The first Spring Naturalist Retreat was held at Sun Mountain Lodge from May 18-21, 1992. It was highly successful and became the prototype for retreats over the next several decades. The luxurious accommodations of Sun Mountain Lodge were attractive, and the instructors were Art Kruckeberg, Bob Pyle, Libby Mills, and Saul Weisberg. Using the Lodge as base camp, participants made forays into the field. May in the Methow Valley was a spectacular setting for studying breeding birds, butterflies, insects, and wildflowers. Fields of yellow balsamroots, a morning chorus of birdsong, Western tiger swallowtails, hawks, and even golden eagles drifting across the sky beckoned the naturalists under the tutelage of these experts. After a good evening meal, a soak in the Lodge's hot tub under the stars would cap off a day of fun and learning.

The Spring Naturalist Retreat became an annual event, attracting an exceptional roster of instructors. In 1993 two sessions were offered. In the absence of regular stalwarts Bob and Saul, Land Steward for the Washington Chapter of the Nature Conservancy and past president of Seattle Audubon Fayette Krause was recruited onto the team, as was author and authority on birds and dragonflies Dennis Paulson. The original team offered this retreat over many years, supplemented by ornithologist David Hutchinson, geologist Scott Babcock, Methow naturalist Dana Visalli, bear biologist Chris Morgan, and ecologist Estella Leopold, among others. These perennially popular spring naturalist retreats were held at Sun Mountain Lodge until 2005. In that year four retreats were offered spread from spring to fall: one in the Methow Valley; another out of the Learning Center, titled "North Cascades Naturalist Retreat: Glaciers, Rivers, Plants and Wildlife"; a third in the Wenatchee Valley; and yet another in the Skagit Valley. This 2005 expansion extended the program too far afield and after this, the Learning Center became its base.

The naturalist retreats were so successful that the format was extended in May 1998 with the first Nature Writer's Retreat at the Sleeping Lady Resort near Leavenworth. Like Sun Mountain Lodge, Sleeping Lady offered a beautiful natural setting and excellent accommodations. The roster of nature writing staff was very high powered, led by prominent novelist Barbara Kingsolver. Bob Pyle, equally famed as both writer and naturalist, was on the team, along with poet Tim McNulty and prolific and popular nature writer Ann Zwinger. Small groups could work with each writer; one catalogue described the process as sharpening "the writer's tools of observation, description, narration, metaphor, analogy, juxtaposition, character development, analysis and argument—and learn[ing] a bit about the ins and outs of getting published." The retreat format for nature writers was a great hit and continued for years, attracting an outstanding faculty. Bob and McNulty would become regulars, and other prominent writers would include Craig Lesly, Molly Gloss, David Peterson, Alison Deming, Bill Kittredge, Annick Smith, Gary Ferguson, Kathleen Dean Moore, Holly Hughes, Rick Bass, Nick O'Connell, Richard K. Nelson, and Ana Maria Spagna. This roster was a veritable Who's Who of local and national nature writing luminaries at the time and, for good reason, proved very popular.

With these successes, the retreat format was extended to the visual arts in 2005 with the opening of the Learning Center. The first of many Diablo Creative Arts Retreats was led by local artists Roxanne Grinstad, Rebecca Meloy, and Barbara VanDyke Shuman. These artists were drawn from contributors to the Institute's visually striking annual catalogues and offered instruction in various media, from pastels to watercolor to block prints. Subject matter around the Learning Center was endless, from mountain vistas to the forest and a multitude of plants and lichens. In 2006, Grinstad returned and Molly Hashimoto and Ruthie Porter joined the instructional team. Ruthie served as an Institute staffer for years, developing field seminars and offering her artistic talents in many ways. Molly, a master of watercolor painting, wrote of her approach to her art:

> When I teach, I start with the skills of representation. I break down the different elements of the landscape based on close observation. The Learning Center provides a landscape of astonishing beauty. We look at the branches and tips of Douglas firs and use a certain wrist motion with a round sable brush to establish that form. On a rainy day, under a shelter, we study the lichens on alders, using masking fluid to preserve areas of lightness. On Diablo Lake where Pyramid and Colonial peaks tower overhead, we wet the paper and stroke in the grays for the edgeless mists. The cloud cover finally gives way to blue sky, and we note how the glacial milky green of Diablo Lake breaks all the rules of water in landscape and is unrelated to any color in the sky. For that rare green hue, we mix opaque cerulean blue with phthalo green.
>
> With these tools, students can begin to articulate their own personal vision. Some may see the landscape as a chaotic world of merging forms and choose a wet-into-paint technique. Others may assert the solidity of individual shapes and paint clearly defined edges. Each is an expression of individuality. When we paint landscapes, we establish the importance of what we view. We say that this place is worthy of our deepest attention and care.[29]

When Molly writes that "students can begin to articulate their own personal vision," and, "We say that this place is worthy of our deepest attention and care," she expresses the goals of all the instructors in the visual and literary art retreats. Their aim was to help students hone their skills of interpretation and expression, and ultimately the goal was "care," the goal expressed by so many from Bob to Molly and her fellow artists.

In 2007, the artist retreat was "Art Afield: A Plein Air Retreat" with Molly, Libby Mills, and Maria Coryell-Martin; in the 2009 retreat Molly taught watercolor, Jocelyn Curry helped participants craft an art journal and fill it with drawings and nature notes, and Kristofer Gilje guided the group in silk painting. In 2010 Melinda West taught "Baskets from Northwest Landscapes" and Porter helped create "Illuminated Field Journals." Retreats like these and others devoted to natural history and writing gave participants an extended exposure to the landscapes of the North Cascades. Everyone had time to interact with instructors and peers around their work, be it writing, painting, or studying birds and butterflies. They could reflect, do a bit of hiking or canoeing, and just settle in for a moment away from the demands of daily lives.

Benj Drummond photo, Courtesy of NCI

Participants in the Spring Naturalist Retreat in the Methow Valley used many tools in their inquiries, here gazing up at hawks and other migrating birds, or even a resident golden eagle.

OTHER ADULT AND FAMILY PROGRAMS

THE OPENING OF THE LEARNING CENTER made possible programs serving clients who needed facilities, and this capability led to other programs like Day Trips, Family Getaways, the Sourdough Speaker Series, Diablo Downtimes, and Base Camp. None of these were on the scale of Mountain School, seminars, retreats, and the various youth programs, but all met needs and provided opportunities. The Family Getaways program was described in chapter seven and met the need described in the program title.

The Sourdough Speaker Series, launched in 2009, was advertised as "intimate gatherings of writers, naturalists and historians to tell their own stories from our remarkable region." Folks checked in on Saturday afternoon, enjoyed a dinner featuring locally grown food, and settled in after for presentations by Sedro Wooley's renowned photographer Lee Mann describing "A Photographer's Journey through the North Cascades"; field biologist and award-winning writer Thor Hanson on "Evolution of Feathers"; or Seattle artist, sculptor, and writer Tony Angell on his work celebrating nature. One of Angell's magnificent bronze sculptures of two eagles and two of his sculptures of otters grace the Learning Center campus, the latter placed along the Diablo Lake shoreline as though they were emerging from the azure waters. After an overnight stay and a continental breakfast on Sunday morning, a naturalist hike offered an exploration of the "wild and scenic neighborhood."

Also beginning in 2009, Diablo Downtimes, like Family Getaways, was conceived as a way for adults who might seek a brief respite from family and other responsibilities. From Friday afternoon through midday Sunday participants could relax, eat wonderful, locally sourced food, participate in naturalist activities, canoe, hike or do yoga if so moved, and simply wind down in a beautiful setting. The "Slow Food" dining part of Downtimes provided staff the opportunity to feature the Institute's Foodshed Project, using local and organic products to teach about food choices, sustainable agriculture, and culturally important foods in the Pacific Northwest. The Foodshed Project presentations integrated into the experience offered an opportunity to educate, which was an essential part of any Institute program.

Base Camp, first offered in 2010, was initially an experiment to see whether more casual visitors could be attracted to the Learning Center. Advertised as the most flexible and affordable offering, the catalogue urged weekend seminar participants to extend their stays. "Gather family and friends and hang out on Diablo Lake participating in fun outdoor activities led by passionate, knowledgeable guides and rangers. Stay with us after your hike in the national park and refuel with delicious meals made with local, organic ingredients, a hot shower and stimulating community." Base Campers could stay as long as they wished but needed to register in advance. This program emerged as a result of a few "drop in" visitors who wondered if they could take advantage of the facilities as one would a resort concession in other National Parks. However, the Institute was not such a resort and would need advanced registration so as to guarantee space around other programs. Base Camp was also seen as an opportunity to fill some beds when they were not being used for other events. Base Campers could choose from learning adventures offered three times a day and varying daily. They could hike the trails, canoe on the lake, and partake in natural history instruction, art activities, campfires, and much more.

SKAGIT TOURS

DIFFERENT FROM OTHER PROGRAMS IS SKAGIT TOURS, which is a service for partner Seattle City Light; most of its tourists only visit the Learning Center for lunch as part of their tour. City Light has offered Skagit Tours since 1928 as a public relations effort to showcase the Skagit hydroelectric project and build support for new dams along the Skagit River corridor among Seattle residents. The utility has operated these tours ever since, with interruptions only during World War II and recently during the COVID-19 pandemic. Gorge Dam sent the project's first electricity to Seattle in 1924. Construction on the second dam, Diablo, commenced in 1927. It was completed in 1930, but delivery of energy to Seattle was delayed by the Great Depression until 1936, when the powerhouse was completed. Ross Dam, initially Ruby Dam, was built in three stages completed in 1937, 1940, and 1953. The original Skagit Tours involved a steam locomotive trip to the company town of Newhalem, dinner at the Gorge Inn, an overnight stay, and another train leg farther upriver to the company town of Diablo. A ride up to the elevation of Diablo Dam on an incline lift delivered the tour groups to Diablo Lake and a barge that would take them to Ross Dam. Later the barge was replaced by other boats, the current one being the 40-person *Alice Ross*.

In 2012, City Light asked the Institute and Park Service to partner on the tours. The Institute now develops and manages the program content and curriculum, trains the staff, registers the tourists, provides meal service, and supervises the operation under a contract with City Light. Park rangers assist with interpretation on the boat. The goal is to tell the story of the North Cascades through the history of the Skagit Hydro Project. As Tracie Johannessen described the curriculum in 2016, "Natural, cultural and hydroelectric history of the watershed weave the storylines, helping participants understand the significance of landscape on human culture."[30] Four times a week from June through mid-September, the *Alice Ross* takes tourists to Ross Dam with lunch included at the Learning Center. Another option is a boat tour without a meal on weekend afternoons, and a third, Newhalem by Night, is a walking tour on Thursday and Friday evenings in July and August with an optional chicken dinner at the Gorge Inn. Skagit Tours introduces new audiences that would not otherwise experience them to the North Cascades and North Cascades Institute. In 2020, the pandemic curtailed this program and it will return as soon as the impacts of the pandemic recede.

RETAIL STORES

IN 2009, NORTH CASCADES NATIONAL PARK Superintendent Chip Jenkins asked Saul if the Institute would be interested in taking on the role of the Park's Cooperating Association partner to manage the six retail book-stores affiliated with the Park. Jenkins explained that the current partner Discover Your Northwest (DYN), which operated retail stores through-out the Pacific Northwest parks and forests, was planning on expanding into regional fundraising and education programs and away from retail stores. Since North Cascades National Park already had strong partners in both these areas (the Institute and Washington's National Park Fund), Jenkins wanted a partner who would focus on continued growth on the retail side of the business. Saul declined, not wanting the Institute to be involved in a conflict between the Park Service and DYN. Later con-versations with the Regional Office of the Park Service led to it creat-ing an interdisciplinary team to review the Institute's and DYN's capac-ity for this partnership role, and their report ultimately convinced the Board to support this new role for the Institute. It began operating the stores in 2010 in a partnership with the Park Service and Mount Baker-Snoqualmie National Forest.

The Institute manages seven stores located at North Cascades Visitor Center (Newhalem), Seattle City Light Information Center (Newhalem), Wilderness Information Center (Marblemount), North Cascades Environmental Learning Center (Diablo), Golden West Visitor Center

(Stehekin), NPS-USFS Headquarters (Sedro-Woolley), and Heather Meadows (USFS). Managing retail stores required a whole new set of business skills for the Institute, including finance, technology, warehousing, and staffing. Jan Healy, a former bookstore manager, was the first retail manager and got things off to a great start. Later, Pat Renau, who managed retail stores at the Mount Baker Ski Area for twenty years, was hired and things really took off. It is a continuing challenge to identify mission-appropriate, high quality, educational products such as books, maps, field guides, art, apparel, and other supplies in the park environment. As education director, Tracie wrote that all merchandise should "reach a variety of visitors and inspire them to experience, enjoy, interpret, share, and *remember* their experiences in North Cascades National Park." Expanding on this, she wrote:

> *Primary goals center around providing exemplary visitor service, information and safety—to help preserve unimpaired the natural and cultural resources and values of the National Park system for the enjoyment, education and inspiration of present and future generations. Secondary goals for North Cascades Institute are to provide educational outreach to a large number of Park visitors through interaction and materials in the stores, and to develop an earned-income revenue stream to support experiential environmental education in the North Cascades. When the stores make a profit, the Institute will be able to realize this goal and provide additional financial support to agency partners.[31]*

Most visitors to the park travel the Highway 20 corridor in their vehicles, often stopping at the Sedro-Woolley Headquarters, the Visitor Center, and City Light Information Center in Newhalem, and perhaps staying in park campgrounds. The *Lady of the Lake* and its sister vessels take visitors up Lake Chelan during spring, summer, and fall to Stehekin for a whirlwind tour of the Lake Chelan National Recreation Area (part of the North Cascades National Park Complex). A stop at the Golden West Visitor Center there is a mandatory part of the tour. While the retail stores cannot deliver an intensive educational experience, the Institute can help introduce and educate a large population through its role as the park's Cooperating Association. In 2016, 104,000 people visited the retail stores, a significant portion of the 980,000 visits to the Park complex (the larger number includes Highway 20 traffic, whether or not it stops anywhere within the Park complex). The Institute has turned what at first seemed a venture marginally related to its mission into an opportunity to serve the public and the park, while generating revenue to support other programs.

CONFERENCES

WHEN THE ENVIRONMENTAL LEARNING CENTER opened in 2005, one new operational challenge the Institute faced was how to support a year-round facility in a seasonal environment. School groups would not be present on weekends, holidays, and school breaks, including a long summer vacation. The "summer season" in the North Cascades was short, with the high country only fully accessible in July, August, and September. The North Cascades Highway closed for the winter, usually in November, a few miles past Diablo Lake. With the opening of the Learning Center the Institute had facility expenses year-round, particularly Center operational and instructional staff. Attracting experienced staff for Center programming and other services required a season long enough to give these people a living wage, which meant extending the tenure of seasonal employees. Superintendent Bill Paleck suggested, as Tracie records, "that these low occupancy times would be ideal to introduce, educate and engage new, diverse and atypical audiences to the National Park. The Learning Center is an excellent facility for convening diverse groups, many of whom do not have opportunities to meet in National Parks."[32] Heeding Bill's advice, the Institute began to offer a suite of opportunities for "Conferences and Retreats" in 2007. These were market-driven programs for non-governmental organizations, for-profit businesses, and government agencies customized to the needs and desires of the groups, while also meeting the Institute's mission to introduce people to and educate them about the ecosystem and the National Park. These adult programs typically meet from one to five days, occasionally overlapping with other Institute programs. In no case did they replace core educational offerings.

In her 2016 Program Overview, Tracie noted that more than 60% of participants in conferences and retreats had not previously visited the park and expressed a desire to return. She described five subsets of the program:

1. *Professional Development and Training: teachers, professional groups, international programs, wilderness and ecosystems management, wilderness medicine, etc.*

2. *Conferences and Planning: educational events for college and universities, professional groups, community leaders, elected officials, youth and schools, etc.*

3. *Lifestyle and Recreation: outdoor recreation and health organizations, hiking clubs, veteran's groups, yoga, meditation, etc.*

4. *Celebrations: Multi-generational, multi-family gatherings: family reunions, green weddings, etc.*

5. *Park and Facility Tours: Tour groups, schools, volunteer organizations, etc.*

All revenue from these programs was allocated to support youth and school programs. As Bill had recognized, the Learning Center provided many groups with a place to meet and be introduced to North Cascades National Park. At the same time, this would provide the Institute with much-needed revenue to keep the school programs going. This allowed some staff to avoid seasonal furloughs, particularly senior operational staff who were difficult to recruit and retain in a remote location like the Learning Center. Conferences and Retreats introduce diverse groups to the park and the Institute and allow groups to meet in a setting where they might get work done and, as Tracie put it, "combine the unique needs and goals of their group with experiential education goals common to all Institute programs." Everyone wins—the group, the Park, and the Institute.

Who has taken advantage of the opportunity to meet in a setting like the Learning Center? The Kinship Conservation Fellowships brought mid-career conservation professionals from Europe, Asia, Africa, North America, and South America to learn from each other and share ideas about conservation and resource management. For many winters, Remote

Medical International has offered wilderness medicine courses to clients from federal agencies, active-duty military, and fire, police, and emergency medical professionals. They come in winter when other programs are impossible. A casual visitor dropping in when one of these courses is underway might wonder what sort of disaster has occurred, as injury simulations are in progress all around the campus. The Interagency Grizzly Bear Committee met to discuss possible reintroduction of the grizzly to the North Cascades and to assess grizzly habitats in the National Park. Sierra Club National Outings made the Learning Center its base camp, shuttling to trailheads to explore the Park and enjoying evening presentations on various natural and cultural history topics. Each year a couple of green weddings occur, often as a result of family members who have been to Institute programs and the Learning Center and think it the perfect place for a family celebration complete with canoeing, hiking, and an array of other activities led by Institute staff.

Courtesy of NCI

Retail stores operated by the Institute in cooperation with the Park Service, Forest Service, and Seattle City Light offer educational materials and memorabilia to visitors to the North Cascades. Shown here is the store at the Skagit Information Center on Highway 20 in Newhalem.

These Conferences and Retreats have generated some controversy, with some Park Service staff disagreeing with the superintendents' views that when the Learning Center is not otherwise occupied with educational programs, it should be used to host other events, keeping staff busy and bringing in revenue to support youth programs. Some skeptics fail to understand that an organization like the North Cascades Institute is a business, and one that must sustain a revenue stream in order to survive. Most Institute revenue comes from philanthropy and tuition, but the Institute, like all businesses, must always be evaluating and seeking business models with multiple funding streams to build reserves for times of weather closures (avalanches, wildfires), government shutdowns, and global pandemics.

Over 35 years North Cascades Institute programs have come and gone, meeting various needs and serving various clientele. Unforeseen circumstances and events have on the one hand frustrated plans, while on the other providing unexpected opportunities. Bureaucratic roadblocks, rockslides, and other troubles delayed the Learning Center, but the Institute found a way to survive and thrive through the long gestation period of that project. The story here is one of deeply committed educators constantly searching for ways to address their mission, adapting to the inevitable ups and downs of any organization, demonstrating resilience in the face of physical and bureaucratic weather, and responding creatively to challenges and opportunities that have appeared. They have been guided by questions: How can we achieve conservation through education? How can we serve the environmental education needs of our region? How can we create programs that are wins for ourselves and our partners? What must we do to survive and thrive as a small nonprofit?

The Institute has grown and served its stated ends in a period of political and economic turmoil and great social change in America. When it began, for instance, the fact of climate change was little known. The political climate was anti-environmentalist and a small-government ideology was squeezing the budgets of the agencies managing America's public lands. The decade of the 1980s did not seem an opportune time to launch a new organization dedicated to conservation, but it turned out that it was a good time to launch the Institute *because* the politics of conservation were squeezing the Park Service and the Forest Service. There is no evidence that the founders of the Institute recognized this dynamic or realized that the federal government was bent on privatizing many services provided by land management agencies, but park officials like John Reynolds and Jon Jarvis certainly did. They saw that developing enduring partnerships could help the park service provide high-quality education, and that a way forward was to engage idealistic and hard-working young people who loved the place and had the background to do that work.

The founders also did not fully understand the scope of the work that needed doing. They joked among themselves that they were out to "save the world," but they were also working to satisfy their own needs, which centered around the opportunity to teach outdoors in a setting like the North Cascades. After they found a way to get started in the face of many hurdles, Saul and the other Institute staff kept finding needs they had not anticipated that they could address, and they found that many in the Pacific Northwest community shared their perception of those needs and were willing to fund efforts to address them. The result was an environmental education enterprise that grew far beyond their initial vision.

Journalist Richard Louv published *Last Child in the Woods: Saving Our Children from Nature-Deficit Disorder* in 2005. In the frontispiece he placed the following quotation from a fourth grader in San Diego: "I like to play indoors better 'cause that's where all the electrical outlets are." The digital age was just beginning to take over the lives of young people when the Institute was founded in 1986. Change in the lives of Americans, adults and children, as a consequence of the digital revolution was profound. It turns out that the need for programs dedicated to playing and teaching in the natural world is greater than it has ever been because of this revolution, a reality that was beyond the imaginations of the founders of the Institute. The story told here is one of a small organization that has responded in a big way to needs it could not foresee.

I think we could do this business well, but I don't know if the business would do well.

Saul Weisberg, letter to Shuksan Institute 1984

XI | HOW THE BUSINESS HAS SUCCEEDED

THIS ACCOUNT OF THE HISTORY OF the North Cascades Institute describes a process of building a not-for-profit organization from two guys with big dreams, carrying their files around in a box in the North Cascades National Park headquarters, to the successful organization that it is today. The Institute's budget in 1986 was $86,000; in 2020 it was over $4 million. So far, the story is one of "what happened." This chapter shifts to a review of how the Institute grew from its humble beginnings to what it is early in the third decade of the 21st century. It is a story of hard work, persistence, good luck, creative people, and ideas. It is a story of risk-taking, adaptability, generosity, dedication, vision, and good organizational processes. So, what factors have allowed the North Cascades Institute to survive and thrive over 35 years?

First, and most obviously, the key to the story is the *people* involved, as the organization's history described so far clearly demonstrates—quality staff, Board members, instructors, partners, and financial supporters. There is no doubt that Saul Weisberg was the most important player over his unusual tenure of 35 years, nearly all of it as executive director. In the beginning he did not see himself as an executive, a director, or a businessman, but he rapidly evolved into these roles while hanging on to the field biologist-educator he set out to be. Over the years he brought outstanding people into the organization, inspired them with his vision and managerial acumen, encouraged them, listened to their ideas and cautions, and supported them during the inevitable ups and downs of the enterprise. Many young non-profit organizations collapse due to conflicts that grow between staff and the board, but that did not happen in the Institute story because Saul and Board leadership oversaw a careful process of staff and Board selection, then worked transparently and collaboratively with everyone. This is not to say there were not issues, but when there were difficulties, problems were worked out without any long-lasting disruption to the organization.

Successful building and sustaining of partnerships were more keys to the Institute's success (more on that later) but nurturing long-term organizational relationships takes patience and skill. Saul often referred to the "normal" frustrations of a "small entrepreneurial nonprofit" working with large agencies like Seattle City Light, the Forest Service, Western Washington University, and the National Park Service. Organizations have cultures and navigating cross-culturally in this organizational sense required skill, insight, and patience. Saul and his colleagues have shown these qualities over the years while coping with the inevitable frustrations that are part of the game.

The Institute's trajectory has been one of sustained growth with blips along the way as the national economy had its ups and downs and other strains came and went. Through all 35 years, Saul provided sustained leadership, his role changing as the organization grew. One essential skill of a leader is delegation, knowing the difference between too much management and too little and being able to trust others to take over responsibilities as demands on leadership change. As the organization grew so did the need for funding, and Saul evolved into an effective fundraiser. He cultivated relationships with supporters which, with the growing leadership of the "Moneyshed" staff, produced a remarkable flow of philanthropic support over the years. Over time he had to relinquish many of his programmatic responsibilities to be an effective fundraiser and the public face of the Institute. Finally, there is something called "founder syndrome" which often appears when an organization becomes very successful, the leader's ego grows, and that gets them into so much difficulty that the viability of the organization is threatened and its board must send the founder packing. As Saul's profile has grown, his ego has not, and that has allowed him to provide leadership over an unusually sustained period.

Saul did not, of course, do this work alone, and without many other key players he could not have sustained the Institute. In the beginning, Superintendent John Reynolds, co-founder Tom Fleischner, and John Miles as the first Board chair played important roles. They were soon joined on the Board by recently retired National Park Service Director Russ Dickenson, and Robyn Dupre and Wendy Scherrer joined the staff with their energy, organization, and ideas. There were three staff members in 1990, nine in 1996, and more than sixty in recent years, especially after the opening of the Learning Center and including seasonal staff. As the Institute grew, the organizational chart changed constantly as new programs and attendant responsibilities were added. An office staff was needed to register and manage both individual participants and schools for an increasing number of programs. A single development staffer grew into the "Moneyshed" team, which has grown to include a director, donor relations manager, grants manager, communications and marketing manager, and graphics coordinator, all focused on raising the funds necessary to support ever-expanding programs.

The path Jeff Giesen took in his decades with the Institute is illustrative of the changes that went with growth. He started in 1999 as an environmental educator, then became watershed education coordinator, then youth and stewardship coordinator, education director, and ultimately associate director. As he succeeded in each role his responsibilities expanded and his title changed. This was the path of many other long-serving staff over the years, like Wendy Scherrer as youth program coordinator and ultimately education director, Kris Molesworth in fundraising, and Kristofer Gilje, who came to the Learning Center to oversee maintenance and operations and ultimately became its director. Tracie Johannessen served in many capacities, growing with the organization but always on the education side of things. An experienced teacher and science educator, she worked first with Wendy and then with other staff to create many youth programs. All of these and legions of others too numerous to mention made the North Cascades Institute the success it has been.

THE BOARD

ALL NONPROFIT ORGANIZATION MUST HAVE A Board of Directors, and over 35 years and the leadership of eleven chairpersons, the Institute Board has been a key to sustained success. As the organization has grown, so has the Board, and its roles have evolved significantly. Early on the small Board helped get the organization started, advising on the writing of bylaws and ensuring that all the necessary legal stuff was done. It approved the salaries of Saul, Tom, and other staff, modest as they were, and provided support to the staff in any way they could, such as helping with fundraising. Former National Park Service Director Russ Dickenson, for instance, offered great advice as a Board member on how to work with the federal bureaucracies as the Institute's partnerships with the Park Service and Forest Service deepened.

When big decisions needed to be made, such as whether to expand beyond the North Cascades in the early days, the Board weighed in and influenced the decision. As the need for fundraising increased, it reviewed, influenced, and approved the strategies proposed by staff. New Board members were carefully and strategically recruited to bring needed expertise to decision-making. The educational expertise of the early Board was supplemented by people experienced in business, fundraising, financial management, communications, government, and public relations. In the history of the Institute the Board never had to select a chief executive officer until Saul retired in 2021, but over the years it regularly assessed Saul's performance, offering critical perspectives as well as approval. After 25 years, for instance, the consensus of the Board was that it was time for Saul to take a break, more than a brief vacation—a sabbatical of at least several months. Saul resisted, but the Board insisted, and Saul took the opportunity to use his six months of paid leave for travel, for reflection, and to advance his writing of poetry as he recharged his batteries. After 35 years the Board did have to select a new executive, as will be described later.

Jan Masaoka, an expert on nonprofit boards, has described a

"governance/support" model for nonprofit boards that captures how the Institute Board and staff have worked over the years. Masaoka writes, "On the one hand, the board, acting as the representative of the public interest, governs the organization. In this role the board has several key responsibilities, including financial oversight, hiring/evaluating the executive director, and making the Big Decisions: on the other hand, board members also act to help—to support—the organization."[33] In the early days, the board did less governing and more supporting. In the 1990s, for instance, a live auction was held annually, and board members helped to solicit donations. As the Institute grew and its budget got bigger, more board governance was necessary while the support role continued.

Courtesy of NCI

A snapshot of key Institute staff in the mid-1990s includes: top left to right, Gail Sterrett, Wendy Scherrer, Intern, Saul Weisberg, Ruthie Porter, Tracie Johannessen; bottom left to right, Don Burgess, Kirsten Tain, Christie Fairchild.

Masaoka writes that often there is confusion about board responsibilities, "between what the board does (as a body) and what individual board members should do." Without knowing what it was called, the Institute Board and staff functioned successfully in this "governance/support" model because common sense suggested that when big decisions needed to be made about finances, planning, or new programs, the Bsoard was boss with input from staff. However, when an individual Board member chipped in to help in various supportive ways, they were comfortable under the direction of staff. A key to this was regular and transparent interaction between Saul, the leadership team, and the Board executive committee, especially the Board chair.

Over the years an evolving Board role has been assisting staff with planning, identifying, and approving strategic and operational goals, and how to measure outcomes in pursuit of those goals. This began in the early 1990s when the Board approved Saul's participation in the City Light mitigation discussions under the aegis of the North Cascades Conservation Council as legal intervenor. When Saul joined Jon Jarvis in proposing an Environmental Learning Center and it ultimately became part of the mitigation package, the need for some serious planning became clear. The Board began having annual retreats. At one in the early 1990s at Colonial Creek Campground, the process of strategic planning began. At first, it was quite informal as everyone began learning what the process involved and what its outcomes should be. Before long it became a very useful tool in determining where the Institute should be going, what was needed to get there, and how progress toward goals was or was not being made. It evolved into quite a rigorous process that helped the organization move forward under the leadership of Board chairs from 1995 to the present.

The Board of the Institute is, of course, a volunteer labor of love. It is a lot of work involving bimonthly meetings of the whole committee, annual retreats, and various sub-committees (Executive, Governance, Finance, Development, Marketing, Audit, and Equity). The dedication of Board members, especially the chairs, over the years has been key to its flourishing. Other volunteers, while not members of the Board, have regularly participated in Board committees in their areas of expertise.

INSTRUCTORS

THE THIRD GROUP OF PEOPLE THAT MUST BE GIVEN great credit for the Institute's success are the instructors, whether they be leaders of field seminars, Mountain School and other youth programs, or special programs like retreats. Over the years the Institute has recruited outstanding experts and practitioners of natural history, regional history, and visual and literary arts. Many had advanced degrees and were regionally and nationally recognized in their fields. They brought passion to their work and none of them were in it for the money, since the remuneration was modest. All instructors loved to teach and believed in the Institute's mission. They especially loved to teach outdoors and experientially which, in their university or conventional education settings, was difficult or impossible. Many, like Bob Pyle, Libby Mills, and Tim McNulty, have taught with the Institute for decades and combined science and art in their work. They had freedom to create in ways often stifled in settings like universities that were organized around disciplines that assiduously guarded their boundaries.

Many of the instructors, of which there have been several hundred over 35 years, have been mentioned in accounts of programs. It would be nice but is impossible to list them all here. Field seminar faculty were recruited by staff based on their reputations, and quite a few came up with program ideas on their own initiative and proposed them to Institute staff. Some catalogues even urged anyone who had a program idea to suggest it, which led to new field seminars and other programs. Many instructors came from university faculties or, like Bob, were independent scholars, writers, and educators. Some came from the Park Service, among them archaeologist Bob Mierendorf, local historian Jim Harris, and utility man "Captain" Gerry Cook. As mentioned earlier, Cook was involved in many North Cascades National Park projects, designed and built the shelters at the Learning Center, and navigated the *Ross Mule* up and down Ross Lake for many summers. He and Mierendorf offered a perennially popular field seminar on "People of the Upper Skagit," and he joined Jeff Muse and later Saul to lead folks up Desolation Peak to celebrate "Beats on the Peaks: Lookout Poets of the North Cascades." Cook had been a lookout himself and understood what inspired writers like Gary Snyder, Philip Whalen, and Jack Kerouac, all of whom had spent time on North Cascades fire lookouts and gone on to distinguished literary careers. A lifetime in the North Cascades imbued Cook with the essence of the place, and after retiring from the Park Service he has continued as a member of the Institute Board and as a mentor to youth program leaders and participants. North Cascades "lifers" like Cook and Jim Harris, who knew the history of the area and served for years as Park Service professionals, brought more than credentials to their instructional roles. They were the embodiment of the place, having lived through its transition from a resource bank from which assets like logs and hydropower were withdrawn to the National Park wilderness which became the Institute's classroom.

Another large group of seasonal instructors became essential after the opening of the Learning Center. They might work as Mountain School instructors in the spring and fall and for the Park Service or Forest Service over the summer. Young outdoor enthusiasts, usually recent graduates in biology or environmental education programs, brought energy and enthusiasm to their tasks, enjoying the chance to live and work in North Cascades National Park. They came from all over the country, many coming back year after year to work for the Institute and develop their instructional and leadership skills as a step toward careers in environmental education. Some who started as Mountain School instructors went on to lead youth programs, spending summers backpacking, canoeing, and working with young people in the park's backcountry. Without them and their willingness to live with their charges, often in challenging conditions (teaching in the rain), many Institute programs would have been difficult or impossible to manage. When the graduate program was launched, the graduate students served as instructors in Mountain School, many of them working in the summers with youth programs as part of their studies.

The Institute also had an amazing ability to attract top instructional talent based on its reputation. The literary and visual arts seminars and retreats were a prime example. Barbara Kingsolver, Ann and Susan Zwinger, Rick Bass, William Kittredge, Alison Deming; all of these were top-notch writers with national reputations. Bob Pyle, Tim McNulty, Kathleen Dean Moore, Ana Maria Spagna, Molly Gloss, Lyanda Lynn Haupt, and other Northwest writers added regional punch to the writing and literary instruction. The same could be said for natural history and visual arts instructors. They were all attracted by the opportunity to teach enthusiastic learners in the North Cascades, to support the Institute and its mission, and to enjoy a few days in the unique environment of the Learning Center.

STAFF

THE STAFF OF THE INSTITUTE, THE WORKHORSES who handle of all the details of day-to-day operations, are the foundation of the enterprise. Without them, there would be no enterprise. Many have been mentioned in this narrative:

Robyn Dure, Wendy Scherrer, Tracie Johannessen, Christi Fairchild, Jeff Giesen, and Kristofer Gilje, among many others. As the Institute grew, three staff groups emerged: administration, programming, and Learning Center operations. Administration included those handling finance, marketing, fundraising, and office functions like registrations. The office staff in Sedro-Woolley were the face of the organization for many participants. They fielded questions about all details of the programs—and there were many—and answered inquiries daily about the Institute. Over the years the office moved around the Park Service/Forest Service building, eventually occupying part of a wing on the first floor of a new building. As office staff increased there was need for an office manager. The first was Kirsten Tain in the 1990s. Debra Brodie, a seasoned veteran manager, succeeded her in that role for many years, ultimately becoming operations director.

Benj Drummond photo   David Snyder photo   Courtesy of NCI

Many Institute instructors taught for decades, among them archaeologist Bob Mierendorf (left), Park Service jack-of-many-trades Gerry Cook (center), and writer and poet Tim McNulty (right).

Most of the staff worked behind the scenes, so they would not be profiled or even featured in catalogues like the field seminar faculty and others offering programs, but they were no less important. Beginning in 1993 development staff worked with Saul on raising money, as has been mentioned in many places in this story. Gale Sterrett was the first, and she filled that role through 1999. Then came Jan Turner, Trish Navare, Laura Bedford, and Kris Molesworth, as the "Moneyshed" expanded and budgetary needs increased. Jodi Broughton has led the fundraising shop most ably in recent years. Budgetary matters required so much oversight that Abbe Rolnick was hired as bookkeeper, followed by Beth Walsh as controller. Jason Revulson, with his extensive background in accounting, has skillfully filled the role of finance director for many years and has been responsible for overseeing professionalism in many areas of the Institute, including retail operations and technology. Marketing was essential, and in the mid-2000s this part of the operation was beefed up and improved by Benj Drummond. It has been managed very effectively by Christian Martin for the past fifteen years.

Technology has certainly evolved and changed the way many staff have done their jobs. The digital age was in its infancy when the Institute was founded. Recall that Saul and Tom moved from desk to desk in Park headquarters so they could use vacant IBM Selectric typewriters. Personal computers were beginning to be available, but were primitive compared to what is being used three and half decades later, and there were no computers in the Institute office for several years. As the Institute and its staff grew, so did their use of technology. One milestone was when Saul got his first Apple computer. Another was when the Institute began using a database and adopted Salesforce as the best database program to meet its needs, as its mailing and fundraising lists grew beyond the Rolodex stage. Then came the need for a website. At first it was contracted out, an approach where cost limited the Institute staff's ability to modify the website on a regular basis. This was ultimately solved by hiring an Internet technology manager. A hallmark of the Institute has been the exceptionally high graphic quality of its printed material, which yielded to digital material in the second decade of the 21st century. Advances in technology have extended the capacity of staff to do necessary work and increase productivity, and has improved efficiency. With the opening of the Environmental Learning Center, regular technical updates for communication, booking, and other functions have been essential.

A second staff group that have appeared in the story are programming staff, changing titles and roles as programs have changed. Managers of Mountain School, Skagit Watershed Education, Youth Leadership Adventures, Adult Field Programs, Conferences and Retreats, the graduate program, and more have worked under the leadership of an education director or program director. That role was filled by Wendy Scherrer and Tracie Johannessen in the early years, then by Jeff Giesen, SuJ'n Chon, and Michel Blackwell.

Decision-making at a rapidly evolving Institute was always collegial, and often challenging. Over time a strong staff leadership team was convened to represent all elements of the organization. This team was led by the executive director and included the associate director and the directors of Education/Program, Finance, Development and Marketing, the Learning Center, and most recently Inclusion and Community Partnerships. Regular meetings allowed the team to keep up to date on all the larger moving parts of the organization. Frequent retreats of Board and staff helped the team to tackle emerging issues and jointly plan budgets and operational goals for the year ahead. Leadership team members attended Board meetings to present and answer questions from the board. Individual program managers also presented to the Board at the annual retreat, so the Board could interact with the people "doing the real work."

David Snyder photo   Courtesy of NPS   Courtesy of NPS

Many National Park Service staff at the North Cascades National Park Complex contributed in myriad ways to the success of the North Cascades Institute over the decades. Representing them here are three who supported the Institute's work: Superintendent Bill Paleck (left), Park Maintenance Worker Mike Brondi (center), and Glaciologist Jon Riedel (right).

The third staff group involved the Learning Center and thus did not appear until 2005, though Don Burgess and Jeff Muse worked on Learning Center matters prior to its opening. Learning Center staff configuration has shifted over the years, but there has always been a facility manager/director, a food service manager, several chefs, and maintenance and housekeeping staff. As Learning Center-based programs grew, the managers and coordinators of these programs (Mountain School, Conferences and Retreats, the graduate program, and Youth Leadership) were all based at the Learning Center. These folks, and the program instructors, have been the core of a close "upriver" community. There has always been a gentle tension between the Learning Center and the "home office" in Sedro Woolley, but communication and coordination between the two offices have worked quite well. Some tension was expected: the Learning Center staff were generally younger and worked long hours with students and participants. They faced the challenges of road closures, forest fires, and students throwing up in the middle of the night. Staff at the Sedro-Woolley office were often older, and while they worked long hours, many worked 9-5 and could go home to their families in the evening. Strong leadership at the Learning Center, especially that provided by Kristofer Gilje, was necessary to ensure that each location was aware and understood the challenges of working together in their different worlds. A true jack-of-all-trades, Gilje found ways to address issues and problems in a calm, thorough, and most effective way.

AGENCY CONTRIBUTORS

FINALLY, A SMALLER GROUP OF PEOPLE ARE VERY IMPORTANT to the story: Park Service and Forest Service leaders. Foremost among them, in terms of their impact on the history of the Institute, are John Reynolds and Jon Jarvis. Without the support John provided to the idealistic young men who were seeking a home for their teaching adventures in the North Cascades, the Institute might not have come to be at all. Had Jarvis not suggested that the Institute reach far beyond its initial aspirations in the Seattle City Light relicensing negotiations and shown a way to do it, there would be no Environmental Learning Center. These two National Park Service leaders made exceptional contributions, and so did superintendents Bill Paleck and Chip Jenkins. Bill solidly supported the Institute in many ways and for many years, and provided excellent counsel. For instance, the path to the Learning Center took fifteen years, as described earlier. After many unforeseen expenses increased the cost of the project from $5 million to $12 million, City Light decided it had done enough and would not complete several of the buildings on the Learning Center campus, leaving foundations without structures. This was, not surprisingly, unacceptable to the Institute and the Park Service, and intense negotiations commenced. Leading the advocacy for the completion of the campus was Bill, ably assisted by Institute Board Chair Jeanne Muir. Bill was a seasoned administrator and able negotiator, and Muir an experienced business leader. They managed to work out a deal to complete the construction of the Learning Center. This was an important moment in Institute history, for how different things would have been with a partially completed Learning Center.

Jenkins succeeded Bill. Just as Bill had suggested that the Institute explore ways to use the Learning Center in the off season that led to conferences and retreats, Jenkins found a way to entice the Institute to become the park's cooperating association. He was especially enthusiastic about youth programs and strongly supported the Path for Youth concept. He regularly attended Board meetings and retreats, and readily contributed his ideas. Jenkins was as solid an advocate within the Park Service for the Institute as his predecessors had been. Other Park Service supporters were, of course, Gerry Cook, Bob Mierendorf, and Jim Harris. Chief of Interpretation Tim Manns saw the Institute's educational initiatives as a great addition to what his small staff could provide and found ways to help. Park personnel contributed to Mountain School from the beginning, and over the years found many ways to assist youth programs.

National Park Service field staff, rangers, and interpreters contributed regularly to many Institute programs. They helped fifth graders understand the nature of a national park, public land, and the North Cascades National Park at early Mountain School programs in the Newhalem Campground and later at the Learning Center. Rangers patrolling Ross Lake might drop in on youth programs traveling the lake and working on service projects. Park Service expertise was always available to contribute to Institute programs, whether about archaeology, history, or wildlife biology. The presence of the National Park Service was palpable at the Environmental Learning Center and in programs conducted in the National Park Complex.

The Forest Service's role in Institute history has been less extensive than that of the Park Service but has been a steady and important part of the story. Early in its history the Institute administrative offices were, as noted earlier, housed in a building shared by several federal agencies, principally the North Cascades National Park Complex headquarters and the USFS Mount Baker Ranger District Office. In the early days of the Institute,

District Ranger Larry Hudson strongly supported the infant organization, regularly attended meetings of the then-small Board, and encouraged use of the national forest for programs. Agreements were worked out with North Cascades National Park and the Mount Baker-Snoqualmie National Forest (and ultimately with other national forests) for use of their lands for Institute programs. Hudson helped negotiate the bureaucratic hurdles to make programs possible and national forests have hosted Institute activities ever since.

Forest Service Skagit River Ranger Jim Chu worked for the Mount Baker-Snoqualmie National Forest until 2004. He moved on to Forest Service International Programs but continued to be a strong advocate for the Forest Service's partnership with the Institute. He helped initiate the Skagit Watershed Education Program and he was convinced that the Forest Service should be supporting educational work like the Institute was doing, especially programs aimed at youth, whether the agency ran them themselves or supported the Institute. In an interview with the Institute's Christian Martin, Chu observed that the Institute was where the real environmental education experts were, and the Forest Service should leverage its meager resources for such programs by working with the Institute when possible. They did so over the years, partnering with the Institute on the Kulshan Creek Program, Eagle Watchers, Mountain Stewards, and River Stewards. In some cases, the Institute helped the programs get established and then moved on, with the Forest Service taking full responsibility. In others, the Institute continued to support them as they conducted programs such as Eagle Watchers and the Kulshan Creek Program.

PARTNERSHIPS

Partnerships have been critical to the Institute's success over the years, as the episodes described here and the people involved have clearly illustrated. Had the Park Service not been the willing partner it was in the beginning, there would likely be no Institute. It has always been a "small entrepreneurial nonprofit," as Saul described it, with some big partners. Early on it became clear that partnering was an essential strategy, and that with the right partners this small organization could leverage its ideas and influence far beyond the direct reach of its staff. The most important partner throughout the story here has unquestionably been the National Park Service. Reynolds, Jarvis, Paleck, and Jenkins all believed their agency could do a better job of education and interpretation in the National Park with the Institute than without it. They immediately saw the advantages for the Park Service and encouraged the partnership. Reflecting on the 23-year partnership in 2009, Bill observed, "I'd seen the way environmental education/interpretation ebbed and flowed in the Service and I saw in the Institute the potential to create some stability in that . . . The capacity could grow, the message could expand, but it was better buffered as a non-profit than the Park Service was, or had been in my experience."[34] The Park Service was a willing partner, seeing how much the North Cascades National Park could benefit as it helped the Institute thrive.

The second most important partnership over the history of the Institute has been that with Seattle City Light, which was not as willing a partner as the Park Service in the early days. It was a forced marriage because, as a public utility, it had to adhere to the environmental mitigation demands of FERC in order to renew its Skagit Hydro Project license. Behind the tiny North Cascades Institute was the federal government in the form of the Park Service, led in negotiations by Jarvis. What emerged was an arrangement where the federal government owned the land on which City Light built the Learning Center and the Institute would run it. Here was the little Institute with two behemoth partners, and while there were many ups and downs, issues, and conflicts over the years with City Light, the trend line was upward in terms of mutual trust and respect, transparency, and real integration and interdependence. The impact of the Learning Center on the Institute's story has been documented here, and without the City Light partnership the story would be much different.

The third major partnership was with Western Washington University's Huxley College of the Environment. Its name has changed several times, and it is now the College of the Environment at Western Washington University. The logic to this partnership was that the University was the leading higher education institution in the North Cascades region, and its environmental studies program embraced environmental education. John Reynolds saw the potential of this relationship right away, and called the Huxley College dean (the author of this history) to ask him if he would serve on the founding board. Dean John Miles ended up serving for eight years as Board chair, and later collaborated with Saul to come up with the graduate program, as described earlier. In the early years the partnership with Western was informal, primarily involving Miles and faculty who served as instructors in many seminars. The graduate program moved the relationship onto more formal ground involving a complex set of interactions. In the end, this partnership yielded much, but foundered when Miles retired and interest in the Institute's approach waned among his replacement and other young University faculty. Trust and respect broke down and, after a good run, the graduate program was terminated.

These three partnerships and that with the Forest Service were of core importance, but as has been seen, dozens of other partners made programs possible over the years. The 2001-2002 *Program Catalogue* listed 60 "Contributing Organizations and Partners" and 41 "Partner Schools and Participating School Districts." This level of interaction with other organizations was typical of the previous two decades of Institute efforts. Schools and school districts were partners from the launch of Mountain School to the present and relationships with them grew over the years, especially with Skagit Valley districts and the Bellingham School District. Some programs, like the Foodshed Project, involved partnering with the regional and local farming community to provide high-quality organic produce and other foods to the Learning Center. Partners have included Blue Heron Farm in Rockport, Silver River Ranch in Concrete, and Breadfarm in Bow. Some programs involved partnering with other conservation organizations like the Skagit Conservation District and the Skagit Fisheries Enhancement Group, and with the Washington Department of Natural Resources. Village Books in Bellingham was an especially strong partner. Its co-owner Chuck Robinson contributed in many ways, serving as a member of the Board and as Board chair. He encouraged and supported the literary side of Institute programming and, along with Kris Molesworth, helped arrange co-sponsorship of major events in Seattle as part of Seattle Arts and Lectures and Book Fare.

At a meeting in 2007 on the topic of "Nonprofit Partnerships: Competition and Collaboration," Saul presented what he had learned about partnering in his career. On the question of what makes partnerships work, he offered several conclusions from his experience: (1) there should be some fun in partnerships if they are to be sustainable; (2) build relationships before going into partnerships; (3) identify where missions overlap and work there; (4) define the audience and ask *them* what they need; (5) identify shared risks and benefits; (6) clarify goals and roles; (7) measure only what's important; (8) accept and learn from conflict; (9) put yourselves in each other's shoes; (10) acknowledge "good problems"; (11) strive for relationships that cut across organizational structures; and (12) develop strong personal relationships between leaders of the partner organizations.[35] This list illustrates the challenges and work that must go into successful partnerships, in Saul's view, and illustrates what he and his staff tried to do in working collaboratively, transparently, and accountably with many partners. The results speak for how well they mastered the art of effective partnering.

Partnerships are like good marriages—both parties must want to be in the relationship, both must commit to it and work for its success, and both must benefit from it. The elements for making partnerships work are not always achieved (in marriages or in organizational partnerships) but having some guidelines to follow, like those Saul laid out in his presentation, helps achieve desired outcomes. There is no question that over the years successful partnerships allowed the Institute to leverage its strengths and resources to achieve the goal "to conserve and restore Northwest environments through education" that would not have been possible without partners.

FUNDRAISING AND FINANCIAL MANAGEMENT

Obviously, no organization can address its mission and flourish without financial resources, the fuel that makes the engine run. In the beginning, the founders didn't give much thought to this reality, but this rapidly changed. They thought they only needed a checkbook to keep track of finances, and fees-for-service paid by field seminar participants would bring in the needed revenue. This naïve approach was short-lived. As business increased, the Board began to exercise its responsibility for financial oversight, and the need to support programs like Mountain School required more than fee-for-service income. The Jackson Foundation and Skagit Environmental Endowment Commission provided a grant to support Mountain School, financial accountability became essential, and fundraising strategies began to grow.

With a high learning curve, Saul managed the financial side of things and his small staff wrote grants, while natural history seminars brought in significant revenue. Annual audits became necessary, and financial transparency was legally required. A need and desire grew to hire more staff as the finances and fundraising challenges intensified, but the difficulty was to grow the financial resources necessary to pay staff to obtain and keep track of those very resources—a classic chicken-and-egg dilemma. Board members with financial and fundraising experience were added and contributed to fundraising efforts. As the organization grew, so too did the fundraising and financial sides of the operation. There is nothing unusual organizationally about this, but it indicates that the Institute responded appropriately and effectively to ensure that its resources matched its aspirations.

The Learning Center brought resources from City Light that helped with the financial impact of opening and operating a major facility. This met some basic needs, but the facility and programs that grew from it required increased fundraising and the "Moneyshed" grew accordingly. A special need that came with program expansion was funding for underserved youth who could not otherwise afford to participate in Institute programs. Staff devoted to fundraising became more specialized, with a development director overseeing the operation, a grant writer studying potential foundation funding and preparing grant proposals, and a donor relations manager building support from individual donors throughout the Northwest. Staff came up with creative ways to cultivate donors, elected officials, and reporters. These included boat trips up Ross Lake with Gerry Cook to visit youth working on projects and learn what they were doing in North Cascades Wild. The youth could wow visitors with their stories and contributions to North Cascades National Park, and the potential for growth in the young participants was clear. This strategy was very fruitful, helping potential donors understand the good work their contributions would support.

Throughout its history the Institute offered fee-for-service programs for those who could afford to pay tuition and scholarship help for those who needed it. In the beginning there were few scholarships, but over the years more resources were directed that way. Youth programs required subsidies and strong scholarship support. Much thought was given to how much to charge for programs. On the one hand, tuition should be low enough to be accessible to participants, but on the other it needed to pay the expenses of seminar faculty, administrative overhead, and whatever other costs might be necessary to mount a program. Prices ranged quite widely. The 2001 four-day Nature Writer's Retreat held at Sun Mountain Lodge cost $650/person (in a triple or quad), $725/person (in a double), or $895/person (in a single) and included accommodations and meals. This was the high end, the program being based out of a luxurious resort. On the facing page of the catalogue presenting the retreat were Skagit Watershed Field Workshops, in which participants were charged $50 for one day in the field with a local expert to learn about salmon habitat restoration. In 2009, the Eleventh Annual Writing Retreat at the Learning Center cost much less than it would have in a facility like Sun Mountain Lodge. The approach was to keep costs to participants as low as possible while meeting costs to the Institute, but there is no doubt that programs were primarily accessible to people with considerable disposable income, with limited help to defer costs for those who could not otherwise afford to attend. Over the years, as fundraising grew, scholarships became available for all Institute programs, with the focus primarily on youth programs.

The prospect of the Environmental Learning Center resulted in a decision to launch a major capital campaign to raise funds for programs and operations, for scholarships, and for an endowment. There was uncertainty about what additional financial burdens would come with the Learning Center. As it turned out, the reluctance of City Light to bear the increasing cost of completing the Center led to considerable unexpected expense for the Institute which, with the Park Service, insisted that the facility be constructed as designed. A consulting firm was hired in 1999 to help design a capital campaign, and the Reach for the Peaks campaign was launched in 2000. Board members Chuck Robinson and Jean Gorton were co-chairs of the campaign; honorary co-chairs were writer Barbara Kingsolver, famed northwest mountaineer Jim Whitaker, and former Seattle mayor Paul Schell. The goal was to raise $3 million "inclusive of annual fundraising." Saul announced the campaign when $1 million in pledges had been secured, and over the three years of the campaign $2.5 million were raised. This allowed the Institute to make the transition to operating a major facility, equipping it, meeting additional financial responsibilities to complete construction as planned, and landscaping the site. Reach for the Peaks was a major milestone in the financial history of the Institute.

There were of course financial ups and downs over the years. Saul wrote to Institute partners and supporters in May 2009 on the subject of "Planning for Uncertainty" to explain how the organization was coping with the Great Recession. Enrollment in all programs was down: Mountain School revenue was down 24%, family and adult programs were down 14%, and response to the 2008 annual fund appeal was down 10%. Investments and endowments were down 15% and 23%, respectively. On the other hand, Saul reported that the Board had consistently "set aside rainy-day funds and, though we don't intend to dip into them this year, we have significant savings in reserve." In response to this downturn, marketing was ramped up, the operating budget downsized, staff reduced, hiring delayed, and two programs eliminated. At the same time, Saul reported the Institute was launching two new programs, Parks Climate Challenge funded by the National Parks Foundation and taking over retail operations of the park stores. The organization responded nimbly to this and other financial challenges, cutting back where necessary and moving ahead at the same time.

Hard work, smart management, and philanthropy have allowed the Institute to thrive over more than three decades. The Pacific Northwest is among the most environmentally conscious regions in America. The Institute tapped into this consciousness, and as its reputation for excellence grew, so did philanthropic support. As Saul would tell graduate students in his course on nonprofit administration, the key to successful fundraising was to convince potential supporters to join the organization in its good and necessary work. He and his staff became masters of this—"Join us in a good and important cause for the benefit of all in the Pacific Northwest community." Soliciting support was not begging for a handout but issuing an invitation, and the list of those who accepted the invitation is a very long one which continues to grow.

OTHER INGREDIENTS OF SUCCESS

Dedicated, visionary people, solid and lasting partnerships, and good management have been major factors in the success of North Cascades Institute, but there have been others. One was a consistent focus on mission and avoidance of mission creep, no small achievement over 35 years. The Institute's 1986 mission was "Conserve and restore Northwest environments through education." In 2017 it was updated to "Inspire environmental stewardship through transformative learning experiences in nature." Coupled with a vision of "healthy Northwest ecosystems where all communities and species thrive," this led to the current *2020-2024 Strategic Plan*. This plan translates the new language into strategic goals that emphasize that "transformative learning experiences in nature include: place-based, environmental education, outdoor recreation, health and wellness, conservation, environmental justice and community engagement." This language indicates a greater focus on stewardship, environmental justice, and community building. "Stewardship" replaces "conservation" as the lead in the mission statement and suggests responsibility for and action to care for the environment more explicitly. All of this is simply to say that while the language of the Institute's mission has changed over the years, its focus on conservation and engagement has not and its mission reflects a considered response to a changing world.

Over the years there have been many debates about whether the Institute should engage in environmental advocacy. Early on, the consensus of the Board was to avoid taking a position on any issue that seemed political, such as the listing of the northern spotted owl as an endangered species in the late 1980s and early 1990s. The Upper Skagit was logging country, and while it would be okay to educate about logging and its impacts on natural systems, it was outside the mission to advocate for owl protection and against logging. This was a fine line to walk.

In 2017, after review and consultation with staff, partners, and funders, the Institute Board embraced a limited advocacy agenda as part of the Institute's conservation toolchest. Recognizing that "government activities, including legislation, policies, permits, and other actions, may impact our ability to achieve our mission . . . the Institute must be prepared to address relevant public policy issues in a timely and effective manner." Therefore, "the Institute may take public positions on government activities at local, state, regional and national levels when these activities may impact our ability or capacity to accomplish our mission." The Institute then spelled out the ways this would be done: "Teach our students how to think critically, and respectfully engage in public discussion and debate on issues that concern them. Actively participate in discussion of selected government activities and present the best available science-based education to our stakeholders, decision-makers and the media. Focus on issues related to conservation, education, and equity as these relate to our current programs, activities, and access to nature. We seek to bring people together and not contribute to increased polarization."

Another contributor to the Institute's success has been its excellent marketing and communications. At first, when finances were tight, catalogues were functional, describing the field seminars, who the instructors were, how much the classes cost, and how to sign up. The writing was good and the black-and-white illustrations attractive, but the marketing was basic. For nearly the first decade the catalogues were in a small 5x7-inch format with lots of text complemented by drawings and sketches. Local artists donated their work, foremost among them Margie Allen, Libby Mills, Laurie McDermott, Jay Haavik, and Sally Hewitt. The cover of the first catalogue featured striking photography by Sedro-Woolley's Lee Mann, considered one of the Northwest's preeminent landscape photographers at the time. That first catalogue was nine pages.

The Institute aimed from the beginning to be excellent in everything it did. These early catalogues offered clear descriptions of the field seminars and highlighted the instructors, who were a Who's Who of Pacific Northwest naturalists. The catalogues grew in length (31 pages by 1991), and more artists like Ramona Hammerly and Ruthy Porter contributed their work. By the late 1990s, photographs began to appear along with the sketches and covers grew more spectacular. Changes in technology and better finances allowed more investment in marketing. Poems by Tim McNulty, Jim Bertelino, and Robert Sund, among others, were featured and testimonials by participants brought added enticements. The 2001–2002 catalogue grew to a larger format that allowed the artwork to be more prominently featured and stayed this size until print catalogues disappeared and marketing and communications went mostly digital. The catalogues are important here because they became much more than just ways to convey information, but grew into expressions of the qualities of the places and the spirit and skills of the people involved in programs. The photos, artwork, and writing featured the beauty, fun, fascination, adventure, and camaraderie that could be experienced in an Institute program. New formats allowed more expression.

Marketing professionalism jumped up several notches when photographer, graphic artist, and filmmaker Benj Drummond became the marketing director and catalogue designer in 2004. He recruited superb wildlife photographer Paul Bannick to contribute some of his work, and watercolorist Molly Hashimoto painted a spectacular double-page cover featuring Mount Baker from the San Juan Islands. Benj moved on after three years and Christian Martin took over marketing and communications; he continues in that role in 2022. The Institute's graphic design team carried on the tradition of artistic excellence in catalogue layout and that of other publications in catalogues until 2012, then took the same standards to the Institute website.

The success of the Institute required smart marketing and good communication strategies, and as the Institute evolved so did these aspects of the operation. Many of the artists and photographers whose works have been featured in the catalogues and on the website have also been faculty for Institute programs. The quality of their work was displayed as an enticement to a public who might wish to learn watercolor painting from Molly, wildlife photography from Paul, or the art of poetry from Tim McNulty. By whomever and however the work was done over 35 years, the word got out that signing up for an Institute program would be a good investment of time and money. Word-of-mouth advertising by satisfied participants was an additional marketing tool beyond control of the staff, except by ensuring that participants enjoyed a quality experience that would motivate them to recommend the Institute to their friends. This was no small factor in bringing in participants.

Finally, in describing some of the factors that have made the Institute a success over the years, a great deal of the credit must go to the spectacular classroom that is the North Cascades ecosystem. From the Salish Sea to the Methow Valley, the Upper Skagit to Glacier Peak and beyond, no place offers more opportunities for adventure and learning than this one. Here is a place to explore a deep history of human interactions with nature stretching back millennia. Here is beauty beyond belief, diversity of life from tidal to tundra, glaciers to giant cedars, mountain goats to wolverines. It is a place of stories. From the Indigenous People to the early settlers to the present day, it is also full of ironies to consider: What if the Skagit hadn't been dammed, no mitigation were required, and no Learning Center were in the picture? Millions of people live close to this mountain landscape and benefit from the ecological services it provides, yet to this day know little about it. The challenge of using this classroom to the best effect continues to inspire.

Most of the story told here recounts what happened over the first three and a half decades of the North Cascades Institute's existence. This brief account of what made it possible for all of this to happen seems inadequate because so much thought, work, dedication, and passion have gone into the effort to make the organization the success it has been. All of the people involved, whether they have been behind a desk in the office, on 24-hour duty at the Learning Center, or camping in the rain in the backcountry with ten novice backpackers, have done what they do because they believe in the mission. For many staff, perhaps most, working for the Institute seems to have been more vocation than job—a lived dedication to the causes of conservation and environmental education. No one has made much money, but all have been richly rewarded with beauty, deep and lasting friendships, and satisfaction at observing the wonder and excitement of Mountain School students or the awe on the faces of young people paddling a canoe on a mountain lake and listening to the call of a loon. The bottom line is that passionate belief in the mission is what has made the Institute's accomplishments possible.

*I live in the Ish River country between two mountain ranges where
many rivers run down to an inland sea.*

Robert Sund, 1979

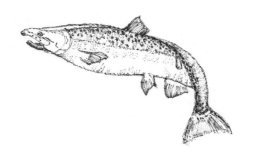

XII | NORTH CASCADES INSTITUTE AT 35: OPPORTUNITIES AND CHALLENGES

THE LAST FEW YEARS LEADING UP TO THE INSTITUTE'S 35TH anniversary and Saul Weisberg's retirement were challenging in several ways. One was that the relationship with North Cascades National Park leadership was strained. A second was that the graduate program, into which much investment had been made, ended. A third involved the movement in American society to fully address issues of equity, diversity, and inclusion (EDI). A fourth was the impact on the Institute of the COVID-19 pandemic, and a fifth was that all of this occurred just as negotiations began for a new FERC Relicensing Agreement for the Skagit Hydro Project. That the only constant is change may be a cliché but is a reality that all people, organizations, and institutions must deal with, and the North Cascades Institute is no exception.

After more than 25 years of strong support from North Cascades

National Park from a succession of strong, partnership-minded superintendents, the relationship between the partners fell on hard times. Superintendent Chip Jenkins left the Park on April 1, 2012 and the position was filled by acting assignments until a new superintendent arrived in March of 2013. During this transition the Park's chief of interpretation and district interpreter, with whom the Institute had worked closely, also left, as did the chief of facility management. All of this turnover compromised the ability of senior Park officials to pass down information regarding the long-standing partnership with the Institute, the leadership of which continued unchanged.

Christian Martin photo, Courtesy of NCI

Launching from the dock at the North Cascades Environmental Learning Center, the beautiful Salish Dancer, a replica of a traditional Northwest Coast seagoing canoe used by Coast Salish tribes, provides a unique way to experience the North Cascades.

The new superintendent, Karen Taylor-Goodrich and her first hire, new Chief of Interpretation Denise Schultz, took positions on the role the Institute should play in Park interpretation and education that challenged long-standing Institute programs supported by previous superintendents. Taylor-Goodrich's style of leadership was not as collaborative as that of her predecessors and she rebuffed Institute efforts to work with her as it had with them, responding to consideration of new initiatives with what Institute Board Chair Sterling Clarren characterized as "bureaucratic explanations that lead to 'no.'" Institute leadership became increasingly frustrated with the situation. After negotiations for a new Cooperative Agreement fell apart in 2015, the Institute Board requested that the NPS regional director establish an interdisciplinary team (IDT) to review and make recommendations on a partnership that seemed on a downward spiral. The IDT was formed, was given its charge, carried out its review, and issued its recommendations in 2017. The regional director issued directives to the parties to begin working on the recommendations immediately. The Institute strongly supported the NPS recommendations but Superintendent Taylor-Goodrich refused to discuss the majority of them, and tensions continued to grow.

The IDT issued 24 recommendations for how the difficulties might be resolved, which involved improving communications and collaborative efforts to resolve the core issues around which there was disagreement. This did not help much because the message conveyed to the Institute by the superintendent was that it was not their job to engage new audiences or to bring people to the park, and their education mission was entirely separate from the park's interpretation mission. Taylor-Goodrich simply rejected several of the IDT's recommendations. One recommendation was that "both parties need to take opportunities to recognize the partnership's successes and values as accomplishing the mission of NOCA and the NPS." Instead, the park removed all Institute marketing material from its Visitor Center and the retail stores the Institute operated. The superintendent did not agree with the IDT's recommendation that "educational" be defined broadly and "not be limited to only that which is provided to organized school groups or includes formal educational experiences, which the team believes aligns with current NPS thinking." [36]

The National Park Service operates in a quite decentralized way and individual superintendents have considerable power to interpret policy and manage their parks as they see fit. This worked to the Institute's benefit with superintendents prior to Taylor-Goodrich but worked to its detriment during her watch. Summarizing the situation regarding the IDT recommendations in a letter to Regional Director Woody Smeck in July 2020, Board Chair Clarren wrote, "The Institute has made a good faith effort to implement these recommendations while Superintendent Taylor-Goodrich has refused to even discuss the majority of them." Despite entreaties to regional directors (four different directors in four years) to take some action to ease the situation, no help came from them. In the letter, Clarren stated that not only had he lost confidence in the possibility of negotiating with Taylor-Goodrich, "we have also lost confidence in the ability of the Regional Office, which, while supportive, has taken no action to follow the recommendations of its own ID Team."[37]

The National Park Service is also not clear and consistent in its policy and guidance. The IDT noted, "Within the Pacific West Region, complicating the situation, different personnel and different branches of the Department of the Interior's Solicitor's office over time have provided changing advice on this matter and sometimes disagreed with certain interpretations of the Regional Director or Superintendent's."[38] In other words, there is discretion in implementing a cooperative agreement like the one between the Institute and North Cascades National Park. Previous superintendents used that discretion in support of Institute programming, while Superintendent Taylor-Goodrich used it in an effort to curtail Institute activities. The Park Service and Institute had operated under a series of Cooperative Agreements for five-year terms. The most recent Cooperative Agreement expired in December of 2014 and in the fraught environment involving the new superintendent, the partners reached an impasse in negotiating a new one. The old Agreement has since been extended through annual agreements by the regional office, but the impasse has continued.

Add to this the fact that in 2017, the Office of the Inspector General of the Interior Department began an audit of the National Park Service "to determine to what extent the NPS ensures that Residential Environmental Learning Centers (RELCs) comply with Department of Interior agreements, statutes, and regulations."[39] It looked at fiscal years 2013-2018 and issued its report in December 2019, finding that the Park Service lacked a specific policy defining what services and activities are appropriate offerings for RELCs, and that it did not ensure that services and activities provided by RELCs were in compliance. Superintendent Taylor-Goodrich seized on this finding, some of which specifically addressed the North Cascades Institute's programs, to argue that she could not address the IDT recommendations until issues were resolved at the national level—more stalling and stonewalling that only exacerbated tensions. She went so far as to direct the Institute to cease many current programs. Learning of this, Park Service officials at the national and regional level informed Clarren that the superintendent's directive "should not be interpreted as a stop work order or as direction to change the status quo." Clarren stated, "We literally do not know where to turn to understand the Superintendent's actions." Finally, in this environment, negotiation of a new Relicensing Agreement for the Skagit Hydro Project began, involving the Park and the Institute.

Little did Saul know, back in 2008 when he commented on the "frustrations" that came with working with powerful partners, how serious and draining those frustrations might be. In his July 2020 letter to Regional Director Smeck, Clarren enumerated the desires of the Institute for the future. It wished to "1) have a positive, collaborative, functional working relationship with NPS and NOCA; 2) move forward with the 2016 NPS IDT recommendations; 3) resolve issues identified in the 2017 OIG RELC audit; 4) collaborate with NPS and Seattle City Light as major partners in the current FERC relicensing of the Skagit Hydroelectric Project; and 5) work creatively within public health guidelines to fulfill our joint missions as best as possible until the Covid-19 crisis has been resolved." The Board and the new executive director certainly face daunting challenges in ensuring that the core partnership that has sustained the Institute for 35 years will continue to be a collaborative relationship that allows both the Institute and the Park to flourish.

CHALLENGES OF SOCIAL JUSTICE

THE PAST TWO DECADES IN AMERICA have seen an increase in campaigns for social justice for Black, Hispanic, and Indigenous Peoples and for gender equity. These include Black Lives Matter, LGBTQ rights, and others. The field of environmental education has recognized that in its many iterations, such as informal programs like the North Cascades Institute, ways must be found to address inequities in American society insofar as possible in pursuit of its primary goal of educating about the environment. This poses a second set of challenges for the Institute today.

Institute leaders have recognized these challenges from the beginning and tried to address them. In the early days, when programs consisted primarily of adult field seminars, the Institute clientele came almost entirely from the relatively well-to-do, educated, white middle class of the Puget Sound Basin. The mailing lists donated to the Institute so word could get out about offerings were from outdoor and conservation organizations, which were mostly white. Prerequisites to responding to the Institute's marketing were interest in and curiosity about the natural history of the North Cascades mountains, and the desire and capability to hike and camp. Such interests, for various reasons, were primarily attributes of the white middle class. Bent on building a foundation for the organization, little thought was originally given to expanding the demographic, racial, and ethnic diversity of program participants. The principal goal was to establish a viable organization.

Mountain School was where this began to change. In the pilot year of the program, one of the three schools participating was Denny Middle School from Seattle. Students in that school were mostly African-American city kids. That first year everything was new to the Institute, and it certainly was to the Seattle students who found themselves sleeping on the ground in tents and expected to engage in learning activities in the rain. Everyone involved learned a lot and a new awareness grew in Institute staff that many assumptions they were making about what would resonate with students needed questioning. Over the years most Mountain School participants came from Skagit and Whatcom counties. Many of the students, especially from Skagit County, were of Hispanic heritage. By its nature, Mountain School began to include new ethnic and racial groups.

Youth programs provided another opportunity to diversify participation. The Institute's success with raising funds allowed them to extend opportunities to young people who could not afford to participate, and this led to subsidized programs that allowed underserved youth to attend the various programs described earlier. Philanthropy made this possible. Over the years, as the Institute and its programs grew, discussions with schools and local communities led to a chance to diversify target audiences for all programs. Efforts to increase the diversity of the Board and staff were also made, but with limited success. The racial and ethnic diversity of the pools from which staff and Board candidates were drawn seemed to be shallow, and the Institute came in for criticism from advocates for social justice who judged it to be inadequately responding to the need for EDI. One source of criticism, as mentioned earlier, involved graduate students and others involved with the graduate program.

Both Western Washington University and the Institute have, throughout their histories, been predominantly white, middle-class institutions, though both have worked to diversify. Growth of racial and ethnic diversity has proved difficult for both given the larger communities they are part of, which historically pushed aside Indigenous People and have been dominantly white. Diversity has increased in recent decades in the wider regional community, with the growth of a Hispanic population attracted by work in agriculture and African-American and Asian communities in the thriving urban centers of Western Washington. Still, institutions like the North Cascades Institute, which have focused on interests and activities more related to the values of the dominant white community, have found increasing diversity quite challenging.

At Western Washington University agitation has grown for a decade, with students expressing dissatisfaction with progress on increasing diversity in all parts of the community. Gene Myers, the M.Ed. graduate program coordinator of Huxley College, wrote in a 2019 memo regarding the proposed moratorium on the program, "While we appreciate the measures NCI has taken to address equity, inclusion and diversity we are wanting to hold ourselves and our students to higher expectations in all aspects of our programs." He did not specify what the "higher expectations" were, and there was no willingness to work with the Institute to determine how the two organizations could collaborate to address them and achieve the desired outcomes. There was little recognition on the part of the University of the efforts and progress the Institute had been making for years to increase EDI. The Institute admitted that efforts to increase the diversity of Institute Board, staff, and clients had fallen short of its goals, but there were reasons for this grounded in diverse cultural preferences that were beyond the ability of the Institute to overcome.

One of these has been that, historically, outdoor recreation and conservation have been interests and concerns of the white Euro-American community, reaching back deep into the 19th century. While wealthy, white, urban Americans were retreating from unhealthy east coast cities into the Adirondacks and White Mountains, Indigenous People and their cultures were being destroyed across the expanding United States. At the same time, African-Americans were subjected to slavery and then to Jim Crow. Well-to-do Americans pressed for parks and for conservation, resulting in the creation of National Parks and forests, the wilderness conservation movement, and growing interest in outdoor recreation. While this was happening, Native Americans were suffering genocide, African-Americans were struggling against systemic racism everywhere, and people of Hispanic heritage in the southwest were struggling to defend their land and culture in the face of a rapidly growing influx of American colonists moving west.

The consequence of all this is that outdoor recreation, conservation, and interest in natural history, all core foci of the Institute, have been more central values of white middle-class Americans than of these other racial and ethnic groups. They have written the narratives around these values. This is not to suggest that minorities have not had interest in them, because they have, but to a lesser degree and in different ways than the dominant culture. Historian Tiya Miles, writing in the *New York Times*, observes, "African-Americans' relationship to the environment is complicated and deep," but there is a "tension in American culture between black people and anything environmental" that has a basis in history. They did not, for instance, go into the forests for pleasure, but to escape persecution and enslavement. This tension is present with Indigenous and Hispanic people as well. None of these racial and ethnic groups participated in major ways in the American conservation movement or embraced outdoor recreation in the late 19th and early 20th centuries. They were often made to feel unwelcome, and Native Americans everywhere resented the appropriation of their ancestral lands for National Parks and forests by conservationists whom they perceived were protecting nature only for their recreational enjoyment. Hispanic people, living primarily in the southwest, felt similarly displaced from what they considered land granted them in the Treaty of Guadalupe being appropriated by the federal government for national forests. All of this has resulted in attitudes and values that are challenging for institutions like the North Cascades Institute. To survive and thrive, it had to market its programs to people who valued public lands and national parks, who were curious about natural history, who enjoyed outdoor recreation, and who had the means to pay for the experiences the Institute was offering.

Over the years the need to work on EDI was increasingly recognized by members of the Institute community. North Cascades National Park archaeologist Bob Mierendorf, a regular Institute instructor and strong supporter, reminded Institute staff that the outdoor classroom of the Upper Skagit region had been the home of Indigenous People since time immemorial, and programs and curricula should make that clear to participants of all ages.

His archaeological work revealed the deep prehistory and more recent history of Indigenous occupation of the region. Mierendorf and Gerry Cook offered a course on "People of the Upper Skagit" which explored "10,000 years of fascinating natural and cultural history." Mierendorf's work revolutionized the archaeology of the North Cascades because earlier archaeologists had dismissed the idea that Indigenous People of the region would venture into the high country in any significant way. They focused their attention on the surrounding lowlands and river corridors, found abundant material documenting a large Indigenous presence along the streams, and concluded that these ancient people traveled across the mountains at various passes but didn't really live in them. Mierendorf did the strenuous work of surveying the high country and revealed that the mountains had indeed been home to Indigenous People for thousands of years.

Despite Mierendorf's urging and that of a few others, a review of Institute programs between 2000 and 2012 shows that most programming continued to focus on the natural history of the North Cascades with little content addressing the deep human history and prehistory of the region. This began to change in the second decade of the 21st century, driven in part by state adoption in 2015 of the *Since Time Immemorial* curriculum, which directed state schools to teach about Indigenous People in grades 3-5. One essential question to be addressed, for instance, was how physical geography affects Northwest Tribes culture, economy, and where they choose to settle and trade. Fifth graders attend Mountain School, offering a golden opportunity to address this question and others, and the curriculum was adjusted to do so.

Rising to this challenge and opportunity, and to observe the 30th anniversary of Mountain School, the Institute began a curriculum redesign that would allow Mountain School to "integrate and organize all program content to align with these new standards." The Institute began to acknowledge more clearly than before that its Learning Center and all its programs occurred on land that was once the domain of Indigenous People who had been removed from it, often violently. A part of this acknowledgement was recognition that Indigenous People living today in the region still hold a strong connection to all the ancestral lands they once occupied. Starting in 2015, the Institute began every program and institutional meeting with a land acknowledgement. Asa Duffee, Marketing and Communications Coordinator for the Association of Nature Center Administrators

(ANCA), cites the North Cascades Institute as a leader in this effort in a blogpost post on the ANCA website titled "Land Acknowledgements: Why and How are Nature Centers Using them?" and uses an Institute acknowledgement as an example:

> *The human story of the North Cascades begins with the original stewards of these lands and watersheds, the Indigenous Nations and their modern descendants. North Cascades Institute acknowledges that our programs take place in the ancestral homelands of Tribes, Bands, and First Nations, including most notably the Upper Skagit Indian Tribe, Sauk-Suiattle Indian Tribe, Swinomish Indian Tribal Community, Samish Indian Nation, Nooksack Tribe, Lummi Nation, Stó:lo Nation, Nlaka'pamux Nation, Colville Confederated Tribes, [and] Syilx/Okanagan Nation.*
>
> *As educators, we have a responsibility to examine our own relationship to the Land we live and teach on and to the local Indigenous communities whose traditions and identities originated in these special places. We acknowledge that the settlement period histories in this place often reflect the detrimental effects of disease, displacement, violence, migration, and loss of tenured land of Indigenous People.*
>
> *We offer this acknowledgement as a first step in honoring their relationship with land we share, and a call toward further learning and action, not in place of authentic relationships with local Indigenous communities, but rather to assist in giving them voice.*[40]

Of such acknowledgements, Saul is quoted as saying, "It's just the barest beginning. The real point of this is to begin a genuine relationship." He goes on to say, "It's a lifelong journey, and we're going to fail, but we fall forward and we get up and keep moving. You can't fail until you get something out there, and you try it." Precisely what justice demands of non-Indigenous People in the 21st century living on lands taken from Indigenous People is much debated, but the Institute has taken the issue seriously and has been working to define what justice demands it do. Land acknowledgement is a step in the right direction. The wider issue of what justice demands of the Institute for adequate attention to the challenges of EDI continues to be a challenge that the Institute acknowledges and pledges to tackle going forward.

In response to the critics who charged that the Institute was not doing enough to tackle the challenges of social justice, the Institute hired the Avarna Group in 2018 to conduct a "culture and climate audit" to help identify perceptions and experiences of the EDI climate in the organization and what resources and actions might be needed to improve in these regards. The Board committed to increasing its efforts on this front and created an EDI Committee to assess what needed to be done, make recommendations, and implement change. The mission statement was reviewed and revised, as noted, and social justice was specifically included in the Strategic Plan and Operational Goals. Programs were revised to respond to increased commitment to EDI—the new Mountain School curriculum is an example. A new leadership team position, director of inclusion and community partnerships, was recruited and hired to lead EDI efforts across the Institute. This is a work in progress, and the Institute is not unique in increasing its attention to this side of its operation—organizations at all scales across the country are responding to calls for more attention to social justice. As calls for progress on this front continue to be heard, the future Institute will be engaged for years to come in this "good trouble," as John Lewis called it.

COVID-19 POSES NEW CHALLENGES

THE YEAR 2020 WAS UNLIKE ANY other in a century due to the widespread impact of the COVID-19 pandemic, which disrupted the normal activity of people across the world. Its impacts on the Institute were many and abruptly resulted in the shutdown of the Environmental Learning Center and nearly all Institute programs. As Saul said, "When your business model involves bringing people together in small, intimate groups, to spend significant amounts of time learning and studying, COVID was a stake into the heart of that business model." Yet the Institute's nimble response provides an example of resilience and adaptation to a very difficult situation. Anticipating a normal year of programming, the plan for 2020 was ambitious. Mountain School started as normal in March, only to be shut down after two weeks as school districts halted in-person learning. Staff had been hired and trained for Mountain School with the prospect of working into June and for the fall sessions, and the Learning Center was stocked with supplies and food. Not only were Institute plans upset but the lives of staff were severely disrupted. On March 19, Saul wrote to the staff announcing the closure of the Learning Center and assuring them that leadership would do everything it could to cushion the blow. He wrote, "Our response, as a community, will define who we are as people, not just as an organization."

Over the next four months, Washington State was hit hard by the virus and the prospect of a brief shutdown faded. Institute leadership responded: On March 24, Saul informed the staff that all spring programs would have to be canceled and 23 staff were furloughed on April 1. Various actions to mitigate the impact on staff included continuation of free housing for hired staff, $1,000 bonuses for staff who were laid off, and all remaining staff, including leadership, being put on reduced work hours. On April 28 the staff was informed that a Cares Act Paycheck Protection Program (PPP) had been approved and would fund salaries for two months of operation. On May 13, the Institute decided to stop planning for summer programs and concentrate on the fall. Summer adult programs were cancelled and Skagit Tours and Youth Leadership would proceed with big changes—without boat tours or backcountry trips. On July 7 they decided to cancel fall Mountain School, since school districts would not know until late August whether they would be allowed to open for in-person learning (and of course, they were not). So it went into 2021 when, with vaccinations revving up, the prospects for restarting began to look better.

With generous support from Seattle City Light, remaining staff developed lessons for "Mountain School at Home" and worked on the revision of the Mountain School curriculum which was to have been launched in 2020. With ups and downs over the course of the pandemic shutdown, staff went from 52 to a low of 23. Mountain School instructors created 16 Mountain School at Home lessons and posted them on the Institute's website. A "History of the Skagit River" video series was produced with funding from Seattle City Light and posted to the website, as were other videos including a series of poetry readings titled "Poetry from the Porch." A smaller, hybrid version of Youth Leadership Adventures was offered for local teens focusing on climate change and culminating in a kayak outing on the Salish Sea. Julie Stone, the Institute's Youth Leadership Manager, said in an interview by *National Parks Traveler*, "It was definitely disappointing to have to cancel our backcountry trips this year, but we never doubted that we would find some new creative ways to work with high school students and keep the program going."[41] Julie captured the essence of the Institute's response to the pandemic disruptions with her comment about finding "new creative ways" to do the work.

Lack of school was especially hard on children who struggled with all-remote learning approaches. In 2019 the Institute became a member of the Whatcom Coalition for Environmental Education, the mission of which was "expanding and deepening access to environmental and sustainability education for every child across Whatcom County." Over the summer of 2020 the various organizations in the coalition worked to figure out how to safely mount learning activities using outdoor spaces that could be delivered in the fall. Out of this came a program called Connections, which tailored programs for three Whatcom County school districts. The Institute led the partnerships that offered Connections in the Blaine and Mount Baker school districts, and Wild Whatcom led the work in Bellingham. The Blaine program involved kindergarteners and first graders, and the Mount Baker program addressed sixth graders from Kendall Elementary School. The Bellingham program focused on supporting English-language learners, migrants, and other students who would benefit most from additional support. Teachers picked students for these programs who they thought would most benefit from joining other children in the outdoors. In Blaine, these were students who had qualified for academic support in the previous school year, were eligible for the federal Free or Reduced Lunch program, had limited access to the outdoors at home, or had low attendance during remote schooling in the spring. These two Connections programs served 32 students in Blaine and 36 in Kendall.

Partnering with 15 other organizations and with local funding, the coalition asserted, "Access to learning is a basic human right, one that the Whatcom Coalition for Environmental Education is committed to protecting for young people across the county. But the needs young people are facing right now extend far beyond just academics. Connections gives young people a respite from feelings of isolation and lack of companionship, and it serves as an opportunity for nonprofit organizations and other stakeholders from across the county to work together to come up with creative solutions to the increased needs of the community during these challenging times."[42] Connections was truly a community effort with many partners committed to environmental education quickly pulling together the funding, logistics, curriculum, and instructional teams to mount a response to school closures due to the pandemic.

Much of the Institute's response to the challenges posed by the pandemic, like that of society at large, involved technology since social distancing and quarantines were part of the response. This was a necessary departure from the Institute's foundational emphasis on experiential learning in the outdoors, but it allowed staff to experiment and develop skills that they might not otherwise have embraced. A question in many minds was what the role of technology might be in Institute programs when the pandemic receded. They discovered, for instance, that online seminars like the one photographer Paul Bannick offered were very popular, his drawing two hundred participants. While participating in such a digital seminar was no substitute for going into the field with Paul, a field seminar enrolled only a dozen students and the online seminar could serve many more. Perhaps both types of seminars could be offered in the future, with the online approach whetting the appetites of participants who would then want to physically go into the field. Technology had been increasingly used as part of programs, with youth program participants recording their experiences and presenting them on blogs and in other ways. One Institute goal was to move young people off their screens and into the natural world, but perhaps if they could use their skills with technology to complement and extend their field experience when they returned home, all the better.

In March 2021, the Institute partnered with Village Books in Bellingham to present a gathering on ZOOM to celebrate popular Writer's Retreat instructor Kathleen Dean Moore's new book, *Earth's Wild Music: Celebrating and Defending the Songs of the Natural World*. Moore led discussion with Saul, Alaska writer Hank Lentfer, pianist Rachelle McCabe and marine biologist Mark Hixon. Moore read from her book, Lentfer shared his magnificent recordings of bird song, McCabe spoke to the music of the wild with her piano, and everyone talked about the wonders of "Earth's wild music." Here was another demonstration of how the Institute and its partners, like Village Books and Moore, could offer programs that brought together experts from far and wide to address a subject. The "Celebrating Earth's Wild Music" event provides another example of how the virtual world of technology can present informative and moving events. In this case, it provided inspiration to get out and listen to the music of the wild.

In 2000 the Institute Board of Directors approved a 2020-2024 strategic plan which will govern strategic goals in the short term. The Vision is of "Healthy Northwest ecosystems where all communities and species survive." Its Mission is "to inspire environmental stewardship through transformative learning experiences in nature." Its Case Statement has three parts:

- *North Cascades Institute is a conservation organization focused on outdoor learning in the mountains, rivers, forests and communities of the North Cascades ecosystem.*

- *"Transformative learning experiences in nature" include: place-based, environmental education, outdoor recreation, health and wellness, conservation, environmental justice and community engagement.*

- *Ecosystems (Communities) thrive when communities (people) have opportunities for meaningful experiences outdoors in nature, from a neighborhood garden to a national park. We have a shared responsibility to open the doors to people of all ages, abilities and backgrounds to ensure their outdoor experiences are powerful and rewarding. When people connect with nature, our communities are strengthened, nature is protected, and we all benefit.*

Finally, the Strategic Plan is built on a set of beliefs:

1. *Nature has intrinsic value.*

2. *Hands-on learning about the environment begins in childhood and lasts a lifetime.*

3. *Intimate contact with nature helps people lead healthy, well-balanced lives.*

4. *Transformative learning lies at the confluence of natural and cultural history, science, humanities, and the arts.*

5. *Everyone benefits when people have equitable access to nature and public lands for education, recreation, and renewal.*

6. *Shared experiences build community.*

7. *Outdoor education, combined with critical thinking and civic engagement, promotes environmental stewardship and conservation.*

The Vision and Mission of the North Cascades Institute have not changed, though the words stating them have. The beliefs have evolved, some growing stronger (such as the first three in this statement), others being added as new needs have been perceived and understanding of them has grown. All of this is a solid foundation for the future of this remarkable organization.

In his letter to Acting National Park Service Regional Director Smeck in July 2020, Board Chair Clarren provided an overview of the North Cascades Institute and what it had accomplished in its 34 years. Writing before the pandemic knocked the Institute back temporarily, he explained that it had a $4 million budget, 65 staff, and a 14-member Board of Directors. He noted that in 2012 the National Park Service Comptroller "held up the NOCA-Institute partnership as a positive model of public-private partnership, with $200,000 of in-kind NPS support leveraging over $2,000,000 in Institute education experiences in the park." Over 34 years, he wrote, the Institute brought in more than $55 million in non-federal funds to support education in the North Cascades. These funds helped more than 157,000 students, totaling nearly a half million learner-days of participation. The story told here provides the details behind these remarkable statistics. Who among the initial Shuksan Institute founders, when they gathered on that Park Service float on Ross Lake in 1981, could have imagined what their dreams would produce? It is an amazing story, but this is of course not the end. It is hopefully and probably only the first chapter. The need for conservation and environmental education is as great as it has ever been on this warming planet, with its burgeoning population and callous disregard for the limitations nature places on all species, of which *Homo sapiens* is only one among billions.

Those presuming to shape the minds that will shape the future must comprehend what the future requires of them.

David Orr, *Earth in Mind*

XIII | FACING THE FUTURE

Saul Weisberg retired on June 30, 2021. After three and a half decades of rewarding, satisfying, and sometimes exhausting work and a year of pondering the idea of stepping aside, he decided it was time for a change of leadership at the Institute. It was also time for him to pursue some of his many other interests in which, with the demands of his work, he had been unable to indulge. Few founding directors last as long as Saul did as leaders of their organizations for various reasons. A tenure of 35 years was a remarkable achievement. Saul grew with the job over those decades, but the last several years of struggles with North Cascades National Park leadership and the onset of the COVID-19 pandemic had sapped his energy and brought the realization that it was time to pass the leadership torch to someone younger, with new ideas and abundant energy. Whoever that might be, they would be faced with many challenges, such as bringing the Institute back to full strength after the pandemic and participating in negotiations for the renewal of the Seattle City Light license for its Skagit Hydro Project, a challenge with many implications for the Institute.

Saul announced his intentions to the Institute Board a year before his retirement so that there would be abundant time for a wide search for his replacement, and hopefully time for him to work with and ease his successor into the job. The first step was for the Board to draft a position description and specifications, in consultation with Saul and other Institute staff. The Board decided to hire a search firm with extensive reach into the parks and conservation communities and settled on the Portrero Group, a prominent executive search firm with an excellent reputation. The firm would advertise the position and screen what was expected to be a large pool of applicants, recommending a top tier of candidates to the Board for final screening and selection.

The Portrero Group posted a visually striking announcement prepared by the Institute Board and staff on its website. The header photograph depicted children paddling the big *Salish Dancer* canoe on a placid Diablo Lake against a forest, with snow-draped Pyramid Peak in the background. The posting announced that "North Cascades Institute seeks our next Executive Director to lead the organization in inspiring environmental stewardship and a community of belonging through transformative learning experiences in nature." Illustrated with additional spectacular photographs, the position announcement featured the typically excellent graphic qualities of all Institute communications. Text presented a background overview of the Institute and its Strategic Goals, Mission, Vision, Values, and the practical responsibilities of the executive director. Along with the usual desired qualities (such as proven leadership skills, extensive management experience, fundraising, and budget management) were the following qualities desired in an executive director: "a practical idealist, curious listener, provocative question asker, and creative problem solver with a demonstrated ability to think strategically and make decisions effectively." The candidate should be "humble, empathetic, and inclusive of various perspectives, able to resolve conflicts and find common ground" and adept at "creating more access for historically marginalized peoples/groups." This was a carefully crafted description of the attributes being sought in the new leader; the Board had clearly reflected deeply on the qualities of its very effective parting executive director and what it anticipated would be required to meet the challenges of "changing times." The new leader would need to pair leadership skills with a "creative, collaborative, and often entrepreneurial approach" to the job.

The Portrero Group posting yielded many applicants who thought they could meet the high standards and expectations presented. Applicants came from across the United States, which was expected (and hoped for) since the North Cascades Institute had a national reputation in its field. The Board had anticipated that processing a large applicant pool was beyond its volunteer capacity and was pleased with the way the professionals of the Portrero Group applied their expertise and winnowed the field to those whom it judged had the greatest potential to fit the extensive and unique specifications.

The search process was complicated for everyone by the COVID-19 pandemic, which made interviewing the top tier of candidates a challenge, but it could be done in the age of ZOOM. The Board ultimately narrowed the field to three finalists, who were closely scrutinized, and offered the position to Bec Detrich. Bec had held several executive positions in the field of environmental education, most recently as the executive director for Trips for Kids Marin in San Rafael, California. In addition to strong academic credentials in environmental science, biology, and business administration, Bec had extensive experience with leading a culturally diverse staff, school-oriented environmental education programs, and working with public land managers, specifically the National Park Service. One of her positions was as a field science education manager for NatureBridge at the Golden Gate National Recreation Area, a unit of the National Park System. In addition to this professional experience, the Board judged that as a person, Bec was the "practical idealist" they were seeking as well as the humble listener and "question asker" sought in the new North Cascades Institute leader.

As hoped, Bec was able to work with Saul for a while prior to his turning over the reins to her. He filled her in on the status of the Seattle City Light relicensing negotiations in which he had been participating. The Institute was already restarting programs as the pandemic receded, and Saul and other staff could explain plans on that front. One of the big challenges already being tackled was rebuilding the staff that had been reduced to cope with pandemic shutdowns. Many who had been furloughed had drifted off to other positions as the pandemic dragged on. Kristofer Gilje had announced in October that he would be retiring after 14 years as the director of the Environmental Learning Center and a search was already underway to fill this critically important position.

Key veterans of Saul's leadership team would continue into the new administration. Jeff Giesen, who had been with the Institute since 1999, would bring deep experience administering the internal operations of the Institute as associate director. Jodi Broughton would continue directing the "Moneyshed" team, assisted by Stephanie Friesen as marketing and design coordinator, Catherine Endicott as donor relations manager, and Christian Martin as director of communication, a position he had ably held since 2006. Jason Revelson would continue in the core role of finance director. These and other Institute veterans would help Bec make the transition to her position.

Committed to increased attention to diversity, equity, and inclusion in all aspects of the Institute, the new position of director of inclusion and community partnerships had been created and funded. Alana (Aazhoganike Noojimo'idizo) Quigley, a member of the Anishinaabe from the Lac Courte Oreilles and St. Croix bands of the Ojibwe people, had been hired to oversee EDI initiatives across the organization. She came on board before Bec assumed leadership, and Institute staff had done much thinking and writing about what might be needed to expand work in the EDI space. This was one of the efforts to which Bec could bring her extensive experience. She and her colleagues filled other positions necessary to build the post-pandemic program, increasing the presence of women in Institute leadership and lowering the overall age of the staff. New staff would bring youthful energy and new ideas, and veteran staff would allow continuity and some mentoring of the new people. Hiring the people needed to open the Learning Center proved challenging due to a post-pandemic shortage of qualified applicants. The Center could not offer food service in the summer of 2022, requiring cancellation of many programs. Other challenges to full reopening were long delays on Highway 20 affecting program schedules.

The most important immediate challenge Bec faced was to represent Institute interests in Skagit Hydro Project relicensing negotiations. Saul had participated in the negotiations in the early 1990s with nothing to lose, but the situation in this round was quite different. The Institute had successfully established itself operating the Environmental Learning Center, with solid cooperation and support (most of the time) from Seattle City

Light and the National Park Service. City Light was very pleased with the way things had gone, but there was new leadership at North Cascades National Park and uncertainty about that relationship. The Park Service's urgent needs at the time of the first relicensing negotiations, which resulted in such strong support for the Institute and the Learning Center, were not present this time around. The new proposed relicensing agreement contained different provisions than had been in the earlier one and would be scrutinized by the Federal Energy Regulatory Commission, which injected another measure of uncertainty into the prospects of continuing and even expanding the Environmental Learning Center and the Institute's role. At the end of the current license, 20 percent of the Institute budget would disappear if the agreement was not renewed. If its role at the Learning Center should end for some unexpected reason, this would significantly change the nature of the organization, which could not be allowed to happen. Beyond ensuring the status quo, some expansion of the Learning Center might be proposed—a boat house, more staff housing, or even another lodge to expand capacity. Contributions to the climate resilience of the Learning Center might be improved, and funding provided for a beefed-up on-site command structure. Bec's goal in the negotiations had to be nothing less than the status quo and to add to the Learning Center to the extent feasible. Support from City Light, the Park Service, and the other intervenors in the negotiations would be necessary to achieve these goals.

On another front, a new Mountain School curriculum framework was proposed in 2020 and was to be piloted starting in the fall. However, the COVID-19 pandemic shut down in-person learning, so no pilot was possible. The new framework would update the curriculum to better reflect the Institute's revised Mission and Vision by advancing authentic science education, expanding programming for climate literacy, embracing EDI, promoting civic engagement, and serving tribal communities responsibly, among other goals. The Institute had been working on all of these across its programming for years, and this new curriculum would more significantly incorporate them into the Mountain School experience.

To achieve these goals, Mountain School would use a relatively new and important curriculum design format being widely adopted in public education called Understanding By Design. The curriculum would continue to embrace its long-standing place-based education approach, incorporate Next Generation Science Standards, and include contributions to the Since Time Immemorial Tribal Sovereignty Curriculum recently mandated by the State of Washington for all public schools. Approaches to instruction would incorporate multicultural education and culturally responsive teaching, as well as student-centered instruction and social-emotional learning. All of this would make curriculum design quite complex and, in some circles, controversial. Incorporating these ingredients into a brief field experience posed many challenges but would continue to make Mountain School a creative, leading-edge practitioner of an environmental education tailored to the needs of the 21st century.

Bec informed the Institute community in early 2022 that "North Cascades Institute entered into 2022 with cautious optimism, as well as excitement for the impact, exploration, joy and connections the year will hold." She reported that the 2021 year finished in a strong financial position thanks to donors and COVID-related government funding. A new leadership team had been formed, the Board had met with new North Cascades National Park Complex superintendent Don Striker after the retirement of his troublesome predecessor, and programming was moving forward. Mountain School was returning with a spring season of "Choose Your Own Adventure Programs." This was described in the Spring Field Notes as such: "Answering the varied needs of local school districts, we're offering options that include a combination of online orientations with a ranger from North Cascades National Park with in-person education at either a park close to the student's school or day trips to the North Cascades Environmental Learning Center." Mountain School was carefully transitioning to a return to full in-person learning as the pandemic slowly receded in the spring of 2022.

Bec also reported that the Institute was taking a leadership role in the Washington Outdoor School Consortium, "a coalition of outdoor science education providers who have launched Outdoor Schools for All to expand outdoor access for all students in Washington as an integral part of school curriculum." The Consortium was working to persuade the Washington Legislature to pass a bill allocating $50 million to make such access possible, something Oregon had done in 2016. The 2022 legislative session provided only $10 million toward the goal, and the legislature pledged to add the other $40 million in the next session. The Consortium celebrated this allocation and pledge and vowed to demonstrate the wisdom of fully funding the request with the amount provided. This promises to be an opportunity for the Institute, the scale of which has yet to be seen.

Jodie Broughton photo, Courtesy of NCI

Bec Detrich became the second executive director of North Cascades Institute in June 2021, bringing extensive experience in environmental education and non-profit leadership to the Institute.

The North Cascades Institute has survived the COVID-19 pandemic in quite good shape thanks to the measures taken under Saul's leadership in 2020, Bec's continuing leadership, generous financial support from the Institute community, and successful and creative interim programming to sustain the support of school districts and other clients. The future is always uncertain, and in 2022 there are more uncertainties than usual. At the time of writing in the late spring of 2022, a new surge of COVID-19 variants seems to be moving across the United States. Cases are up, hospitalizations are up, and deaths are down. How the country will respond to further COVID-19 challenges is uncertain, but it seems unlikely to be as draconian and impactful as was necessary at the beginning of the pandemic. Other uncertainties involve climate change, the future of democracy, a struggling domestic and global economy, and energy policy. The Institute is part of a volatile world in the second decade of the 21st century.

As the story of the first 35 years of the North Cascades Institute demonstrates, creative, realistic, collaborative, and sustained responses to societal change allow an organization like this, with strong leadership, to survive and prosper. The need for the work the Institute does has never been greater, whether that need derives from social unrest and divisiveness, dysfunctional modern lifestyles, environmental degradation, or the existential threats of biodiversity loss and climate change. The Institute's stated goals of ecosystem and climate literacy, community, diversity, belonging, and civic participation and stewardship are appropriate and necessary responses to the crises of the 21st century in the Pacific Northwest and beyond. The Institute has not and cannot in the future reach these goals by itself, as it has always realized. With its partnerships and example, it can lead toward positive outcomes both short- and long-term for all beings that share the blessings of the Earth.

AUTHOR'S NOTE

IF YOU READ THE INTRODUCTION TO THIS STORY, you know that the author is the same John Miles who appears occasionally in it. I feel compelled to make clear that this work is not that of an objective observer. I bring to this account a strong bias—I think the North Cascades Institute is and has been a wonderful organization, a leader in the field to which I dedicated much of my professional career, environmental education. I initially decided to pull this history together because I thought the story remarkable in many ways: young people with a vision bringing it to fruition; a community of educators adhering around a set of beliefs about nature, conservation, and how learning about them might be best achieved; and a remarkable array of partners working together to accomplish shared goals of conservation and education.

I began this work several years ago, but life drew me off in other directions, so progress was slow. When I learned that Saul Weisberg was retiring, I decided it was time to get this done, to recount how the Institute grew through his tenure as executive director. The Institute's story of storms weathered and successes achieved is a testimony to the hard work, dedication, creativity, and deep conviction about the Institute's mission of many people. Some of them are mentioned in this account, and many are not—there are simply too many to credit them all. It is especially a testimony to Saul's leadership. He would be the first to say that he could not have built and sustained the Institute without all who helped along the way, and he will modestly refuse to say that he is the glue that has held the organization together all these years, but I think he is.

I count many of the people in this story as my friends, and it has very difficult to refrain from injecting myself into it, to express opinions and share personal stories. I have probably not entirely succeeded, at least on the opinion side, but I have tried. Pouring through Institute catalogues, hundreds of blogs, and piles of documents has been great fun, a journey at times through my personal history with the Institute. Before undertaking this project, I did not have the big picture of how the organization evolved, even though I was present for parts of it. I finish this work even more impressed with the Institute and the people that made it than I was when I began. It has been a pleasure and an honor to have made this journey.

ACKNOWLEDGMENTS

THIS ACCOUNT OF NORTH CASCADES INSTITUTE's first 35 years was made possible by my relationships with key players in the story over most of that time. They, of course, are the story, but they also taught me much as I shared the journey with them. Foremost among the staff in this regard over the years were Saul Weisberg, Jeff Giesen, Tracie Johannessen, Kristofer Gilje, Jason Ruvelson, Christian Martin, Tanya Anderson, and Kris Molesworth. From them, I learned what I know about how an educational non-profit can evolve and succeed. National Park Service Superintendents John Reynolds, Bill Paleck, and Chip Jenkins gave me many insights into their agency and how creative and flexible administrators can make partnerships like that between the small Institute and large federal agencies thrive. Other North Cascades National Park staff Bob Mierendorf, Tim Manns, Gerry Cook, and Mike Brondi shared much of their knowledge with me over the years. As I served on the Institute Board, colleagues Chuck Robinson, Jeanne Muir, and Brian Scheuch broadened my understanding of how boards should function and, as veterans of the business world tempered idealism with pragmatic insights into what was necessary to make viable an organization like the Institute.

As I worked on this project, my greatest Institute supporter was Saul Weisberg whom I interviewed and queried often over five years. He read the entire manuscript several times and offered suggestions that greatly improved and corrected it. Other Institute staff who helped in the preparation were Jodi Broughton, Christian Martin, Stephanie Friesen, and Kim Nelson. Thanks to them all.

The publishing team at Village Books agreed to publish Teaching in the Rain as a Chuckanut Edition, and shepherd it through the final stages. Thanks to Paul Hanson, Chloe Hovind, Jessica Moreland, and everyone else involved. I appreciate their patience and expertise.

Finally, my wife and partner in many projects, Susan Morgan, has read the manuscript many times and offered much helpful advice. She has supported me in every way, and I thank her for all that she does to keep me going.

NOTES

1   Samuel P. Hays, *Beauty, Health and Permanence: Environmental Politics in the United States, 1955-1985. New York: Cambridge University Press*, 1987.

2   Arthur R. Kruckeberg, *The Natural History of the Puget Sound Country.* Seattle: University of Washington Press, 1991, p. 131.

3   United States, 64th Congress, First Session, August 25, 1916. *U.S. Statutes at Large,* 39:535.

4   Stephen Mather, Reports of the Dept. of the Interior for the Fiscal Year Ended June 30, 1917.

5   Lane in Robert Sterling Yard, *The National Parks Portfolio*, Washington D.C.: Dept. of Interior, 1917.

6   Memorandum, Dickenson to Regional Directors and Superintendents, March 2, 1982, quoted in Barry Mackintosh, "Interpretation in the National Park Service: A Historical Perspective," p. 101.

7   John Reynolds interview in Tracie Johannessen, "Partnering for Success," NCI, 2009, p. 4.

8   Brian Scheuch interview with Christian Martin, 2011.

9   Robert Michael Pyle interview with Christian Martin, 2011.

10   Thomas Lowe Fleischner interview with Christian Martin, 2011.

11   Jon Jarvis interview in Tracie Johannessen, "Partnering for Success," 2009. p. 4.

12   Jon Jarvis, in Tracie Johannessen, "Partnering for Success," NCI, 2009, p.7.

13   Dean Shumway, www.Seattle.gov/light/skagit/license.asp.

14   John Reynolds, in Tracie Johannessen, "Partnering for Success," NCI, 2009, p. 9.

15   Settlement Agreement on Recreation and Aesthetics, p. 36. http://www.seattle.gov/light/skagit/docs/Recreation%20and%20Visual%20Quality%20settlemnt%20AGREEMNT.pdf

16   David Hall, interview with Christian Martin, 2011.

17   Skagiteec.org/about/high-ross-treaty.

18   North Cascades Institute Statement of Beliefs and Core Themes, n.d.

19   Rachel Carson, *The Sense of Wonder*. New York: Harper and Row, 1965, p. 45.

20   Henry Beston, *The Outermost House*. New York: Henry Holt, 1928, p. 217.

21   Scott Slovic in Robert Michael Pyle, *Walking the High Ridge: Life as a Field Trip*. Minneapolis, MN: Milkweed Editions, 2000, p. 127.

22   Bob Pyle interview with Christian Martin, 2011.

23   Stephen R. Kellert, "Experiencing Nature: Affective, Cognitive, and Evaluative Development in Children," in Peter H. Kahn, Jr. and Stephen R, Kellert, eds., *Children and Nature: Psychological, Sociocultural, and Evolutionary Investigations*. Cambridge, MA: The MIT Press, 2002, p. 136.

24   Megan McGinty comment to Elizabeth Keating in NCI Blog Archive #91, July 23, 2009.

25   Cascade Climate Challenge participant quotes are from Elizabeth Keating Blog post, NCI Blog Archives 83 and 84, September 20 and 24, 2010.

26   Kate Rinder, "A Confluence of Young Leaders," NCI Blog Archive #81, Nov. 17, 2010.

27   Mollie Behn, "Fueling the Fire: North Cascades Institute Path for Youth," *Clearing*, 2012. Accessed at http://www.clearingmagazine.org/NCI-FuelingTheFire.html.

28   Tracie Johannessen, "2016 Program Overview," NCI, p. 17.

29   Molly Hashimoto, "Mists, Forests and Glacial Lakes," NCI Catalogue, Spring/Summer 2006, p. 22.

30 Tracie Johannessen, "2016 Program Overview," NCI, p. 16.

31 Tracie Johannessen, "2016 Program Overview," NCI, p. 19.

32 Tracie Johannessen, "2016 Program Overview," NCI, p. 14.

33 Jan Masaoka, "The Governance/Support Model for Nonprofit Boards," http://blueavocado.org/board-of-directors/the-governance-support-model-for-nonprofit-boards/

34 Tracie Johannessen, "Case Study: Partnering for Success," NCI, 2009, p. 7.

35 Saul Weisberg, "Nonprofit Partnerships: Competition and Collaboration," presentation to Whatcom Council of Nonprofits, May 3, 2007.

36 National Park Service Interdisciplinary Team, "North Cascades National Park Complex and North Cascades Institute Partnership Review," November 3, 2016, p. 25.

37 Sterling Clarren letter to Acting Regional Director NPS Region 9 Woody Smeck, July 30, 2020.

38 IDT Report, p. 15.

39 Office of the Inspector General, U.S. Department of the Interior, "The National Park Service Need to Improve Oversight of Residential Environmental Learning Centers," December 2019.

40 Asa Duffee, "Land Acknowledgements: Why and How are Nature Centers Using Them?" http://blog.ncascades.org/odds-and-ends/land-acknowledgements-why-and-how-are-nature-centers-using-them/

41 "Tomorrow's Leaders Concerned About Climate Change at North Cascades." https://www.nationalparkstraveler.org/2020/11/tomorrows-leaders-concerned-about-climate-change-north-cascades.

42 NCI Blog Post, "Connections: Outdoor Learning During a Pandemic," http://blog.ncascades.org/mountain-school/connections-2020.

INDEX

Figures are indicated with italic locators. Acronyms are used in subheadings. All acronyms are listed as main headings and spelled out.

NUMBERS

2021 Emergency Response Procedures (NCELE), 98

A

A Natural History Backpack in the Glacier Peak Wilderness Area, 63
acknowledgments, land, 193–194, 217
ADA accessibility (Americans with Disabilities Act), 90
Adirondacks (NY), 191
administration, nonprofit, 77, 78, 178
adult programming, 143–157
    conferences, 153–157
    Diablo Downtimes, 149
    Elderhostel programming, 143–145
    Family Getaways, 91, *94*, 104, 149
    retail stores, 151–153
    retreats, 145–148
    seminars, 31, 103, 139, 168
    Skagit Tours, 150–151
advocacy, conservation, 16, 20–21, 179–180
aesthetics of place, 7, 8, 49, 63, 64
African Americans, 190–192
agency training, 34–35
Alaska National Interest Land and Conservation Act, 35
Alice Ross (vessel), 150, 151

Allen, Margie, 16, 180
alpine ecology, 5, 134, 139
Alpine Lakes Wilderness, 2
Americans with Disabilities Act (ADA), 90
amnesia, ecological, 9, 104–105, 157
amphibian ecology, 122
ANCA (Association of Nature Center Administrators), 193–194
Anderson, Tanya, 80
Angell, Tony, 149
Anishinaabe Peoples, 206
Annual Writing Retreat, 177
anti-environmentalism ideology, 156–157
Antioch College (OH), 12
Antioch University (Seattle), 13
Art Afield: A Plein Air Retreat, 147
Arthur Carhart Wilderness Training Center, 113–114, 115
Artist Point, 59
art/writing at NCI
    adult seminars, 60–61, 63
    Art Afield: A Plein Air Retreat, 147
    Base Camp and, 150
    catalogs, NCI, 180
    COVID-19, 196
    Diablo Creative Arts Retreats, 146–147
    Drawing from Nature: Blending Art and Science in the Classroom, 140

art/writing at NCI (*continued*)
    Earth's Wild Music: Celebrating and Defending the Songs of the Natural World (Moore), 198
    instructors of, 60, 147–148, 166
    Nature Writers Retreat, 146
    Sourdough Speakers Series, 92, 148–149
    Writing Retreat, Annual, 177
Association for Experiential Education, 26
Association of Nature Center Administrators (ANCA), 193–194
Audubon Society, National, 16
Avarna Group, 195

B
Babcock, Scott, 23, 146
backpacking *see* hiking
Baker, Mount *see* Mount Baker
Baker Lake/River, 122, 131, 161
bald eagles, 58–59, 62, 66, 82, 110, 130
Bald Eagles of the Upper Skagit, 66
Bannick, Paul, 181, 198
Base Camp, 148, 149
Baskets from Northwest Landscapes, 148
Bass, Rick, 146, 166
bears, 18, 63, 81–82, 120, 121, 155
Beats on the Peaks: Lookout Poets of the North Cascades, 165
Beauty, Health and Permanence: Environmental Politics in the United States, 1955-1985 (Hays), 215
Bedford, Laura, 167
Behn, Mollie, 125
    "Fueling the Fire: North Cascades Institute Path for Youth," 216
Belcher, Jennifer, 35
Bellingham
    public schools, 136–138, 174
    University of, 74
    Village Books, 25, 174, 198
    Waterbirds of Bellingham Bay, 66
Bennett, Stephanie, 80
Berry, Wendell, 61
Bertelina, Jim, 180
Beston, Henry, 61
Big Beaver Creek/Camp, 109

Big Canoe and You, The, 91
birds
    Birds, Bugs, and Load-bearing Llamas, 106–107
    Birds of the North Cascades, 20
    Eagle Festival, 59
    Eagle Watchers, 58, 60, 62, 172
    eagles, bald, 58–59, 62, 82, 110, 130
    eagles, golden, 145, *148*
    Eagles, Swans, Seals & You: An Outdoor Adventure on a Northwest Shore, 144
    hawks, 145, *148*
    "know a wren" (teaching concept), 104–105
    loons, 110
    mergansers, 82, 110
    Migratory Bird Festival, 130
    osprey, 110
    owls, 20–21, 57, 82, 179
    ravens, 106
    snow geese, 63
    study of, 145
    swallows, 110
    trumpeter swans, 63
    Water Birds of Bellingham Bay, 66
    White Birds of Winter, 63
    Wings over the Methow: Birds and Butterflies from Sagebrush to Snow, 63
Birds, Bugs, and Load-bearing Llamas, 106–107
Birds of the North Cascades, 20
black bears, 81–82
Black Lives Matter, 189
Blackwell, Michel, 168
Blaine School District, 197
Blue Heron Farm, 94, 174
Blue House, 83
Board of Directors
    advocacy, environmental, 179
    Allen, Margie, 16
    Clarren, Sterling, 186
    Cook, "Captain" Gerry, 165
    Cooperative Agreement, 187
    Dickenson, Russ, 22

Board of Directors (*continued*)
  Dupre, Robyn, 161
  EDI and, 190–191, 195
  Fleischner, Tom, 161
  founding, 16–17
  Gorton, Jean, 177
  governance/support model, 163–164
  Markworth, Peg, 40
  Miles, John, 34
  mission of NCI, 29
  mitigation, education as, 40–41
  Muir, Jeanne, 171
  NCELC construction, 51
  retail stores, 151
  retreats, 169
  Reynolds, John, 16
  Robinson, Chuck, 174
  role in NCI, 162–164
  Scheuch, Brian, 31
  staff and, 160, 169
  Strategic Plan, 2020-2024, 199–200
  Weisberg replacement, 204–205
  youth programming, 125
  see also budgeting, NCI; business of
    NCI; finances/fundraising
Bogne, Grace, 124
Book Fair (Seattle), 174
Boston Basin, 122
Bowerman, CeCe, 70
Braaten, Anne, 121
Breadfarm, 94, 174
British Columbia, 20, 44, 55
Brodie, Debra, 167
Brondi, Mike, 121, *169*
Broughton, Jodi, 167, 206
Brower, David, 8
Brown, Amy, 84–85, 114, 115–116, *116*
Brown's Farm, 67
budgeting
  Cascade Climate Challenge, 121
  comparison 1986 vs. 2020, 159
  expansion of NCI, 31–32
  Great Recession, 177, 178–182
  Moneyshed, 68, 160, 161, 167, 176, 206
  Mountain School, 55–56
  NCELC, 89–90

  oversite of, 167–168
  youth programming, 103–104
Burgess, Don
  Cascade Climate Challenge, 121
  graduate program, 73
  Mountain School, 82
  NCELC staff, 68, 72, *163*, 169
  Spring Ornithology (NCI), 66
business of NCI
  Board of Directors, 162–164
  Conferences and Retreats, 153–157,
    168–170
  contributors, agency, 170–172
  Elderhostels, 144
  instructors, 164–166
  nonprofit status, 16
  office work, 25
  overview, 159–162
  partnerships, 172–175
  retail stores, 151–153
  Scheuch, Brian, 22
  staff, 31, 166–170
  success, 178–182
  technology, 168
  youth education, 103
  see also budgeting; finances/fundraising
Butterflies of the South Cascades, 63

C
canoeing
  Canoe Camp, Discovery, 85, 107, 108–
    111, 114, 115
  Cascade Climate Challenge, 122
  Diablo Lake, 91, 108, 109
  Family Getaways, 155
  Learning Center Day Trips, 92
  North Cascades Naturalist Retreat,
    90–91
  risk management, 99
  Ross Lake, *116*
Canopy Crane, Wind River, 140
Capen, Peter, 63
Cares Act Paycheck Protection Program
  (PPP), 196
Carson, Rachel, 61, 128
Casa de San Jose (WA), 130

Cascade Climate Challenge, 104, 117, 120, 121–124
Cascade Crest, 23
Cascade Divide, 5
Cascade Pass, 74, 80, 122
Cascadia Weekly, 134–135
"Case Study: Partnering for success" (Johannessen), 217
catalogs, NCI/NCELC
    Base Camp (2010), 149
    bird seminars (1994 and 1997), 66
    Contributing Organizations and Partners (2001-2002), 174
    Elderhostel courses (2000-2001), 144
    Family Getaways (2005), 91
    food at NCELC (2007), 94
    Learning Center Experience (2007), 93
    marketing/communications, 180–181
    Mountain Camp (1992), 105–106, 107
    Nature Writers Retreat (1998), 146
    NCELC opening (2005), 90
    North Cascades Discovery (2002), 110–111
    Sourdough Speakers Series (2009), 149
    Wind River Canopy Crane (2002), 140
Catholic Housing Services of Washington, 130
Cedar Summer, 106
cedar trees, 4, 5, 106, 109
Celebrating Earth's Wild Music, 198
Celebrating Wildflowers, 60
Celebrating Wildflowers: Educator's Guide to the Appreciation and Conservation of Native Plants (Scherrer, Johannessen), 140
Centrum (Port Townsend, WA), 26
challenges/opportunities, current, 185–200
Chelan National Recreation Area, 4, 17, 49, 152
Chelan Sawtooth Wilderness, 80
Children and Nature: Psychological, Sociocultural, and Evolutionary Investigations (Kahn and Kellert), 216
Chon, SuJ'n, 168
Choose Your Own Adventure Programs, 208

Chu, Jim, 58, 172
City Light *see* Seattle City Light
Claasen, Charles, 91, 92, 93
Clarren, Sterling, 186–189, 200
Clear Creek/Lake Camps, 32
Clearing: A Resource Journal of Environmental and Place-based Education, 125, 216
climate change, 104, 117–124, 156, 196, 209
climax forest, 105
Clipper canoes, 109, 115
Cole, David, 34
Coleman Glacier, 6
College of the Environment at Western Washington University *see* Huxley College of Environmental Studies
Colonial Creek Campground, 105, 106, 108, 164
Colonial Peaks, 81, 147
Columbia River Indians and Their Land, 63
Colville Confederated Tribes, 194
Coming to Know the Land: The Natural History of Puget Sound Country, 63
communications *see* marketing/ communications
community and school programming
    Concrete Summer Learning Adventure, 104, 132–134
    Forest School, 136–138
    Kulshan Creek Neighborhood Youth Program, 130–132
    teacher education, 139–141
    various programs, 134–136
    see also Mountain School
Community Health Outreach Program, United General Hospital, 132
Concrete Summer Learning Adventure, 104, 132–134
conferences/retreats, 145–148, 153–157, 168–170
"Confluence of Young Leaders, A" (Rinder), 216
Congress, U.S. 64th, 215

Connections (Whatcom Co. School District program), 197–198
conservation, environmental
  advocacy, 16, 20–21, 179–180
  Alaska National Interest Land and Conservation Act, 35
  EDI and, 191–192
  founders, NCI, 7
  Reagan, Ronald, 16
  recycling/sustainability, 46, 50, 90, 94–95
  wilderness, 2, 29, 114, 191
  see also North Cascades Conservation Council (NCCC); Skagit Watershed Education Project (SWEP)
construction, NCELC
  avalanche, rock, 74–75
  Burgess, Don, 73
  finances, 41
  LEED and, 50
  NPS support, 170–171
  Reach for the Peaks (capital campaign), 177
  remediation, site, 95
  schedule, 50–51, 68
  Seattle City Light, 46–47
Cook, "Captain" Gerry
  adult seminars, 66–67
  fundraising efforts, 176
  Indigenous Peoples studies, 193
  instructor, 167
  NCELC career, 165
  NCI relationship, 171
  remediation, 115
  Ross Mule, 110, 122
  shelters, NCELC, 79, 97, 99
core beliefs/themes of programming, 54, 61, 64–65
Corkran, Ned, 93
Cornet Bay, 130
Cornet Bay Environmental Learning Center, 67
Coryell-Martin, Maria, 147
COVID-19, 134, 150, 185, 189, 195–200, 205, 207–209
Craters of the Moon National Monument, 43

creeks see rivers/creeks
cultural history
  core beliefs/themes of programming, 54, 61, 64
  Elderhostel programming, 144
  field seminars, 21
  graduate program, 74
  Kulshan Creek Neighborhood Youth Program, 130
  North Cascades Discovery, 111
  People of the Upper Skagit, 193
Curry, Jocelyn, 147

D
dams
  Diablo Dam, 40, 108, 150
  environmental impact, 97, 122
  Gorge Dam, 39, 150
  risk management, 98
  Ross Dam, 40, 41, 55, 108–109, 150–151
  see also relicensing of Skagit Hydroelectric Project; Skagit Hydroelectric Project; Skagit River
Day Trips, 92, 148, 208
Deadhorse Point, 24
Dean, Eric, 92, 96
Deer Creek/shelter, 49, 90, 96, 97
deficit disorder, nature, 9, 104–105, 157
DeLeon, Mark, 64
Deming, Alison, 146, 166
Denny Middle School (Seattle), 190
Denver Service Center (NPS), 37, 41
Department of Fish and Wildlife, Washington, 58
Department of the Interior Office of Inspector General, U.S., 217
Department of Transportation, Washington, 58
Depression, Great, 150
design process, NCELC, 47–48
Desolation Peak, 122, 165
Detrich, Bec, 205–209
Devil's Creek, 110
Devil's Junction Campsite, 109
Dewey, John, 32

Diablo Creative Arts Retreats, 146–147

Diablo Dam, 40, 108, 150

Diablo Downtimes, 149

Diablo Lake, 5, 49, 75, 91, 108, 109, 147, 204

Diablo Lake Resort, 41–42, 45, 46, 48, 95

Dickenson, Russ, 19, 22, 31, 161, 162, 215

digital seminars, 198

Diobsud Creek, 83

Discover Your Northwest, 151

Discovery Canoe Camp, 85, 107, 108–111, 114, 115

Discovery Dayhikes, 20

diversity *see* equity, diversity, and inclusion

Douglas fir, 4–5, 106, 147

Drawing from Nature: Blending Art and Science in the Classroom, 140

Drawing the Details, 92

Drum, Ryan, 63

Drummond, Benj, 124, 168, 180–181

Drummond, David, 66, 144

Duffee, Asa, 193–194

"Land Acknowledgments: Why and How are Nature Centers Using Them?" 217

Dupre, Robyn, 30, 67, 161, 167

Dyer, Polly, 4

E

Eagle Festival, 59

Eagle Watchers, 58, 60, 62, 172

eagles, bald, 58–59, 62, 82, 110, 130

eagles, golden, 145, *148*

Eagles, Swans, Seals & You: An Outdoor Adventure on a Northwest Shore, 144

Earnst, John, 37, 42, 43–44

Earth in Mind (Orr), 202

Earthcorps, 124

Earth's Wild Music: Celebrating and Defending the Songs of the Natural World (Moore), 198

East Bank Trail, 122

Easton Glacier, 6, 59, 112, 122

Eco-Geographic Basis for Lepidoptera Conservation, The (Pyle), 61

ecological amnesia, 9, 104–105, 157

ecology

  alpine, 5, 134, 139

  amphibian, 122

  Cascade Crest, of, 23

  forest, 5, 121, 140

  insect, 140, 145

  stream, 106, 118

  tidal, 144

  tree canopy, 140

ecosystem management, 21, 36–37, 56

ecosystems, North Cascades

  forest ecosystems, 5

  management, 21, 36–37, 56

  mission of NCI, 44–45, 153

  place, aesthetics of, 3

  programming, NCI and NCELC, 16, 19, 20, 21, 37, 89, 137

EDI (equity, diversity, and inclusion), 114, 124, 185, 189–195, 206, 207

Educator's Guide to the Samish and Padilla Bay Watersheds, An (Johannessen), 140

Eisinger, Ann, 144

Elderhostel programming, 64, 66, 143–145

Emergency Medical Technicians, 100

Emergency Response Procedures, 2021 (NCELC), 98

Emmons Glacier, 112

endangered species, 20–21, 57, 121, 179

Endicott, Catherine, 206

environmental advocacy, 16, 20–21, 179–180

Environmental Architecture: Green Building Design and Operation, 95–96

environmental education *see* programming, NCI and NCELC; youth programming

Environmental Education in the Classroom and Field: A Workshop for Teachers, 66

environmental generational amnesia, 9, 104–105, 157

equity, diversity, and inclusion (EDI), 114, 124, 185, 189–195, 206, 207

Evans, Dan, 34
Evergreen State College, 12
"Everyone lives in a watershed"
        (educational concept), 56
Evolution of Feathers, 149
executive director search, 204–205
expansion of NCI, 31–37
*Experiencing Nature: Affective, Cognitive
        and Evaluative Development in
        Children* (Kellert), 216
experiential learning
    Association for Experiential Education,
        26
    description, 2–3
    Dewey, John, 32
    graduate program, 76–79
    instructors, NCI, 23, 61–62

F

Facing Climate Change (Drummond and
        Steele), 124
Fairchild, Christie, 68, 109, 138, *163*, 167
Family Getaways, 91, *94*, 104, 148
Family Nature Programs, NCI, 20
Fawn Shelter, 97
Federal Energy Regulatory Commission
        (FERC), 40, 41, 43, 173, 185, 207
Federal Power Commission, 40
Ferguson, Gary, 146
field seminars
    adult seminars, 23–25, 29, 60–64,
        143–145
    art/writing at NCI, 92
    digital, 198
    EDI and, 189
    focus of NCI, early, 22
    graduate program, *79*
    initial catalog, 16, 19–20
    instructors, 164–165, 167
    online education, 198
    revenue, 31, 175
    risk management, 98
    teacher education, 139
    youth programming, 103
finances/fundraising
    auctions, 163

Board of Directors, 25, 104, 162, 175–
        176, 177–178
    executive director, 55
    Mountain School, 56
    NCELC, 47, 89
    programming, 42
    retail stores, 151
    staff, 167
    technology and, 168
    youth programming, 104, 176
    see also budgeting
Fire and Ice, 106
Fish and Wildlife, Washington
        Department of, 58
Fleischner, Tom, 1–2, 11–14, 15–17, *25*,
        26, 161
Fluharty, Dave, 39–41, 42
Fodor, Paul, 35
food at NCELC, 92, 93–94, 100, 149, 169,
        174, 206
Foodshed Project, 94, 100, 149, 174
forest ecology, 5, 78, 121, 140
Forest School, 104, 134, 136–138
Forest Service *see* U.S. Forest Service
Forest Service International Programs, 172
Forest Stewardship Council, 95
Foresta Institute, 13
Fort Casey (WA), 130
founding of NCI, 1–2, 11–26, *12*
Four Winds Camp, 67
Fourth of July Pass, 105
Free or Reduced Lunch (federal program),
        197
Friesen, Stephanie, 206
From Stream to Sea: the Story of the
        Northwest Salmon, 63
From the Ground Up in the Wind River
        Canopy Crane, 140
*Fueling the Fire: North Cascades Institute
        Path for Youth* (Behn), 216
fundraising *see* finances/fundraising

G

genocide, 192
Geological Survey, U.S., 111
Geology of the North Cascades, 20

Giesen, Jeff, 138, 161, 167, 168, 206
Gifford Pinchot National Forest, 140
Gilje, Kristofer, 99, 147–148, 161, 167, 170, 205–206
Girard, Chris Kiser, 79
Girls on Ice, 85, 111–113
Glacier National Park, 117
Glacier Peak Wilderness, 2, 4, 80, 111, 181
glaciers
    Coleman Glacier, 6
    Easton Glacier, 6, 112, 119, 122
    Emmons Glacier, 112
    Girls on Ice, 111–113
    Glacier Peak Wilderness, 111
    Mount Jack, 110
    Mountain Camp, 106
    Pleistocene era, 121
    recession of, 117, 118, 122
    South Cascade Glacier, 111
Gloss, Molly, 146, 166
Goat Wall, 62
golden eagles, 145, 148
Golden Gate National Recreation Area, 205
Golden West Visitor Center, 151, 152
Goldsworthy, Pat, 4
Gordon Carter Environmental Education Site, 137, 138
Gorge Dam, 39, 150
Gorge Inn, 150, 151
Gorton, Jean, 177
"Governance/Support Model for Nonprofit Boards, The" (Masaoka), 217
governance/support model of Board of Directors, 163–164
graduate program, 20, 71–86
    challenges and opportunities, 80–85
    development, 71–74
    early years, 74–76
    EDI and, 190–191
    end of, 85–86, 185
    experiential learning, 76–79
    field study, 79
    Huxley College of Environmental Studies, 174
    management, 169–170

Nonprofit Leadership and Administration, 77–78
    outdoor classroom, 79–80
    staff, 168
    teacher education, 141
Grand Teton National Park, 3
Great Depression, 150
Great Recession, 177
Great Smoky Mountains National Park, 3
Green Building Council, U.S., 50, 95
Grinstad, Roxanne, 146–147
grizzly bears, 18, 63, 155
Grumbine, Ed, 1–2, 11–14, 32

H
Haavik, Jay, 180
habitat restoration, 95, 115, 122, 130, 132, 177
Hall, David, 48–49, 50, 95–96
Hambleton, Jeff, 134–135
Hamblin, Codi, 138
Hammerly, Ramona, 180
Hanson, Thor, 149
Hardesty, Jeff, 1–2, 11–14
Harris, Jim, 165, 171
Harts Pass, 23
Hashimoto, Molly, 92, 147, 181
    "Mists, Forests and Glacial Lakes," 216
Haupt, Lyanda Lynn, 166
hawks, 145, 148
Hays, Samuel P., Beauty, Health and Permanence: Environmental Politics in the United States, 1955-1985, 215
Healy, Jan, 152
Henry, Eric, 136, 139
Henry Klein Partnership, 48, 95–96
Henry M. Jackson Foundation, 32
Hewitt, Sally, 67, 180
Higgins, Joe, 34
hiking
    adult and family programming, 21, 24, 149–150
    Cascade Climate Challenge, 121–122
    communities, 19
    Discovery Dayhikes, 20

hiking (*continued*)
Girls on Ice, 111
I'm Lichen Hikin', 91
Mountain School, 105
NCELC, 92–93
Path for Youth Initiative, 126
place, emersion in, 77
Railroad Grade, 6
Sourdough Speakers Series, 149
stewardship programs, 59
Hispanic Peoples, 130, 189, 190–192
history, natural *see* natural history
History of the Skagit River (video series), 196
Hixon, Mark, 198
Hounsell, Elaine, 15
Howard, Benjie, 124
Hudson, Larry, 36, 172
Hughes, Holly, 146
Hulmes, Doug, 26
Hunn, Eugene, 64
Hutchinson, David, 146
Huxley College of Environmental Studies, 17, 31, 72–73, 76, 117, 173–174, 191
hydroelectric power, 46, 118–119, 150–151, 165–166
see also relicensing of Skagit Hydroelectric Project; Skagit Hydroelectric Project

I
IDT (interdisciplinary team), 187–188
Illuminated Field Journals, 148
I'm Lichen Hikin', 91
Incident Command System, 98
inclusion *see* equity, diversity, and inclusion
Inclusion and Community Partners, 169
Indigenous Peoples
Colville Confederated Tribes, 194
cultural destruction, 191
EDI and, 189, 191–194
environmental tension, 192
Lummi Nation, 194
NCI mission, 207
Nlaka'pamux Nation, 194

Nooksack Tribe, 194
North Cascades inhabitation, 7, 54, 106, 109, 193
Samish Indian Nation, 194
Sauk-Suiattle Indian Tribe, 194
Sto:lo Nation, 194
Swinomish Indian Tribal Community, 194
Syilx/Okanagan Nation, 194
Upper Skagit Indian Tribe, 194
insect ecology, 140, 145
Inspector General, U.S. Department of the Interior Office of, 217
Inspiring Girls Expeditions, 113
instructors, NCI, 164–166
art/writing at NCI, 60, 147–148, 166
core beliefs/themes of programming, 65
experiential learning, 23, 61–62
Girls on Ice, 111
graduate program, 76–77
initial faculty, 16
interpreters, NPS, 32
Mountain School, 33, 56, 82, 83, 84, 196
retreats, 145
risk management, 98, 100, 109
volunteer, 136, 138
see also bears
Interagency Grizzly Bear Committee, 155
interdisciplinary team (IDT), 187–188
International District Housing Alliance Wild, 123
interpretation (educational approach), 18–19, 30, 61, 96, 106, 121, 123, 150, 186
Interpretation in the National Park Service: A Historical Perspective (Mackintosh), 215
Ish River, 184
Island Ethnobiology by Kaya, 63

J
Jack Mountain, 109
Jackson Foundation, 175
Jarvis, John
anti-environmentalism, 156–157
expansion of NCI, 30
NCELC relationship, 41–43, 44, 47

Jarvis, John (*continued*)
  NCI relationship, 170, 173
  North Cascades as ecosystem, 21
  NPS and NCI partnership, 38, *43*
  Parks Climate Challenge, 117
Jefferson, Anne, 64
Jenkins, Chip, *43*, 84, 117, 125, 151, 170–171, 173, 185
Jim Crow, 191
Jipson, Lansia, 93
Johannessen, Tracie
  "Case Study: Partnering for Success," 217
  Celebrating Wildflowers: Educator's Guide to the Appreciation and Conservation of Native Plants, 140
  Concrete Summer Learning Adventure, 132–133
  Conferences and Retreats, on, 153–154
  educational programs, 161–162
  Educator's Guide to the Samish and Padilla Bay Watersheds, An, 140
  Forest School, 138
  graduate program, 84
  Mountain School, 32, 53, 72
  Partnering for Success, 215, 216
  program director, 168
  retail stores, 152
  Sharing the Skagit: An Educator's Guide to the Skagit River Basin (Weisberg, Riedel, Johannessen, Scherrer), 140
  Skagit Tours, 150–151
  Skagit Watershed Education Project Teacher Handbook, 140
  staff and, *163*, 167
  teacher education, 140
John Day Fossil Beds National Monument, 144
Jordan, Tim, 1–2, 11–14

K
Kahn, Peter H. Jr. and Stephen Kellert, *Children and Nature: Psychological, Sociocultural, and Evolutionary Investigations*, 216
kayaking, 63, 85, 109, 196
Keating, Elizabeth, 118, 122, 216

Kellert, Stephen, 107
  Children and Nature: Psychological, Sociocultural, and Evolutionary Investigations (with Peter H. Kahn Jr.), 216
  "Experiencing Nature: Affective, Cognitive and Evaluative Development in Children," 216
Kendall Elementary School, 197
Kerouac, Jack, 61, 165
Kingsolver, Barbara, 61, 67, 101, 146, 166, 177
Kinship Conservation Fellowships, 154
Kittredge, Bill, 146, 166
"know a wren" (teaching concept), 104–105
Kodner, Robin, 135
Koppes, Michele, 111
Kovalicky, Tom, 34
Kraus, Fayette, 145
Kruckeberg, Art, 5, 6, 61, 62, 63, 139, 145
  Natural History of the Puget Sound Country, The, 77, 215
Kulshan Creek Neighborhood Youth Program, 104, 129, 130–132, 172
Kuntz, Rusty, 144
Kurko, Keith, 45

L
La Conner Country Inn, 144
Lac Courte Oreilles band (Ojibwe people), 206
Lady of the Lake (vessel), 152
Laitner, Bill, 41, 43
Lake Whatcom, 137
lakes
  Baker Lake, 122, 131, 161
  Chelan, Lake, 4, 17, 49, 152
  Diablo Lake, *5*, 49, *75*, 91, 108, 109, 147, 204
  Ross Lake, 11, 66, 108, *112*, 122, 171
  Whatcom, Lake, 137
  see also rivers/creeks; Skagit River
land acknowledgments, 193–194, 217
"Land Acknowledgments: Why and How are Nature Centers Using Them?" (Duffee), 193–194, 217
Lane, Franklin, 18

Last Child in the Woods:Saving Our Children from Nature-Deficit Disorder (Louv), 104, 157
leadership development, 113–114, 115–116, 195
Leadership in Energy and Design (LEED), 50, 95
Learning Center Day Trips, 92
Leavenworth (WA), 60, 67, 89, 146
Lentfer, Hank, 198
Leopold, Estella, 146
Lesly, Craig, 146
Lester, Bill, 14, 15, 20, 34
Lewis, John, 195
LGBTQ rights, 189
Lightning Creek Campsite/Float, 11, 110
Lily Shelter, 97
Living with Mountains: A Guide for Learning and Teaching about Mountain Landscapes (Scherrer, Weisberg), 140
logging
    advocacy, environmental, 179
    industry and NCI, 35–36
    Mount Baker-Snoqualmie National Forest, 20–21
    North Cascades, 2, 5
    timber wars, 37
Louv, Richard, 104, 142
    Last Child in the Woods: Saving Our Children from Nature Deficit Disorder, 157
    Nature Principle, The, 142
Luckmann, Chuck, 68
    Sharing the Skagit: An Educator's Guide to the Skagit River Basin (Weisberg, Riedel, Johannessen, Scherrer), 140
    Voices Along the Skagit: Teaching the History of the First People in the Skagit Watershed, 140
Lummi Basketry, 64
Lummi Nation, 7, 134, 194

M

Mackintosh, Barry, *Interpretation in the National Park Service: A Historical Perspective,* 215

Major, Ted, 3
management
    ecosystem, 21, 36–37, 56
    natural resources, 7, 8, 21, 36
    risk, 98–100, 109, 112, 115, 131, 138, 175
    wilderness, 34–35, 37
Mann, Lee, 16, 149, 180
Manning, Harvey, 4
Manns, Tim, 44, 84, 171
Marblemount Wilderness Office, 15, 98
Marin, Christian, 104
marketing/communications
    Board of Directors, 164
    Drummond, Benj, 168
    executive director search, 190
    graduate program, 78
    Moneyshed, 161, 206
    NCELC, 47, 178
    staff leadership, 169
    Taylor-Goodrich, Karen, 187
Markworth, Peg, 39
Martin, Christian, 168, 172, 181, 206, 215
Masaoka, Jan, 162–163
    "Governance/Support Model for Nonprofit Boards, The," 217
Mather, Stephen, 18, 215
Matthews, Daniel, 63
McCabe, Rachelle, 198
McDermott, Laurie, 180
McGinty, Megan, 117–118, 121, 123, 216
McNulty, Tim, 60, 67, 146, 165–166, *167,* 180–181
McWilliams, Doug, 21, 36–37
Meloy, Rebecca, 146
Memoranda of Understanding, 36
Mesa Verde National Park, 18
Methow River, 45
Methow Valley, 63, 66, 144–146, *148*
middle class, white, 191–192
Mierendorf, Bob, 20, 66, 165, *167,* 171, 192–193
Migratory Bird Festival, 130
Miles, John
    Board of Directors, 17, 31, 34, 161
    graduate program, 72–73, 80–81, 86

Miles, John (*continued*)
  Huxley College of Environmental
    Studies dean, 173–174
  NCCC and, 39–41
  resources, natural, 35–36
Miles, Tiya, 192
Miller, Joe, 42
Miller, Keith, 13
Mills, Libby
  art/writing at NCI, 61, 62, 92, 147
  catalog art, 180
  Elderhostel programming, 144
  field seminars, 63, *65*
  instructor, 165
  retreats, 145
mission of NCI
  driving force of organization, 182
  EDI and, 195, 207
  evolution, 29–37, 200
  future of, 209–210
  "mission creep," 144–145, 178–179
  NCELC and, 45, 51, 63, 100
  North Cascades ecosystem, 44
  NPS and, 187
  retail stores, 152–153
  risk management, 99
  Strategic Plan, 2020-2024, 179, 199–200
  teacher education, 139
"Mists, Forests and Glacial Lakes"
    (Hashimoto), 216
mitigation
  education as, 39–44, 45, 47, 51
  environmental impact, 39–40, 42, 164,
    173
Molesworth, Kris, 92, 161, 167, 174
Moneyshed, 68, 160, 161, 167, 176, 206
Moore, Kathleen Dean, 146, 166
  *Earth's Wild Music: Celebrating and
    Defending the Songs of the Natural
    World*, 198
Morgan, Chris, 146
Morris, Doug, 35
Mount Baker
  aesthetics of place, 7
  environmental impact, 59
  Forest School, 104, 134

glaciers, 6, 112, 122
logging, 57
Railroad Grade, 118
Ranger District, 20, 57–58, 59, 130,
  136, 171–172, 197
school districts, 136, 197
Ski Area, 59, 134–135, 152
Snow School, 104, 134
Mount Baker Ranger District, 57–58, 59,
  130, 171–172
Mount Baker School District, 136, 197
Mount Baker Ski Area, 59, 134–135, 152
Mount Baker Snow School, 104, 134
Mount Baker-Snoqualmie National Forest
  educational programs, 129
  logging, 20–21
  Memoranda of Understanding, 36
  NCI relationship, 172
  retail stores, 151
  Snow School, 134
  spotted owl, 58
  youth leadership programming, 123
Mount Rainier, 112, 114, 144
Mount Rainier National Park, 34
Mount Shuksan, 59
Mount Vernon (WA), 48, 53, 54, 98, 130, *132*
Mountain Camp, 56, 85, 104, 105–108, 110
Mountain School
  COVID-19, 195–196, 207
  EDI and, 190
  expansion of NCI, 31–34
  food at NCELC, 94–95
  funding, 175, 177
  graduate program, 72–75, 78–81,
    83–84
  instructors of, 166
  management, 169–170
  National Park Service, 171
  NCELC and, 48, 49, 96–98
  NCI partnerships, 174
  overview, 53–56
  Path for Youth Initiative, 125–126
  school curricula, 134, 193, 207–208
  staff, 168
  teacher education, 139
  youth programming, 104

Mountain Stewards, 59, 172
Mountain Wildflowers, 20
Muir, Jeanne, 171
Muir, John, 8
Muse, Jeff, 68, 92, 96, 99, 165, 169
Myers, Gene, 72, 191

N

National Audubon Society, 16
National Forests
  Gifford Pinchot National Forest, 140
  Mount Baker-Snoqualmie National
    Forest, 20–21, 36, 58, 123, 134, 151,
    172
  Okanogan National Forest, 5, 21, 36, 90
  Wenatchee National Forest, 5, 36, 90
National Oceanic and Atmospheric
    Administration, 40
National Outdoor Leadership School, 13
National Park Fund (WA), 33, 151
National Park Service (NPS)
  career opportunities, 124
  Forest Service relationship, U.S., 21, 35
  logging, 2
  NCELC relationship, 40–42, 90
  NCI relationship, 3, 15–21, 36–37, 43,
    44–45, 84, 117, 160, 170–171, 173
  North Cascades Wild, 115
  Parks Climate Challenge, 119
  Path for Youth Initiative, 125–127
  retail stores, 152
  Ross Lake campsites, 109–110
  Washington Park Service, 34
  youth education, 8, 32
National Parks Foundation, 117, 119
National Wild and Scenic Rivers Act, 58
National Wilderness Preservation System,
    2, 34
National Wildlife Federation, 61
Native Plants of the Eastslope Cascades,
    140
natural history
  art/writing at NCI, 148
  Base Camp, 150
  Discovery Canoe Camp, 110
  eagles, 58, 62

EDI and, 192–193
field seminars, 60–61, 63, 175
Fleischner, Tom, 26
Methow Valley, 66
Mountain Camp, 106
*Natural History of the Puget Sound
  Country, The*, 77, 215
NCI initial focus, 7–8, 13
*Natural History of the Puget Sound
  Country, The* (Kruckeberg), 77, 215
natural resources
  agencies, 35, 57, 117, 174
  Kulshan Creek Neighborhood Youth
    Program, 131
  management, 7, 8, 21, 36
Nature Conservancy Washington Chapter,
    145
nature deficit disorder, 9, 104–105, 157
Nature Interpretation (UWA), 61
Nature Perception and Protection (UWA),
    61
Nature Principle, The (Louv), 142
Nature Writers Retreat, 67, 146, 177
NatureBridge, 205
Navare, Trish, 167
NCCC (North Cascades Conservation
    Council) *see* North Cascades
    Conservation Council
NCELC (North Cascades Environmental
    Learning Center) *see* North
    Cascades Environmental Learning
    Center
NCI (North Cascades Institute) *see* North
    Cascades Institute
Nelson, Richard K., 146
New Perspectives on Natural Resources
    Management on State Lands
    (workshop), 35–36
New Wilderness Project, 124
Newhalem by Night, 151
Newhalem Campground (Park Service)
  Mountain School, 32, 49, 53, *55*, 73–74,
    78, 171
  NCELC and, 97, 113
  NCNP Visitor Center, 41, 45
Next Generation Science Standards, 137, 208

Nlaka'pamux Nation, 7, 40, 194
nonprofit administration, 77–78, 178
Nonprofit Leadership and Administration, 77–78
"Nonprofit Partnerships: Competition and Collaboration" (Weisberg), 174, 217
Nooksack River, 45, 135
Nooksack Tribe, 7, 194
North Cascades Conservation Council (NCCC), 4, 39–41, 42, 45, 47, 164
North Cascades Discovery, 110–111
North Cascades ecosystem, 20, 21, 36–37, 44–45, 89, 181–182
North Cascades Environmental Learning Center (NCELC)
   community and school programming, 129–141
   design process, 47–48
   facility, 89–101
   family education, 91, *94*, 104, 149
   landscaping, 95
   NCI mission, 100
   opening, 75, 100–101
   opposition to, 133–134
   staff, 67–68, 154
   see also construction, NCELC; origins of NCELC
North Cascades Institute (NCI)
   accomplishments, 200
   adult programs, 143–157
   agency training, 34–35
   challenges/opportunities, current, 185–200
   community and school programs, 129–141
   COVID-19, 185, 189, 195–198, 209
   growth of, 29–37
   land acknowledgments, 193–194
   leadership, 203–210
   mission, 29–31, 144, 157, 200, 209–210
   opposition to, 155–156
   reputation, 35, 44
   technology and, 198
   see also Board of Directors; business of NCI; catalogs, NCI; graduate program; origins of NCI; programming, NCI and NCELC; youth programming

North Cascades Landscape Watercolors, 92
North Cascades National Park (NCNP)
   climate change, 117, 120
   complex, park, 4, 11
   educational programs, 19, 66, 123, 129
   establishment, 34
   Kulshan Creek Neighborhood Youth Program, 130
   NCELC and, 47, 90
   NCI relationship, 13–14, 15, 172, 185–187, 206–207
   Skagit river dams, 108
   staff at NCI, *169*
   visitor center, 41, 45, 54, 60, 74, 123
North Cascades Naturalist Retreat: Glaciers, Rivers, Plants and Wildlife, 90–91, 146
North Cascades Visitor Center, 41, 45, 60, 74, 123, 151, 187
North Cascades Wild, 104, 113–116, 130, 131
North Cascades Youth Leadership Conference, a Confluence of Young Leaders, 123–124
Northwest Avalanche Center, 134–135, 136
Northwest Indian College, 136

O
Obama administration, 43, 117
O'Connell, Nick, 146
Office of the Inspector General of the Interior Department, 188
Okanogan Archaeology, 64
Okanogan National Forest, 5, 21, 36, 90
old-growth forests, 5, 105, 140
Olympic Mountains, 114
Olympic National Park, 13–14, 19, *25*, 34
operations (NCELC), 89–101
opportunities/challenges, current, 185–200
origins of NCELC, 39–51
   concept, 44–47
   mitigation, education as, 39–44, 45, 47, 51
   see also construction, NCELC

origins of NCI, 1–26
  aesthetics, 7–8
  business aspects, 25–26
  cultural elements, 6–7
  field seminars, 23–25
  formation, 11–26
  founders, 1–2, 11–14
  launching, 14–17
  leadership, 22–23
  National Park Service support, 17–21
  place, 3–6
  program concepts, 9
  timing, 2–3
Orr, David, *Earth in Mind*, 202
Outdoor Schools for All, 208
Outermost House, The (Beston), 61

P
Pack Forest (UWA), 36
Palleck, Bill, 43–44, 50, 153, *169*, 170–171, 173
Parelskin, Michael, *116*
Park Service *see* National Park Service
Park Service Interpretive Rangers, 32
Parks Climate Challenge, 104, 117–120, 122
"Partnering for Success" (Johannessen), 215, 216
Pasayten Wilderness, 2, 4, 80, 107
Passing of the Paddle, *75*
Path for Youth Initiative, 125–127
Paul Allen Family Foundation, 121
Paulson, Dennis, 62, 145
People of the Mountain World, 20
People of the Upper Skagit, 66, 165, 193
Peterson, David, 146
Pettit, Erin, 111, 112–113
Photographer's Journey through the North Cascades, A, 149
place, aesthetics of, 7, 8, 49, 63–64
place-based education, 77, 84, 125
Planning for Uncertainty (Weisberg letter), 177
Poetry from the Porch (video series), 196
Port Susan Bay, 144
Porter, Joshua, 80
Porter, Ruthy, 68, 147, 148, *163*, 180

Portrero Group, 204
PPP (Cares Act Paycheck Protection Program), 196
Prescott College (AZ), 26
primary education programs, 56–57, 64, 74, 76, 85
programming, NCI and NCELC, 53–68
  adult education, 143–157
  Big Canoe and You, The, 91
  Cascade Climate Challenge, 104, 117, 120, 121–124
  Celebrating Wildflowers, 60
  concepts, early, 4, 9
  Conferences and Retreats, 153–157, 168–170
  core beliefs/themes of programming, 54, 61, 64–65
  Discovery Canoe Camp, 85, 107, 108–111, 114, 115
  Drawing the Details, 92
  Eagle Watchers, 58, 62, 172
  Environmental Architecture: Green Building Design and Operation, 95–96
  Family Getaways, 91, *94*, 104, 149
  formats, exploration of, 65–67
  Girls on Ice, 85, 111–113
  I'm Lichen Hikin', 91
  Learning Center Day Trips, 92
  Mountain Camp, 85, 105–108
  North Cascades Landscape Watercolors, 92
  North Cascades Naturalist Retreat, 91
  North Cascades Wild, 113–116
  Parks Climate Challenge, 104, 117–120, 122
  People of the Upper Skagit, 66, 165, 193
  primary education programs, 56–57, 64, 74, 76, 85
  Sourdough Speakers Series, 92
  staff, 67–68
  stewardship programs, 57–60
  Summer Wilderness Adventures, 85
  see also field seminars; Mountain School; Skagit Watershed Education Project; youth programming

Puget Sound, 2, 4, 64, 66, 89
Pyle, Robert Michael "Bob"
    art/writing at NCI, 61–62, 67, 146, 166
    Eco-Geographic Basis for Lepidoptera Conservation, The, 62
    extinction of experience, 9
    instructor, as, 23, *65*
    retreats, 145
    teacher education, 139
    Thunder Tree, The, 62, 104
    Walking the High Divide: Life as a Field Trip, 62
Pyramid Peak, 81, 147, 204

Q
Quigley, Alana (Aazhoganike Noojimo'idizo), 206

R
racism, systemic, 192
Railroad Grade, 6, 59, 118, 122
Rainier, Mount, 112, 114, 144
Rasar State Park, 131
Reach for the Peaks (capital campaign), 177
Reagan, Ronald, 2, 16
Recession, Great, 177
recycling/sustainability, 46, 50, 90, 94–95
RELC (Residential Environmental Learning Centers), 188
relicensing of Skagit Hydroelectric Project
    approval, 44–45
    COVID-19, 185
    Detrich, Bec, 205, 206–207
    Discovery Canoe Camp, 108
    history of license, 39–40
    mitigation, environmental impact, 173
    NCELC and, 170
    NCI future, 204
    NCI-NCNP negotiations, 189
Remote Medical International, 154–155
Renau, Pat, 152
Residential Environmental Learning Centers (RELC), 188
resources, natural *see* natural resources
restoration, habitat, 95, 115, 122, 130, *132*, 177

retail stores, 151–153, *155*
retreats/conferences, 145–148, 153–157, 168–170
Return to Mountain Camp, 106
Revelson, Jason, 168, 206
Reynolds, John
    anti-environmentalism, 156–157
    black bears, 170
    Board of Directors, 161
    departure from NPS, 37
    expansion of NCI, 30, 144
    Huxley College of Environmental Studies and, 173
    Memoranda of Understanding, 36
    North Cascades as ecosystem, 20
    NPS superintendent, as, 15
    support of NCI, *18*, 19, 44, 45, 84, 173
Riedel, Jon, 6, 118, *119*, 122, 140, *169*
Rinder, Kate, 124, 216
risk management, 98–100, 109, 112, 115, 131, 138, 175
Risk Tolerance Statement (NCELC), 99–100
River Stewards, 172
rivers/creeks
    Baker River, 122, 131, 161
    Big Beaver Creek, 109
    Clear Creek/Lake Camps, 32
    Deer Creek, 49, 90, 96, 97
    Diobsud Creek, 83
    Ish River, 184
    Kulshan Creek, 130–131
    Lightning Creek Campsite/Float, 11, 110
    Methow River, 45
    Nooksack River, 45, 135
    Sauk River, 121–122
    Sourdough Creek, 49, 96, 97
    Suiattle River, 74
    Thunder Creek, 77, 105
    Twisp River, 80
    see also Kulshan Creek Neighborhood Youth Program; Skagit River
Road Scholars, 143–144
Robinson, Chuck, 25, 174, 177
Rockport State Park, 106
Rolnick, Abbe, 168

Rosemary Lodge, 34
Ross Dam, 40, 41, 55–56, 150
Ross Lake, 11, 66, 108, *112*, 122, 171
Ross Lake National Recreation Area, 4, 11
Ross Lake Resort, 109
Ross Mule (vessel), 66, 110, 122, 165

S
Salesforce (software), 168
Salish Dancer (vessel), *186*, 204
Salish Sea, 4, 6, 67, 181, 196
salmon, 119, 131, 177
Salmon Run Game, 131
Salmonberry Dining Hall, 96
Samish Indian Nation, 194
San Juan Islands, 67
Santa Cruz, UC, 13
Sauk Mountain, 121
Sauk River, 121–122
Sauk-Suiattle Indian Tribe, 7, 40, 194
Savoian, Sasha, 131
Schell, Paul, 177
Scherrer, Wendy
  Board of Directors, 161
  *Celebrating Wildflowers: Educator's
    Guide to the Appreciation and
    Conservation of Native Plants*, 140
  *Living with Mountains: A Guide
    for Learning and Teaching about
    Mountain Landscapes*, 140
  Mountain Camp, 105
  Mountain School, 53
  program director, 168
  school programming, 138
  *Sharing the Skagit: An Educator's Guide
    to the Skagit River Basin* (Weisberg,
    Riedel, Johannessen, Scherrer), 140
  staff, *163*, 167
  teacher education, 140
  *Teaching for Wilderness: A Guide
    for Teaching about Wilderness and
    Wildlands*, 140
  youth programming, 31
Scheuch, Brian, 22, 25, 31, 103–104, 110,
  215
Schneider, Erin, 95

scholarships, 106, 107, 113, 176–177
Schreibers Meadow, 59
Schultz, Denise, 186
Science, Technology, Engineering, and
  Mathematics education (STEM),
  136
Seattle Arts and Letters, 174
Seattle City Light
  Base Camp, 150
  construction, NCELC, 48–50
  COVID-19 response, 196
  graduate program, 73
  Information Center, 151
  NCELC and, 39–47, 176
  NCI relationship, 89, 160, 173
  Parks Climate Challenge, 118–119
  SEEC and, 55–56
  see also construction, NCELC;
    relicensing of Skagit Hydroelectric
    Project; Skagit Hydroelectric Project
Seattle Mountaineers, 16
Seattle Times, 51
Sedrow-Woolley (WA), 20, 21, 24, 74, 148,
  167
Selan, James, 63
seminars, field *see* field seminars
Sense of Wonder, The (Carson), 61, 128
Sequoia National Forest, 12
Sequoia-Kings Canyon National Park, 19, 35
*Sharing the Skagit: An Educator's Guide to
  the Skagit River Basin* (Weisberg,
  Riedel, Johannessen, Scherrer),
  140
shelters, NCELC, 79, 90, 96–97, *99*, 165
Shuksan, Mount, 59
Shuksan Institute, 9, 10, 14, 17, 26, 139,
  158
Shuman, Barbara VanDyke, 146
Shumway, Dean, 43, 216
Sierra Club National Outings, 155
Sierra Institute, 13, *25*, 26
Silver River Ranch, 174
Since Time Immemorial Tribal
  Sovereignty Curriculum, 193, 208
Skagic Fisheries Enhancement Group, 130
Skagit Conservation District, 174

Skagit Environmental Endowment
    Commission (SEEC), 55–56, 133,
    175
Skagit Fisheries Enhancement Group, 174
Skagit Flats, 63
Skagit Gorge, 92
Skagit Hydroelectric Project
    Skagit Tours, 150–151
    youth programming, 118–119
    see also relicensing of Skagit
    Hydroelectric Project
Skagit Information Center, 155
Skagit Land Trust, 83
Skagit River
    aesthetics of place, 7
    dams, 39–40, 108, 110, 118
    eagles, 130
    History of the Skagit River (video
    series), 196
    Kulshan Creek Neighborhood Youth
    Program, 130–131
    Mountain Camp, 106
    Mountain School, 54, 78, 97
    National Wilderness Preservation
    System, 58
    NCELC and, 97
    Sauk river confluence, 121–122
    scenic river designation, 58
    Skagit Tours, 150–151
    stewardship programs, 60
    see also relicensing of Skagit
    Hydroelectric Project; Skagit
    Hydroelectric Project; Skagit
    Watershed Education Project (SWEP)
Skagit River Hydroelectric Project
    licensing see relicensing of Skagit
    Hydroelectric Project
Skagit River Stewards, 60
Skagit Tours, 150, 196
Skagit Valley
    bird watching, 59, 63
    Cascade Climate Challenge, 121
    graduate program, 75
    Kulshan Creek Neighborhood Youth
    Program, 130
    Mountain Camp, 106

Mountain School, 56
naturalist retreats, 146
NCELC and, 92
NCI and, 89, 133
Ross Dam, 55
Ross Lake, 108
school districts, 174
youth programming, 44
Skagit Valley Farm, 94
Skagit Valley School District, 174
Skagit Watershed Education Project
    (SWEP), 56–57, 60, 67–68, 104,
    168, 172, 177
Skagit Watershed Education Project
    Teacher Handbook (Johannessen),
    140
Skagit Watershed Field Workshops, 172
Slate Peak, 24
slavery, 191
Sleeping Lady Resort, 67, 146
Slovic, Scott, 62
Slow Food, 149
Smeck, Woody, 187, 189, 200
Smith, Annick, 146
Smith, Lanette, 107
Snow School, 134, 137
Snyder, Gary, 61, 165
social justice, 189–195
Song of the Sea: Marine and Tidal
    Ecology, 144
Sourdough Creek/Shelter, 49, 96, 97
Sourdough Mountain, 5, 109
Sourdough Speakers Series, 92, 148
South Cascade Glacier, 111
Southern Ute Tribe, 12
Spagna, Ana Maria, 146, 166
Spring in the Cascades: The Natural and
    Cultural History of the Methow
    Valley, 144
Spring Naturalist Retreat, 66, 145–146,
    148
Spring Ornithology, 66
St. Croix band (Ojibwe people), 206
staff
    Board of Directors, 164
    COVID-19, 195–196, 205

staff (*continued*)
  interpersonal relations, 170
  leadership, 169
  mid-1990s, *163*
  NCELC, 169–170
  seasonal furloughs, 154
  technology and, 168
State Patrol, Washington, 58
Steele, Sara Joy, 124
Stehekin (WA), 17, 80
STEM (Science, Technology, Engineering, and Mathematics education), 136
Stephen Mather Wilderness, 80
Sterrett, Gail, 56, 68, *163*, 167
stewardship, 57–58, 113, 130, 131, 179
Stewart, Brandi, *75*
Sto:lo People, 7, 194
Stone, Julie, 196–197
"strategic opportunities," 30, 41, 44–47, 117
Strategic Plan, 2020-2024, 179, 199–200
stream ecology, 106, 118
Stream Scene, 106, 107
Striker, Don, 208
Student Conservation Association, 124
subalpine meadows, 6, 59
Suiattle Pass/River, 74
Summer Wilderness Adventures, 85
Summer Youth Programs, 111
Sun Mountain Lodge, 62, 66, 67, 144, 145, 146, 177
Sund, Robert, 180, 184
Sussman, Abbey, 134–135, 136
sustainability/recycling, 46, 50, 90, 94–95
Sweeney, Aneka, 117–118, 121, 123
SWEP (Skagit Watershed Education Project) *see* Skagit Watershed Education Project (SWEP)
Swinomish Indian Tribal Community, 7, 40, 194
Syilx/Okanagan Nation, 194
systemic racism, 192

T
Table Mountain, 59
Tain, Kirsten, 68, *163*, 167

Taylor, Ron, 23
Taylor-Goodrich, Karen, 186–189
teacher education, 139–141
Teaching for Wilderness: A Guide for Teaching about Wilderness and Wildlands (Scherrer, Weisberg), 140
Tenmile Campsite, 110
Teton Science Schools, 3, 13, 83
Thaler, Toby, 45
Thorpe, Sylvia, 16–17
Thunder Creek, 77, 105
Thunder Tree, The (Pyle), 62, 104
tidal ecology, 144
Tiffany Mountain, *79*
timber wars, 37, 57–58
Tobin, Jim, 15
"Tomorrow's Leaders Concerned About Climate Change at North Cascades," 217
trail system, NCELC, 96–98, *99*, 121
transfer of experience, 46, 116–117, 122
Treaty of Guadalupe, 192
Treetop Science, 140
Trips for Kids Marin, 205
tundra, alpine, 5
Turner, Jan, 167
Twisp River, 80

U
UC Santa Cruz, 13
underserved youth, 85, 113–114, 125, 176, 190
Understanding By Design curriculum, 207–208
United General Hospital Community Health Outreach Program, 132
University, Antioch (Seattle), 13
University, Western Washington *see* Western Washington University
University of Alaska, 113
University of Bellingham, 13, 74
University of Washington (Univ. of WA), 5, 35, 61
University of Wyoming, 83
Upper Skagit Indian Tribe, 7, 40, 194

U.S. 64th Congress, *U.S. Statutes at Large,* 39:535, 215
U.S. Department of the Interior Office of Inspector General, 217
U.S. Forest Service (USFS)
  career opportunities, 124
  Kulshan Creek Neighborhood Youth Program, 130
  mitigation, environmental impact, 40, 42
  National Park Service relationship, 21, 35
  NCI relationship, 59, 64, 90, 160, 171–172
  Parks Climate Challenge, 119
  Path for Youth Initiative, 125–127
  retail stores, 152
  timber wars, 58
  Washington Park Service workshop, 34
  youth education, 8
U.S. Geological Survey, 111
U.S. Green Building Council, 50, 95
U.S. Statutes at Large, 39:535 (U.S.64th Congress), 215
UWA (University of Washington), 5, 35, 61

V
Van Almkerk, William, 107, 113
Village Books (Bellingham), 174, 198
Visalli, Dana, 107, 144, 146
VISTA (Volunteers in Service to America), 133
Voices Along the Skagit: Teaching the History of the First People in the Skagit Watershed (Luckmann), 140
Volunteers in Service to America (VISTA), 133

W
Wahl, Terry, 20
Walking the High Ridge: Life as a Field Trip (Pyle), 62
Wallace, Bill, 36
Walsh, Beth, 168
War Creek Pass, 80
Warm Beach/Conference Center, 66, 144
Washington, DC, 118, 119

Washington Chapter, Nature Conservancy, 145
Washington Conservation Corps, 124, 136
Washington Department of Fish and Wildlife, 40
Washington Department of Natural Resources, 35–36, 174
Washington Department of Transportation, 58
Washington Forest Practices Board, 35
Washington Legislature, 208
Washington National Park Fund, 33
Washington National Park Wilderness Act, 35
Washington Outdoor School Consortium, 208
Washington Park Service workshop, 34
Washington Park Wilderness bill, 34
Washington State Patrol, 58
Washington State Science Learning Standards, 137
Washington University, Western *see* Western Washington University
Water Birds of Bellingham Bay, 66
Watershed Festival, 57
watersheds
  Skagit Tours, 151
  Skagit Watershed Field Workshops, 172
  Snow School, 135
  Watershed Festival, 57
  see also Kulshan Creek Neighborhood Youth Program; Skagit Watershed Education Project (SWEP)
Watt, James, 2, 19
Webber, Bert/Sue, 67
Weisberg, Saul
  administrator, 25, 26, 48, 160–161, 175–176
  business of NCI, 158
  COVID-19, 195–196
  founder of NCI, 1–2, 11–17
  land acknowledgments, 193–194
  Living with Mountains: A Guide for Learning and Teaching about Mountain Landscapes, 140
  National Park Service, 43

Weisberg, Saul (*continued*)
  Nonprofit Partnerships: Competition and Collaboration, 217
  North Cascades Conservation Council, 39–41
  partnerships, 174–175
  retirement, 162, 185, 203–204
  Sharing the Skagit: An Educator's Guide to the Skagit River Basin (Weisberg, Riedel, Johannessen, Scherrer), 140
  Sierra Institute, 25
  staff, 67, 81, *163*
  teacher education, 139, 140
  Teaching for Wilderness: A Guide for Teaching about Wilderness and Wildlands, 140
Weisberg, Shelley, 139, 144
Weiser, Russ, 95–96
Wenatchee National Forest, 5, 36, 90
Wenatchee Valley, 89, 146
West, Melinda, 148
Western Washington University
  Cascade Climate Challenge, 124
  EDI and, 190–191
  graduate program, 71–75, 85
  Huxley College of Environmental Sudies, 17, 31, 72–73, 76, 117, 173, 173–174, 191
  Miles, John, 17
  NCI partnership, 83, 160, 173–174
  professors as NCI instructors, 20, 23
  Scherrer, Wendy (graduate), 31
  Snow School, 135, 136
Wet and Wild, 106
Whalen, Philip, 61, 165
Whatcom, Lake, 137
Whatcom Coalition for Environmental Education, 197
Whatcom Museum, 66
Whidbey Island, 66, 130
Whitaker, Jim, 177
White Birds of Winter, 63
white middle class, 191–192
Whitford, Lee, 131
Wilborn, Maketa, 124
Wild Ginger Library, 96

Wild Whatcom, 197
wilderness
  Alpine Lakes Wilderness, 2
  Arthur Carhart Wilderness, 111
  Chelan Sawtooth Wilderness, 80
  conservation, environmental, 2, 191
  education, 77, *79*, 80, 114, 125, 155
  Glacier Peak Wilderness, 2, 63, 80, 111
  hiking community, 19
  management, 34–35, 37
  Marblemount Wilderness, 15
  Methow Valley and wilderness movement, 24
  National Park Service Wilderness Workshop, 36
  National Wilderness Preservation System, 2, 34
  New Wilderness Project, 124
  Olympic National Park, 19
  Pasayten Wilderness, 2, 4, 80, 107
  Sequoia-Kings Canyon National Park, 19
  South Cascade Glacier, 111
  Stephen Mather Wilderness, 80
  timber wars, 57
  Washington Park Wilderness bill, 34
  Wilderness Act of 1964, 34
  Wilderness First Responders, 100
  Wilderness Information Center, 151
  youth programming, 108
  see also North Cascades National Park (NCNP)
Wilderness Act of 1964, 34
Wilderness First Responders, 100
Wilderness Information Center, 151
wildfire, 100, 118, 156
wildflowers, 6, 63, 145
Wind River Canopy Crane, 140
Wings over the Methow: Birds and Butterflies from Sagebrush to Snow, 63
Winter Ethnobotany of the Island Landscape, 66
Winter Wildlands Alliance, 134
Wrangell-St. Elias National Park, 43
writing at NCI *see* art/writing at NCI

Writing Retreat, Annual, 177
Wyoming, University of, 83

Y
Yellow Aster Buttes, 77
Yellowstone National Park, 17–18, 19
Yosemite Institute, 3
Yosemite National Park, 19
Youth Ambassadors, 126
Youth Conservation Corps, 123
youth environmental education *see* youth
      programming
Youth Leadership Adventures, 104, 117,
      123–124, 126, 131, 168–170, 196
youth programming
  Board of Directors, 125
  Cascade Climate Challenge, 104, 117,
    120, 121–124
  Choose Your Own Adventure
    Programs, 208
  Discovery Canoe Camp, 85, 107, 108–
    111, 114, 115
  EDI and, 190
  Girls on Ice, 111–113
  instructors, 166
  low-income youth, 53
  Mountain Camp, 106–108
  North Cascades Wild, 113–117
  Parks Climate Challenge, 104, 117–120,
    122
  Path for Youth Initiative, 125–127
  philosophy, 123
  Stream Scene, 106
  underserved youth, 113–114, 190
  see also Mountain School; Youth
    Leadership Adventures

Z
Zalesky, Laura/Phil, 4
Zoom (videoconferencing app), 198, 205
Zwinger, Ann, 61, 67, 146, 166
Zwinger, Susan, 166

JOHN C. MILES IS PROFESSOR EMERITUS of Environmental Studies at the College of the Environment, Western Washington University. He taught at Western for four decades where he focused his work on environmental education and environmental humanities, especially history of the US national park system. He served as dean of the college from 1985-1992. His books include *Koma Kulshan*; *Guardians of the Parks*; *Wilderness in National Parks*; and *Impressions of the North Cascades*. He and his wife Susan Morgan live at the foot of the Sangre de Cristo Mountains near Taos, New Mexico.

Printed in the USA
CPSIA information can be obtained
at www.ICGtesting.com
JSHW070228220923
48672JS00002B/2